MARQUEE SERIES

Microsoft®

PowerPoint®

2016

Nita Rutkosky
Pierce College Puyallup
Puyallup, Washington

Audrey Roggenkamp
Pierce College Puyallup
Puyallup, Washington

Ian Rutkosky
Pierce College Puyallup
Puyallup, Washington

St. Paul

Senior Vice President	Linda Hein
Editor in Chief	Christine Hurney
Director of Production	Timothy W. Larson
Production Editors	Rachel Kats, Jen Weaverling
Cover and Text Designer	Valerie King
Copy Editor	Sarah Kearin
Senior Design and Production Specialist	Jaana Bykonich
Assistant Developmental Editors	Mamie Clark, Katie Werdick
Testers	Desiree Carvel; Ann E. Mills, Ivy Tech Community College of Indiana, Indianapolis, IN
Instructional Support Writer	Brienna McWade
Indexer	Terry Casey
Vice President Information Technology	Chuck Bratton
Digital Projects Manager	Tom Modl
Vice President Sales and Marketing	Scott Burns
Director of Marketing	Lara Weber McLellan

Cover Photo Credits: © whitehoune/Shutterstock.com; © Bohbeh/Shutterstock.com.

ISBN 978-0-76386-723-2 (print)
ISBN 978-0-76386-724-9 (digital)

875 Montreal Way
St. Paul, MN 55102
Email: educate@emcp.com
Website: ParadigmCollege.com

Printed in the United States of America

24 23 22 21 20 19 18 17 16   1 2 3 4 5 6 7 8 9 10 11 12

Contents

Introducing

PowerPoint® 2016

Create colorful and powerful presentations using PowerPoint, Microsoft's presentation program that is included in the Office 2016 suite. Use PowerPoint to organize and present information and create visual aids for a presentation. PowerPoint is a full-featured presentation program that provides a wide variety of editing and formatting features as well as sophisticated visual elements such as images, pictures, SmartArt, WordArt, and drawn objects. While working in PowerPoint, you will produce presentations for the following six companies.

First Choice Travel is a travel center offering a full range of traveling services from booking flights, hotel reservations, and rental cars to offering travel seminars.

The Waterfront Bistro offers fine dining for lunch and dinner and also offers banquet facilities, a wine cellar, and catering services.

Worldwide Enterprises is a national and international distributor of products for a variety of companies and is the exclusive movie distribution agent for Marquee Productions.

Marquee Productions is involved in all aspects of creating movies from script writing and development to filming. The company produces documentaries, biographies, as well as historical and action movies.

Performance Threads maintains an inventory of rental costumes and also researches, designs, and sews special-order and custom-made costumes.

The mission of the Niagara Peninsula College Theatre Arts Division is to offer a curriculum designed to provide students with a thorough exposure to all aspects of the theatre arts.

In Section 1 you will learn how to

Prepare a Presentation

Prepare a presentation using a template provided by PowerPoint or create a presentation and apply formatting with a design theme. Preparing a presentation consists of general steps such as creating and editing slides; adding enhancements to slides; and saving, previewing, printing, and closing a presentation and running a slide show. When running a slide show, the way in which one slide is removed from the screen and the next slide is displayed is referred to as a *transition*. Interesting transitions can be added to slides as well as transition sounds to a presentation.

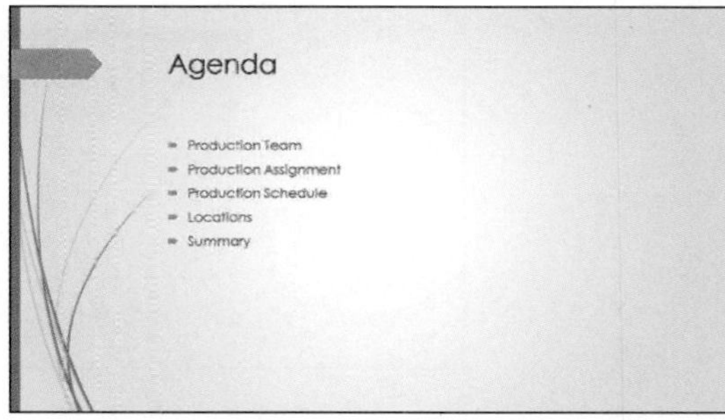

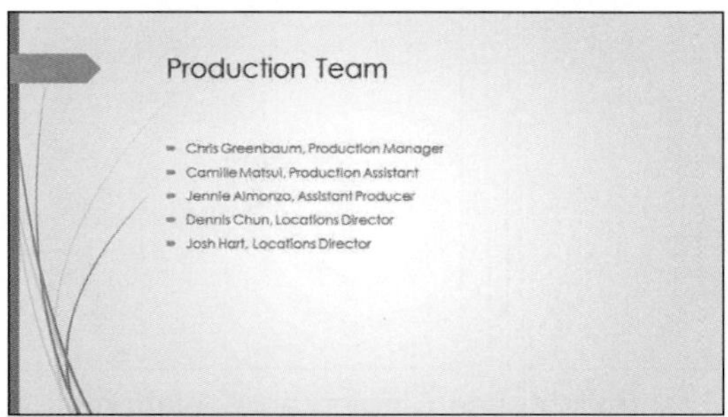

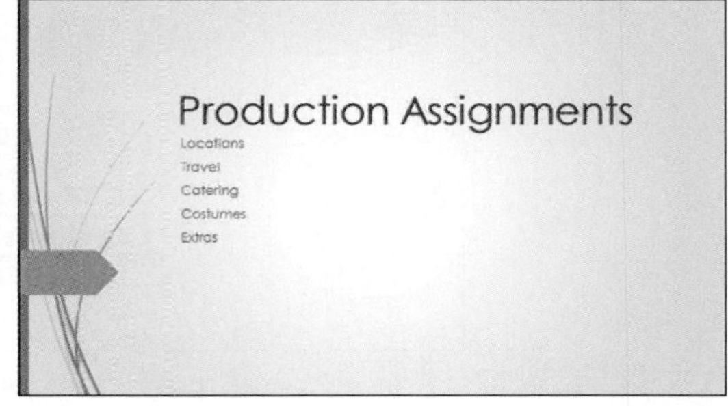

Create presentations using PowerPoint design themes and apply various slide layouts to change the appearance of slides.

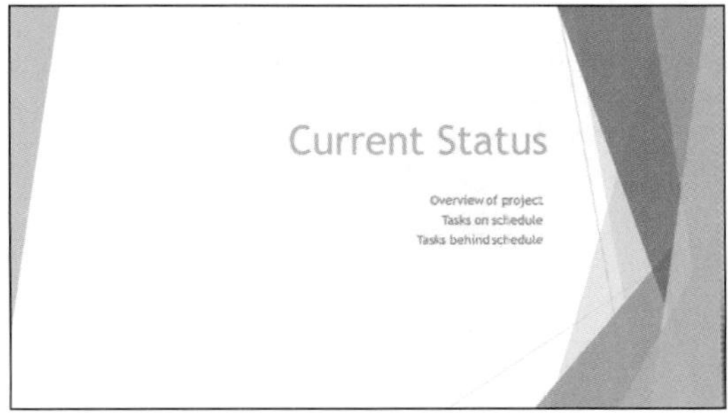

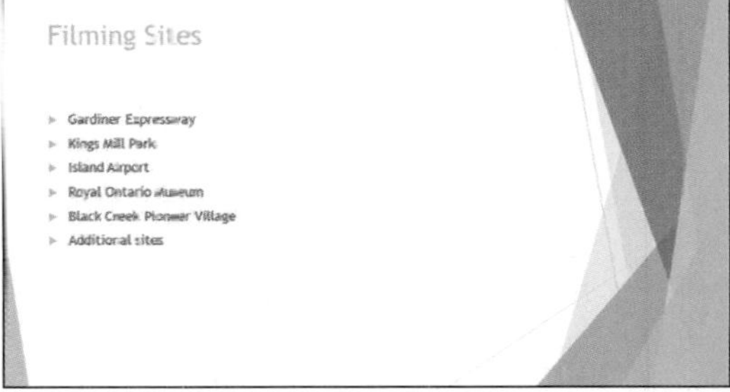

In Section 2 you will learn how to

Edit and Enhance Slides

Edit slides and slide elements in a presentation to customize and personalize the presentation. Editing can include such functions as rearranging and deleting slides; cutting, copying, and pasting text; changing the font, paragraph alignment, and paragraph spacing; and changing the design theme, theme color, and theme font. Add visual appeal to a presentation by inserting images, pictures, and SmartArt organizational charts and graphics.

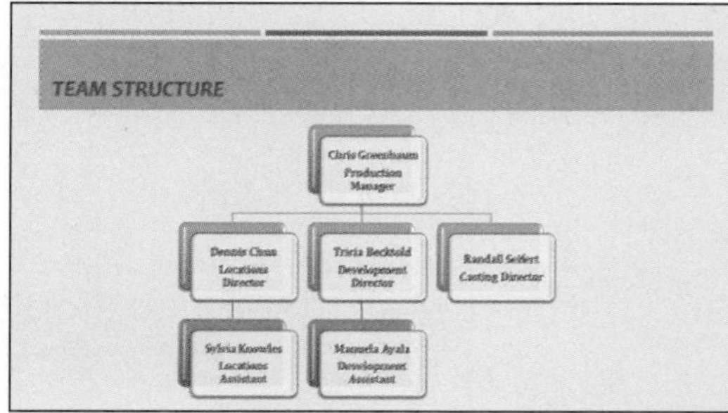

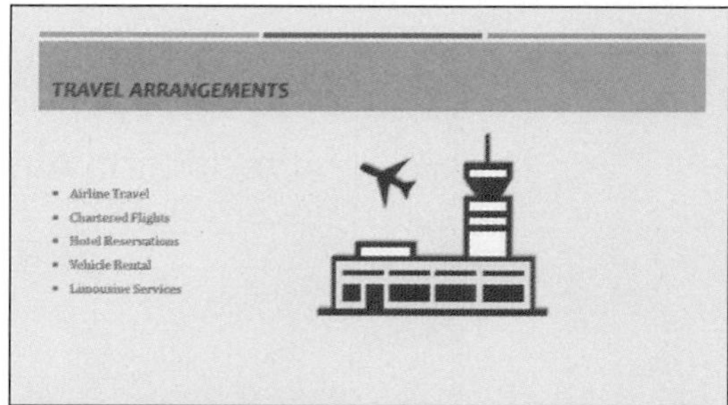

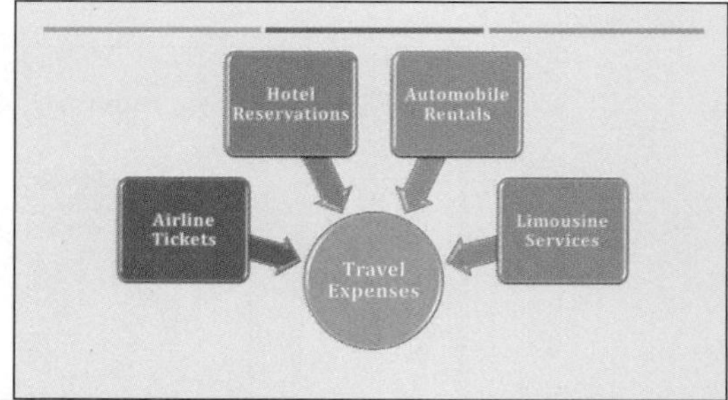

Edit slides by performing such actions as rearranging and deleting slides and changing slide size. Perform editing tasks on text in slides such as changing the font, paragraph alignment, and spacing. Enhance the visual appeal of a presentation by inserting such elements as a company logo, image, an organizational chart, and a graphic.

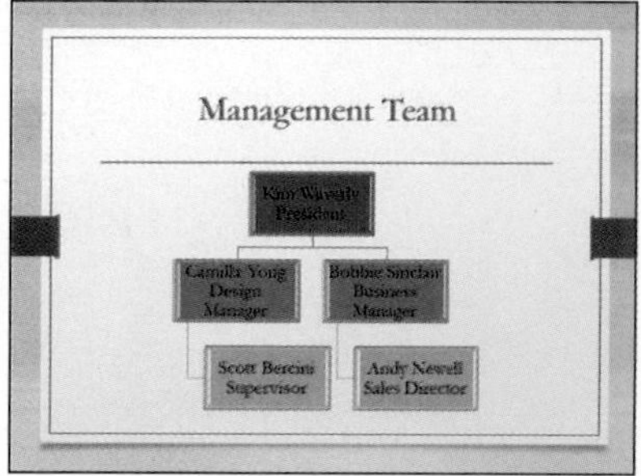

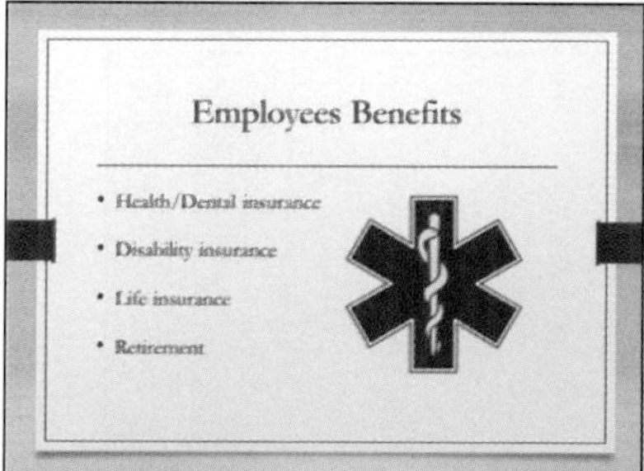

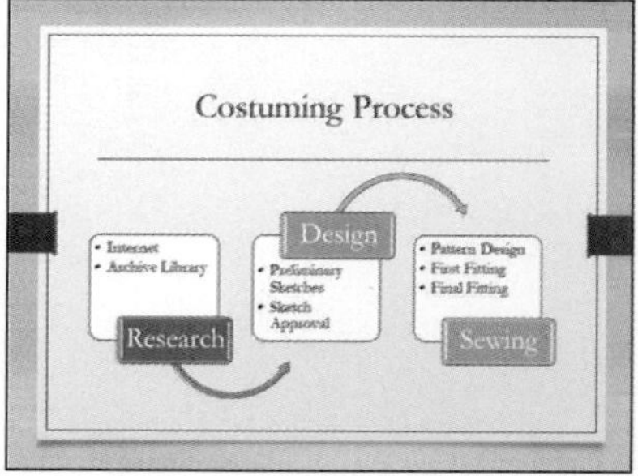

In Section 3 you will learn how to

Customize Presentations

Customize a presentation with the WordArt feature and by drawing and formatting objects and text boxes. Additional features for customizing a presentation include using the Clipboard; inserting and formatting a table; inserting actions buttons, hyperlinks, and headers and footers; and inserting audio and video files.

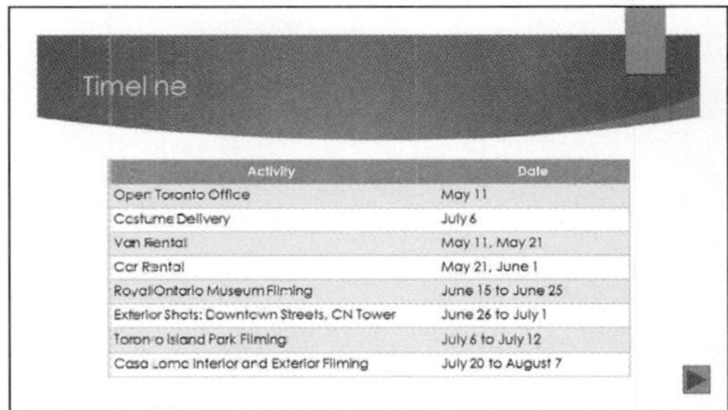

Further customize presentations with features such as headers and footers, audio and video files, WordArt, shapes, text boxes, and tables.

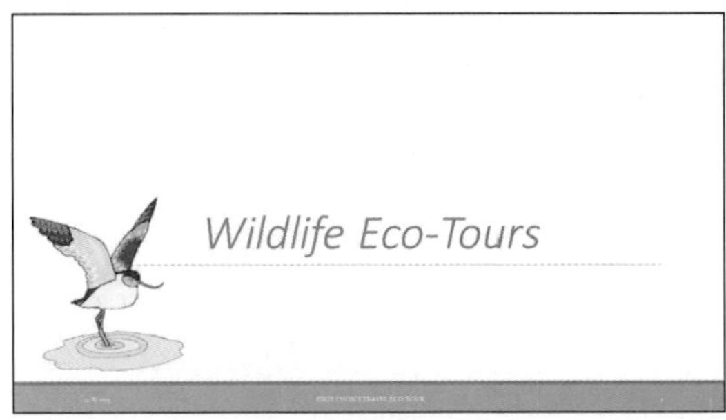

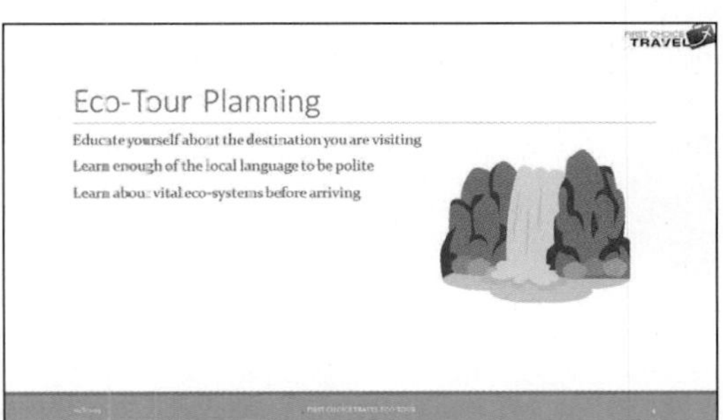

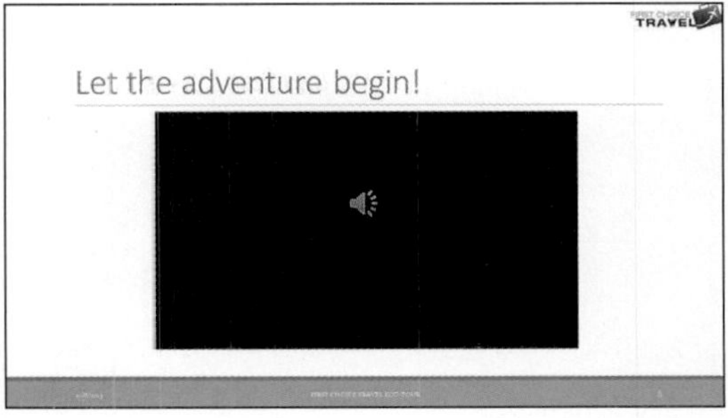

Getting Started

Adjusting Monitor Settings, Copying Data Files, and Changing View Options

Skills

- Set monitor resolution
- Modify DPI settings
- Copy files from OneDrive
- Copy files from a network location
- Change view options
- Display file extensions

The Microsoft Office product line has evolved over time, becoming available on Apple computers, tablets, phones, and through the Internet. This textbook and the accompanying ebook were written using a typical personal computer (tower/box, monitor, keyboard and mouse) or laptop. While you may be able to perform some of the activities in this textbook on a different operating system or tablet, not all of the steps will work as written and may jeopardize any work you may be required to turn in to your instructor. If you do not have access to a compatible computer, explore what options you have at your institution such as where and when you can use a computer lab.

One of the evolutions of the Microsoft Office product is that it is now offered in a subscription-based plan called Microsoft Office 365. An advantage of having a Microsoft Office 365 subscription is that it includes and incorporates new features or versions as they are released, as long as your subscription is active. For example, when Microsoft released Office 2016, any Office 365 users with the Office 2013 version were automatically upgraded. This new direction Microsoft is taking may impact section activities and assessments. For example, new features and tweaks may alter how some of the steps are completed. The ebook will contain the most up-to-date material and will be updated as new features become available.

In Activity 1 you will customize your monitor settings so that what you see on the screen matches the images in this textbook. In Activity 2 you will obtain the data files you will be using throughout this textbook from OneDrive. Activity 3 includes instructions on how to change the view settings so that your view of files in a FIle Explorer window matches the images in this textbook.

Activity 1 Adjusting Monitor Settings

Before beginning projects in this textbook, you may need to customize your monitor's settings and turn on the display of file extensions. Projects in the sections in this textbook assume that the monitor display is set at 1600 x 900 pixels, the DPI is set at 125%, and that the display of file extensions is turned on. Adjusting a monitor's display settings is important because the ribbon in the Microsoft Office applications adjusts to the screen resolution setting of your computer monitor. A monitor set at a high resolution will have the ability to show more buttons in the ribbon than a monitor set to a low resolution. The illustrations in this textbook were created with a screen resolution display set at 1600 × 900 pixels. In Figure GS1 at the bottom of the page, the Word ribbon is shown three ways: at a lower screen resolution (1366 × 768 pixels), at the screen resolution featured throughout this textbook, and at a higher screen resolution (1920 × 1080 pixels). Note the variances in the ribbon in all three examples.

What You Will Do Adjust the monitor settings for your machine to match the settings used to create the images in the textbook. If using a lab computer, check with your instructor before attempting this activity.

1. Right-click a blank area of the desktop and then click the *Display settings* option at the shortcut menu.
2. At the Settings window with the *Display* option selected, scroll down and click the Advanced display settings hyperlink.
3. Scroll down and look at the current setting displayed in the *Resolution* option box. For example, your screen may be currently set at 1920 × 1080. If your screen is already set to 1600 × 900, skip ahead to Step 7.

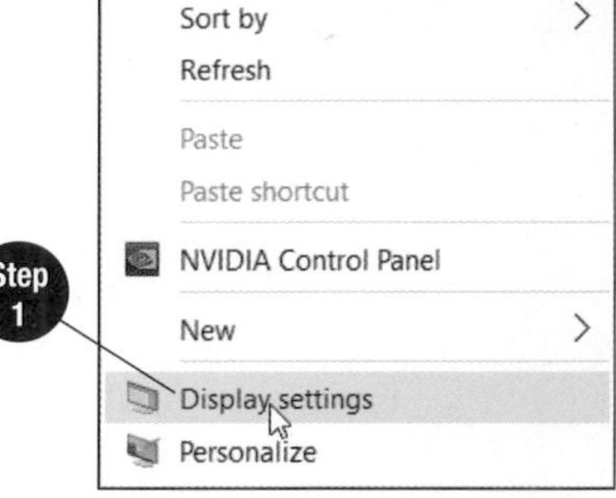

Screen resolution is set in pixels. Pixel is the abbreviation of picture element and refers to a single dot or point on the display monitor. Changing the screen resolution to a higher number of pixels means that more information can be seen on the screen as items are scaled to a smaller size.

Figure GS1 Word Ribbon at Various Screen Resolutions

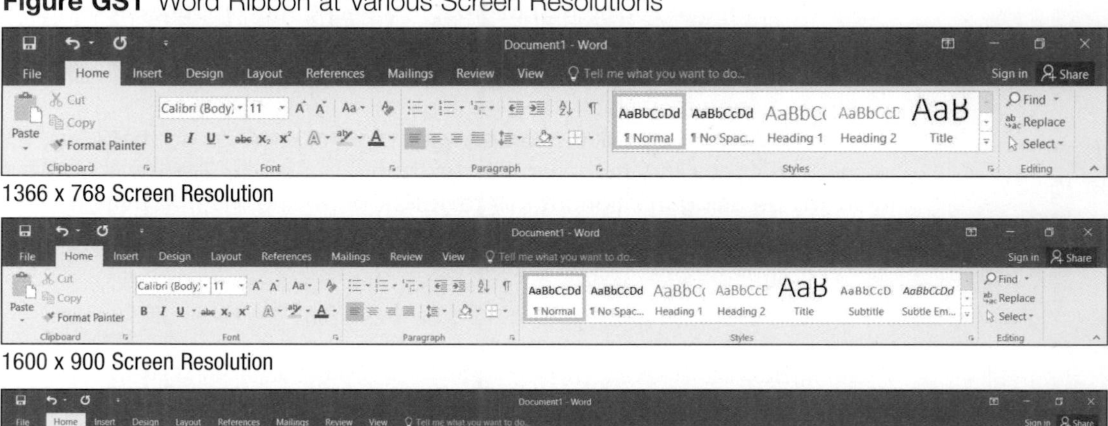

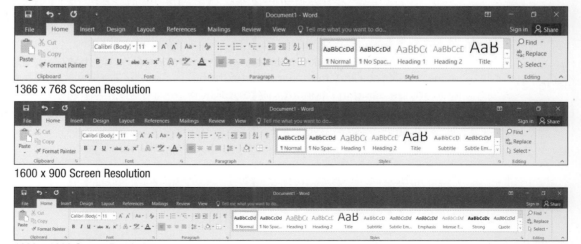

1366 x 768 Screen Resolution

1600 x 900 Screen Resolution

1920 x 1080 Screen Resolution

4. Click the *Resolution* option box and then click the 1600 × 900 option. If necessary, check with your instructor for alternate instructions. ***Note: Depending on the privileges you are given on a school machine, you may not be able to complete these steps.***

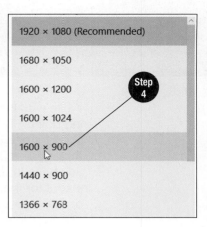

   If the machine you are using has more than one monitor, make sure the proper monitor is selected. (The active monitor displays as a blue rectangle.)

5. Click the Apply button.
6. Click the Keep changes button at the message box asking if you want to keep the display settings.

   Some monitor settings will render the computer unusable because objects on the desktop or in a window will become inaccessible and hidden. In this case, Windows will automatically revert the settings to the previous configuration after 30 seconds.

7. Click the Back button.
8. At the Settings window with the *Display* option active, look at the percentage in which the size of text, apps, and other items currently display (also known as the DPI setting). For example, items on your screen may display at 100%. If the percentage is 125%, skip to Step 12.

   As the resolution on monitors has increased, text, application windows, buttons, options, and so on start to appear smaller and smaller on the screen. To counter this, Windows allows you to increase the size of these objects by changing the DPI setting. The computers used to create the images in this textbook uses the 125% DPI setting, which slightly increases the size of text, applications, buttons, and options.

9. Click and hold down the left mouse button on the button on the slider bar below the text *Change the size of text, apps, and other items*, drag the slider button until *125%* displays, and then release the mouse button.

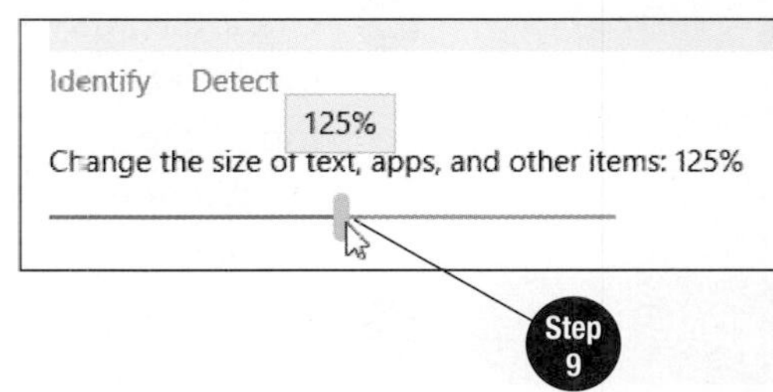

10. Click the Apply button.
11. At the message indicating that you must sign out of your computer, click the Sign out later button.

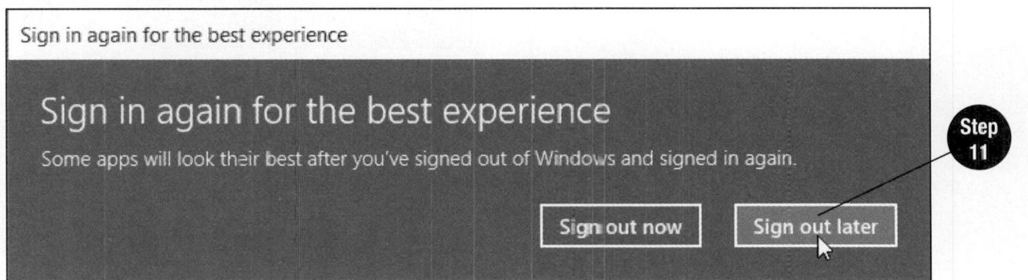

12. Click the Close button.

Activity 2 Retrieving and Copying Data Files

While working through the activities in this book, you will often be using data files as starting points. These files need to be obtained from OneDrive or other locations such as your school's network drive. All of the files required to complete the bookwork are provided through OneDrive, which you can access through links in the textbook's ebook. Make sure you have Internet access before trying to retrieve the data files from OneDrive. Ask your instructor if alternate locations are available for retrieving the files, such as a network drive or online resource such as Angel, BlackBoard, or Canvas. Retrieving data files from an alternate location will require different steps, so check with your instructor for additional steps or tasks to complete.

What You Will Do In order to complete the activities in this textbook, you will need to obtain the data files from OneDrive. Make sure you have access to OneDrive or an alternate location containing the files.

1. Insert your USB flash drive into an available USB port.
2. Navigate to this textbook's ebook. If you are a SNAP user, navigate to the ebook by clicking the textbook ebook link on your Assignments page. If you are not a SNAP user, launch your browser, go to https://paradigm.bookshelf.emcp.com, log in, and then click the textbook ebook thumbnail. ***Note: The steps in this activity assume you are using the Microsoft Edge browser. If you are using a different browser, the following steps may vary.***
3. Navigate to the ebook page that corresponds to this textbook page.
4. Click the Ancillary Links button in the menu. The menu of buttons may be at the top of the window or along the side of the window, depending on the size of the window.

Data Files

5. At the Ancillary Links dialog box that appears, click the Data Files: All Files hyperlink.

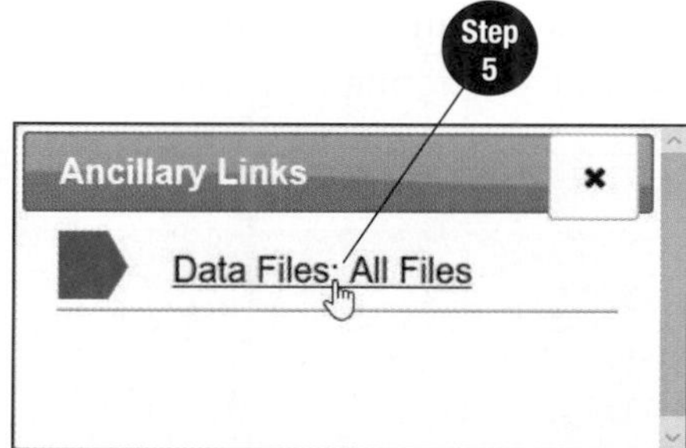

6. Click the Download hyperlink at the top of the window.

   A zip file containing the student data files will automatically begin downloading from the OneDrive website.

7. Click the Open button in the message box saying that the DataFiles.zip has finished downloading.

8. Right-click the *ExcelS2* folder in the Content pane.
9. Click the *Copy* option at the shortcut menu.

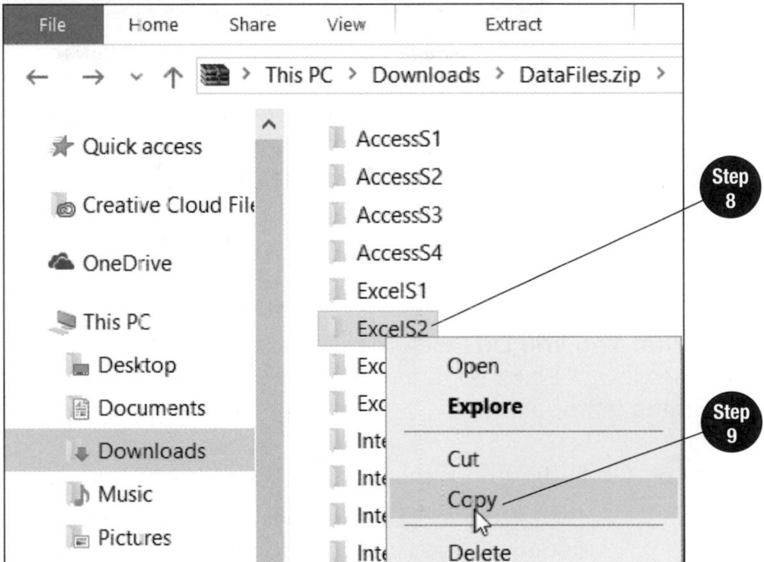

10. Click your USB flash drive that displays in the Navigation pane at the left side of the File Explorer window.

11. Click the Home tab and then click the Paste button in the Clipboard group.

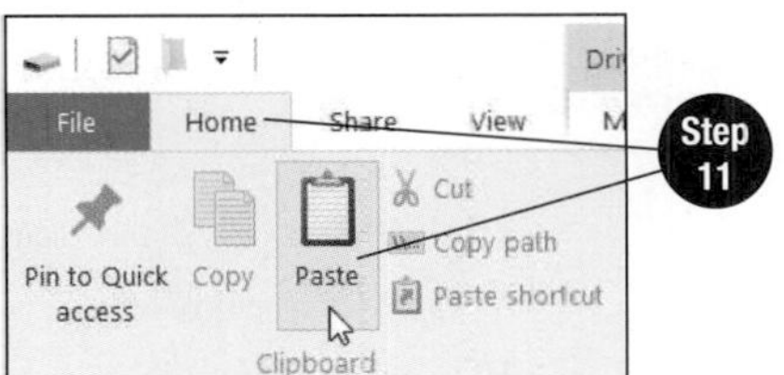

12. Close the File Explorer window by clicking the Close button in the upper right corner of the window.

Activity 3 Changing View Options

You can change the view of the File Explorer window to show the contents of your current location (drive or folder) in various formats, including icons, tiles, or a list, among others. With the Content pane in Details view, you can click the column headings to change how the contents are sorted and whether they are sorted in ascending or descending order. You can customize a window's environment by using buttons and options on the File Explorer View tab. You can also change how panes are displayed, how content is arranged in the Content pane, how content is sorted, and which features are hidden.

What You Will Do Before getting started with the textbook material, you need to adjust the view settings so that items in the File Explorer window appear the same as the images in the textbook.

1. Click the File Explorer button on the taskbar.

   By default, a File Explorer window opens at the Quick access location, which contains frequently-used folders such as Desktop, Documents, Downloads, Pictures and so on. It also displays recently used files at the bottom of the Content pane.

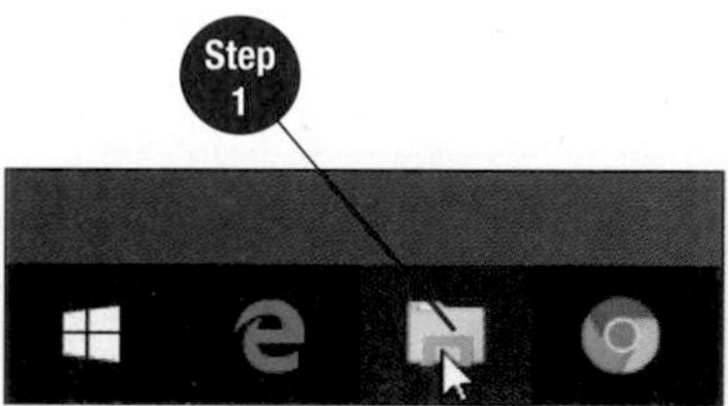

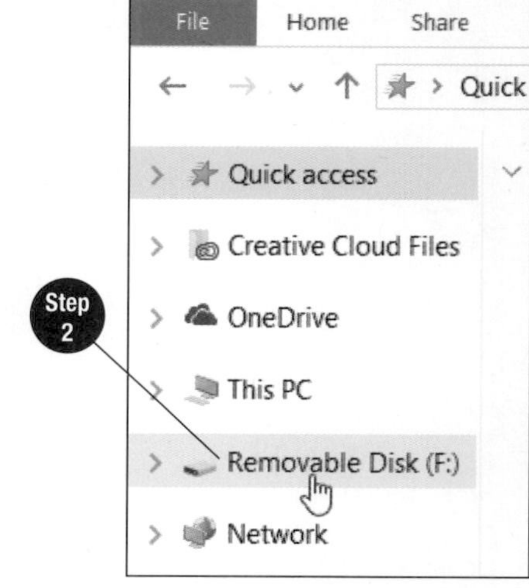

2. Click the drive letter representing your storage medium in the Navigation pane.
3. Double-click the *ExcelS2* folder in the Content pane.
4. Click the View tab below the Title bar.
5. Click the *Large icons* option in the Layout group.

   After you click an option on the View tab, the View tab collapses to provide more space in the File Explorer window.

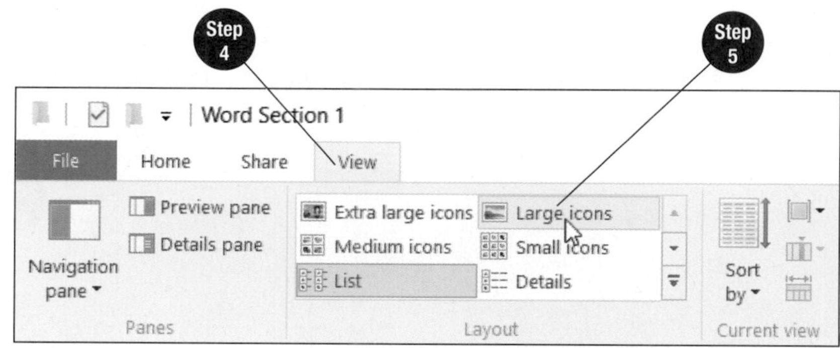

6. Click the View tab.
7. Click the *Details* option in the Layout group.

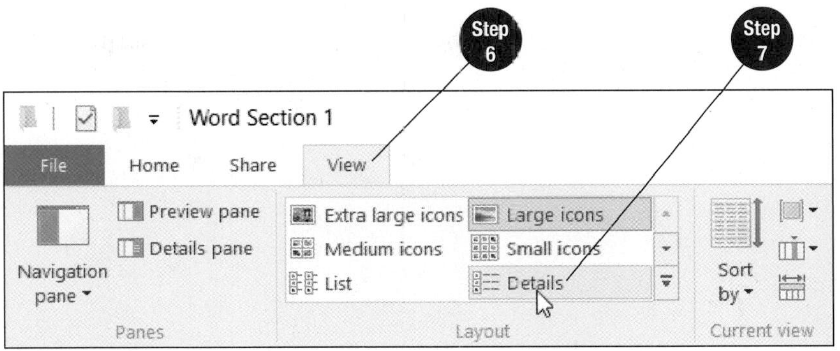

8. With files now displayed in Details view, click the *Name* column heading to sort the list in descending order by name.

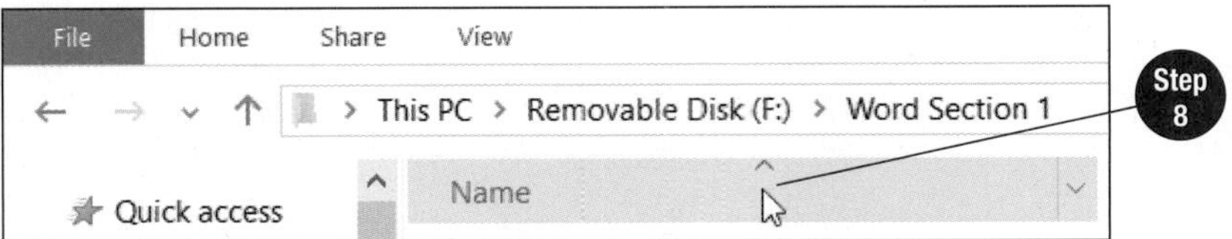

9. Click the *Name* column heading again to restore the list to ascending order by name.
10. Click the View tab and then click the *File name extensions* check box in the Show/hide group to insert a check mark. ***Note: If the check box appears with a check mark in it, then file extensions are already turned on—skip this step.***

    Inserting a check mark in a check box makes the option active. The files in the File Explorer window will now display any files with a file extension.

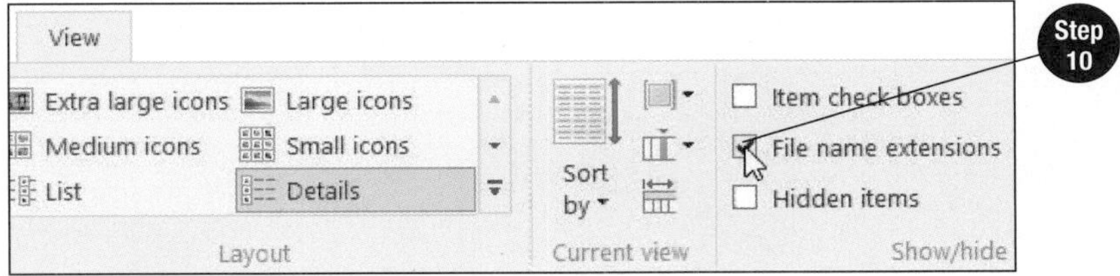

11. Close the File Explorer window by clicking the Close button in the upper right corner of the window.

In Addition

Changing the Default View for All Folders

You can set a view to display by default for all folders of a similar type (such as all disk drive folders or all documents folders). To do this, change the current view to the desired view for the type of folder that you want to set. Next, click the Options button on the View tab and then click the View tab at the Folder Options dialog box. Click the Apply to Folders button in the Folder views section and then click OK. Click Yes at the Folder Views message asking if you want all folders of this type to match this folder's view settings.

PowerPoint SECTION 1

Preparing a Presentation

Data Files Before beginning section work, copy the PowerPointS1 folder to your storage medium and then make PowerPointS1 the active folder.

Skills

- Open, save, and close a presentation
- Run a slide show
- Choose a design theme
- Add a new slide to a presentation
- Navigate in a presentation
- Insert a slide in a presentation
- Change the slide layout
- Change the presentation view
- Rearrange, delete, and hide slides
- Use the Tell Me and Help features
- Check spelling in a presentation
- Use Thesaurus to display synonyms for words
- Run a slide show and use the pen during a slide show
- Use ink tools
- Add transitions and transition sounds to a presentation
- Print and preview a presentation

Precheck Check your current skills to help focus your study of the skills taught in this section.

Projects Overview

Use an installed template to prepare a presentation about the new features in PowerPoint 2016; prepare a movie production meeting presentation and a location team meeting presentation.

Prepare an executive meeting presentation for Worldwide Enterprises.

Prepare a presentation containing information on the accommodations and services offered by The Waterfront Bistro.

Prepare a presentation on Toronto, Ontario, Canada.

Prepare a presentation for a costume meeting.

If you are a SNAP user, launch the Precheck and Tutorials from your Assignments page.

Model Answers Preview the model answers for an overview of the projects you will complete in the section activities.

Activity 1.1 Opening, Saving, and Closing a Presentation; Running a Slide Show

PowerPoint is a presentation graphics program you can use to organize and present information. With PowerPoint, you can create visual aids for a presentation and then print copies of the aids as well as run the slide show. To open a predesigned PowerPoint template, open the PowerPoint program, click the desired template, and then click the Create button. The presentation screen contains a variety of features for working with a presentation, such as the Title bar, Quick Access Toolbar, ribbon, and Status bar. After creating a presentation, save the presentation so it is available for future use. Save a presentation at the Save As backstage area.

What You Will Do You are an employee of Marquee Productions and Office 2016 has just been installed on your computer. You need to prepare a presentation in the near future so you decide to open a PowerPoint file and experiment with running the slide show.

Tutorial Opening a Presentation Based on a Template

Tutorial Exploring the PowerPoint Screen

Tutorial Running a Slide Show

Tutorial Saving to a Removable Disk

Tutorial Closing a Presentation and Closing PowerPoint

1. At the Windows 10 desktop, click the Start button and then click the PowerPoint 2016 tile at the Start menu.

   Depending on your system configuration, these steps may vary.

2. At the PowerPoint 2016 opening screen, click the *Welcome to PowerPoint* template.

   If this template is not visible, you will need to search for it. To do this, click in the search text box, type Welcome to PowerPoint, and then press the Enter key.

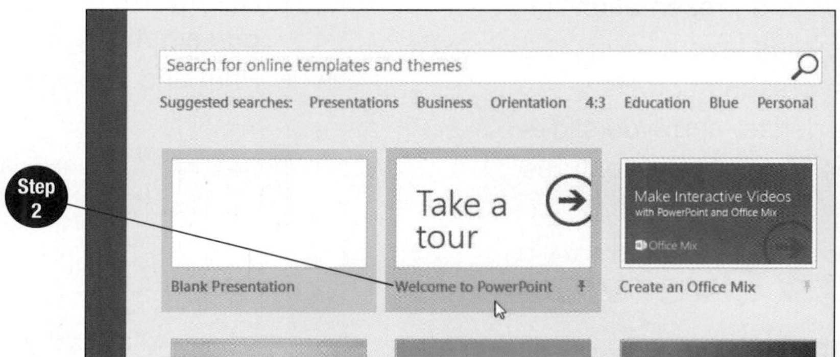

3. Click the Create button.

   The Welcome to PowerPoint template opens in the PowerPoint window. What displays in the PowerPoint window will vary depending on what type of presentation you are creating. However, the PowerPoint window contains some consistent elements, as those identified in Figure 1.1. Refer to Table 1.1 for a description of the window elements.

4. Run the slide show by clicking the Start From Beginning button on the Quick Access Toolbar.

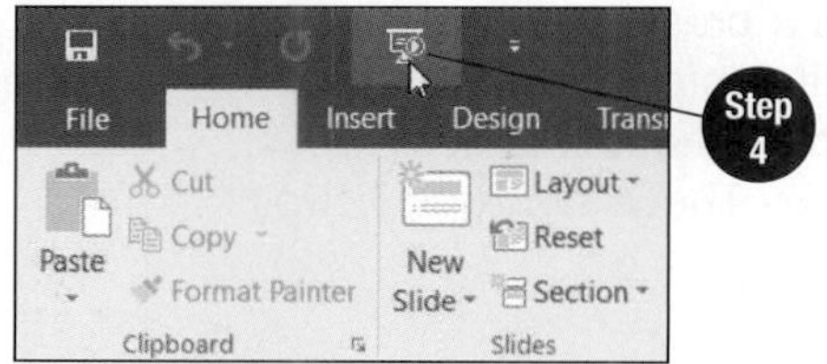

5. When the first slide fills the screen, read the information and then click the left mouse button. Continue reading the information in each slide and clicking the left mouse button to advance to the next slide. When a black screen displays, click the left mouse button to end the slide show.

FIGURE 1.1 PowerPoint Window

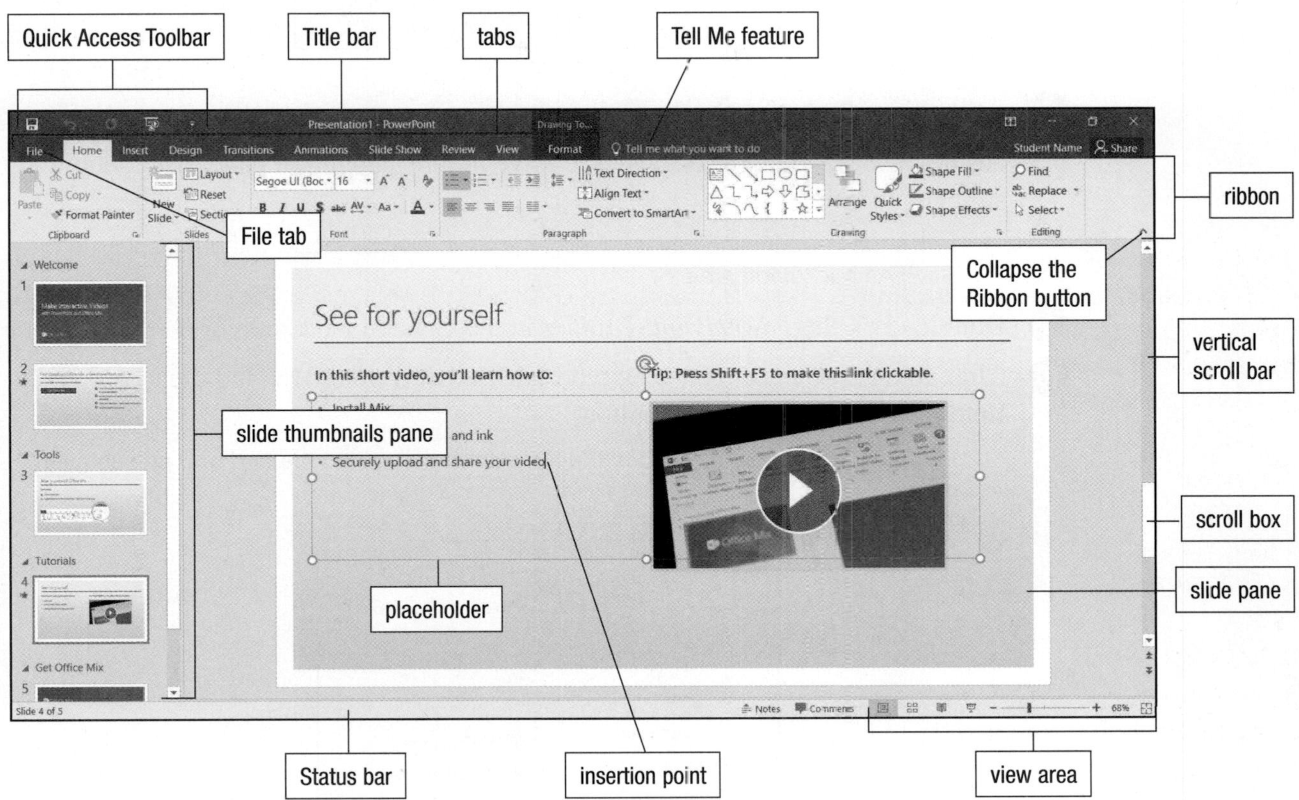

Table 1.1 PowerPoint Window Elements

Feature	Description
Collapse the Ribbon button	when clicked, removes ribbon from screen
File tab	when clicked, displays backstage area that contains options for working with and managing presentations
I-beam pointer	used to move insertion point or to select text
insertion point	indicates location of next character entered at keyboard
Tell Me feature	used to look up features and provide options for using them
placeholder	location on slide with dotted border; holds text or objects
Quick Access Toolbar	contains buttons for commonly used commands
ribbon	area containing tabs with options and buttons divided into groups
scroll box	used to scroll through slides in presentation; click and hold mouse button on scroll box to indicate slide number and title
slide pane	displays slide and slide contents
slide thumbnails pane	left side of screen; displays slide thumbnails
Status bar	displays slide number, view buttons, and Zoom slider bar
tabs	contain commands and buttons organized into groups
Title bar	displays presentation name followed by program name
vertical scroll bar	used to display specific slides
view area	contains buttons for changing presentation view

6 Save the presentation by clicking the Save button on the Quick Access Toolbar.

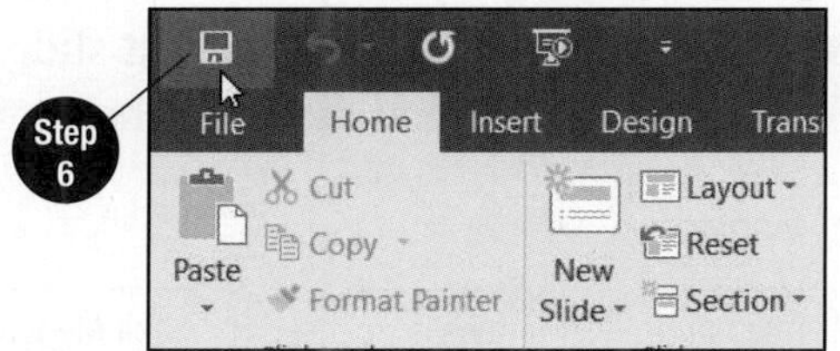

7 At the Save As backstage area, click the *Browse* option.

8 At the Save As dialog box, click the drive in the Navigation pane that contains your storage medium.

Press the F12 function key to display the Save As dialog box without displaying the Save As backstage area.

9 Double-click the *PowerPointS1* folder in the Content pane.

10 Click in the *File name* text box, type 1-MPPowerPoint2016, and then press the Enter key (or click the Save button).

PowerPoint automatically adds the file extension *.pptx* to the end of a presentation name.

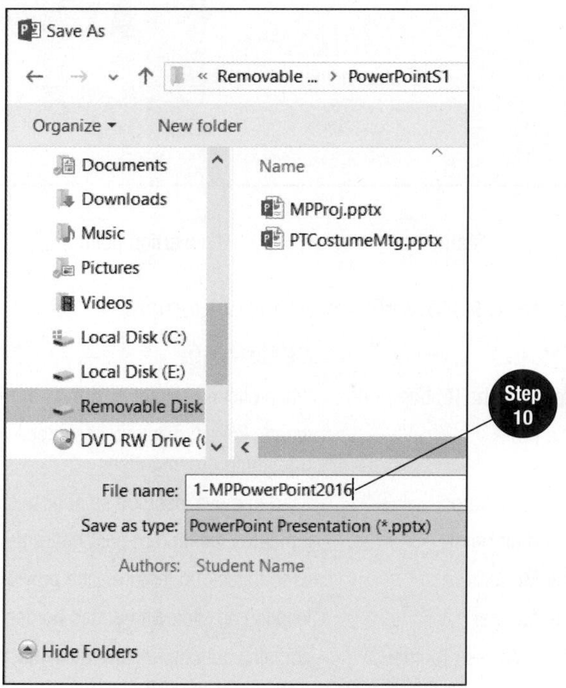

In Brief

Create Presentation with Installed Template
1. Click File tab.
2. Click *New* option.
3. Click template.
4. Click Create button.

Save Presentation
1. Click Save button on Quick Access Toolbar.
2. Click *Browse* option.
3. Navigate to location.
4. At Save As dialog box, type presentation file name.
5. Press Enter.

Run Slide Show
1. Click Start From Beginning button on Quick Access Toolbar.
2. Click left mouse button to advance slides and to end slide show.

Print Presentation in Outline Layout
1. Click File tab.
2. Click *Print* option.
3. Click second gallery in *Settings* category.
4. Click *Outline*.
5. Click Print button.

Close Presentation
1. Click File tab.
2. Click *Close* option.

11. At the PowerPoint window, print the presentation information in outline layout by clicking the File tab and then clicking the *Print* option.

    The File tab is in the upper left corner of the screen at the left side of the Home tab. When you click the File tab, the backstage area displays with options for working with and managing presentations.

12. At the Print backstage area, click the second gallery in the *Settings* category (the gallery containing the text *Full Page Slides*) and then click *Outline* in the *Print Layout* section of the drop-down list.

13. Click the Print button. ***Note: If working in a lab, check with your instructor before printing.***

14. Close the presentation by clicking the File tab and then clicking the *Close* option.

    If a message displays asking if you want to save the presentation, click Yes.

15. Close PowerPoint by clicking the Close button that displays in the upper right corner of the screen.

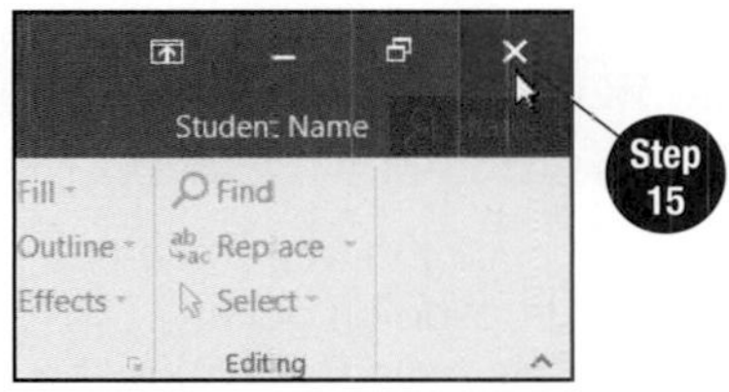

Check Your Work Compare your work to the model answer to ensure that you have completed the activity correctly.

In Addition

Using Tabs

The ribbon area displays below the Quick Access Toolbar. The buttons and options in the ribbon area vary depending on the tab selected and the width of the window displayed on the screen. PowerPoint features are organized into tabs that display in the ribbon area. Commands and buttons are organized into groups within a tab. For example, the Home tab, which is the default tab, contains the Clipboard, Slides, Font, Paragraph, Drawing, and Editing groups. When you hover the mouse pointer over a button, a ScreenTip displays with the name of the button, a keyboard shortcut (if any), and a description of the purpose of the button.

Activity 1.2 Applying a Design Theme and Inserting Text

Create a PowerPoint presentation using an installed template as you did in the previous activity or begin with a blank presentation and apply your own formatting or a slide design theme. To display a blank PowerPoint presentation, use the keyboard shortcut Ctrl + N, or click the File tab, click the *New* option, and then click the *Blank Presentation* template in the New backstage area. A PowerPoint presentation screen displays in Normal view with the slide pane in the center and the slide thumbnails pane at the left side of the screen.

What You Will Do Chris Greenbaum, production manager for Marquee Productions, has asked you to prepare slides for a movie production meeting. You decide to prepare the presentation using a design template offered by PowerPoint.

Tutorial Opening a Blank Presentation

Tutorial Applying a Design Theme

Tutorial Inserting and Deleting Text in Slides

Tutorial Inserting a New Slide

1. Open PowerPoint.
2. At the PowerPoint 2016 opening screen, click the *Blank Presentation* template.
3. At the PowerPoint window, click the Design tab.
4. Click the More Themes button in the Themes group.

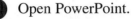

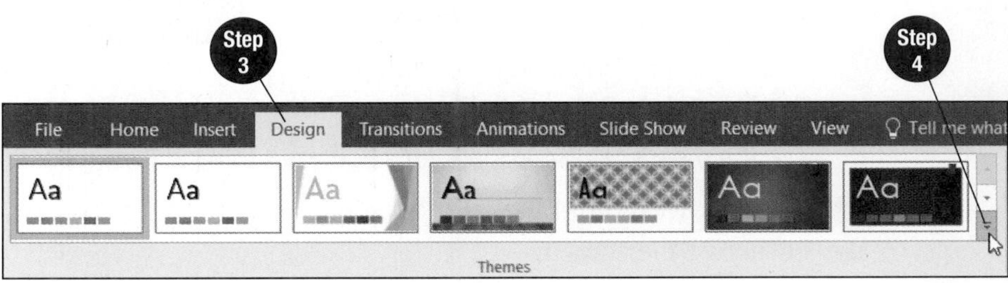

5. Click the *Wisp* option in the *Office* section of the drop-down gallery.

   When you click the More Themes button, a drop-down gallery displays. This gallery contains the live preview feature. When you hover your mouse pointer over one of the design themes, the slide in the slide pane displays with the design theme formatting applied. With the live preview feature, you can view a design theme before actually applying it to the presentation.

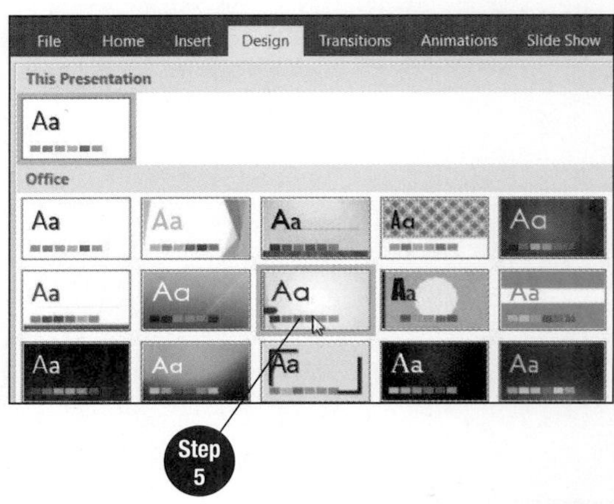

6. Click the second option from the left in the Variants group.

   This changes the tab at the left side of the slide to a dark gold color.

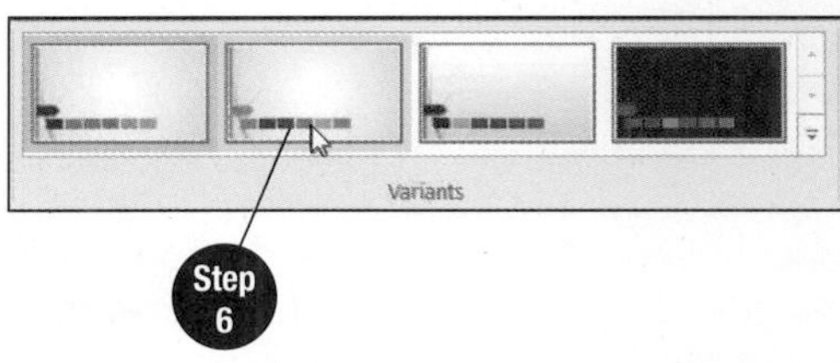

7 Click anywhere in the *Click to add title* placeholder that displays in the slide in the slide pane and then type Marquee Productions.

A placeholder is a location on a slide that is marked with a border and holds text or an object.

8 Click anywhere in the *Click to add subtitle* placeholder that displays in the slide and then type Movie Production Meeting.

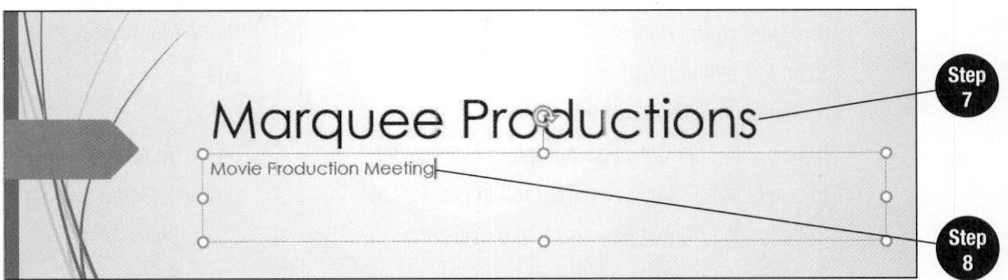

9 Click the Home tab and then click the New Slide button in the Slides group.

When you click this button, a new slide displays in the slide pane with the Title and Content layout. You will learn more about slide layouts in Activity 1.3.

10 Click anywhere in the *Click to add title* placeholder that displays in the slide and then type Agenda.

11 Click anywhere in the *Click to add text* placeholder that displays in the slide and then type Production Team.

12 Press the Enter key and then type the following agenda items, pressing the Enter key after each item except the last one: Production Assignments, Production Schedule, Locations, and Summary.

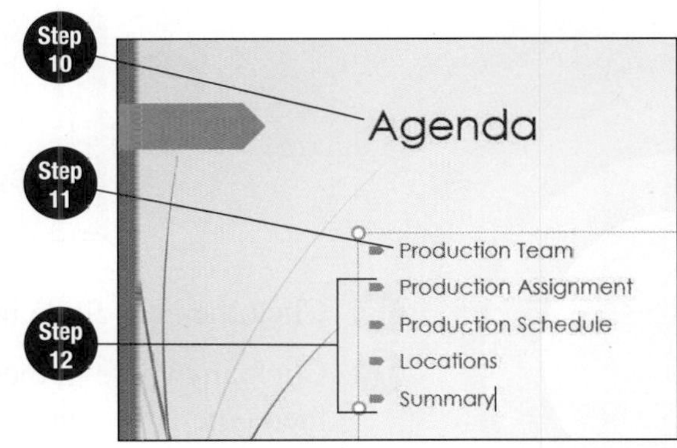

You can use keys on the keyboard to move the insertion point to various locations within a placeholder in a slide. Refer to Table 1.2 on the next page for a list of insertion point movement commands.

13 Click the New Slide button in the Slides group on the Home tab.

Table 1.2 Insertion Point Movement Commands

To move insertion point	Press
One character left	Left Arrow
One character right	Right Arrow
One line up	Up Arrow
One line down	Down Arrow
One word to the left	Ctrl + Left Arrow
One word to the right	Ctrl + Right Arrow
To end of a line of text	End
To beginning of a line of text	Home
To beginning of current paragraph in placeholder	Ctrl + Up Arrow
To beginning of previous paragraph in placeholder	Ctrl + Up Arrow two times
To beginning of next paragraph in placeholder	Ctrl + Down Arrow
To beginning of text in placeholder	Ctrl + Home
To end of text in placeholder	Ctrl + End

14. Click anywhere in the *Click to add title* placeholder that displays in the slide and then type Department Reports.

15. Click anywhere in the *Click to add text* placeholder that displays in the slide and then type the bulleted text as shown in the slide below. Press the Enter key after each item except the last one.

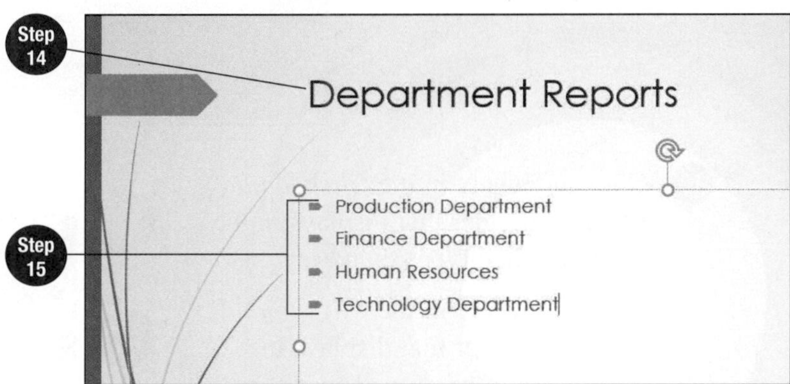

16. Click the New Slide button in the Slides group on the Home tab.

17. Click anywhere in the *Click to add title* placeholder that displays in the slide and then type Locations.

18. Click anywhere in the *Click to add text* placeholder that displays in the slide, type Studio Shoots, and then press the Enter key.

19. Press the Tab key, type Vancouver Studio, and then press the Enter key.

    Pressing the Tab key demotes the insertion point to a second-level bullet, while pressing Shift + Tab promotes the insertion point back to the first level.

20. Type Los Angeles Studio and then press the Enter key.

In Brief

Choose Design Theme
1. Click Design tab.
2. Click More Themes button.
3. Click theme at drop-down gallery.

Insert New Slide
1. Click Home tab.
2. Click New Slide button.

21. Press Shift + Tab, type Location Shoots, and then press the Enter key.
22. Press the Tab key, type Stanley Park, and then press the Enter key.
23. Type Downtown Streets.

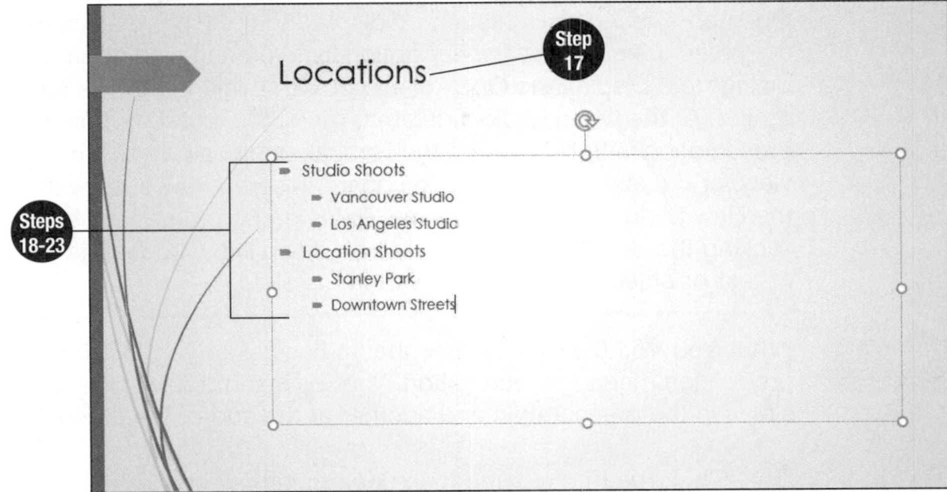

24. Click the Save button on the Quick Access Toolbar.
25. At the Save As backstage area, click the *Browse* option.
26. At the Save As dialog box, click the drive in the Navigation pane that contains your storage medium.
27. Double-click the *PowerPointS1* folder in the Content pane.
28. Click in the *File name* text box, type 1-MPProdMtg, and then press the Enter key (or click the Save button).
29. Close the presentation by clicking the File tab and then clicking the *Close* option.

Check Your Work Compare your work to the model answer to ensure that you have completed the activity correctly.

In Addition

Planning a Presentation

Consider the following basic guidelines when preparing content for a presentation:

- **Determine the main purpose.** Do not try to cover too many topics. Identifying the main point of the presentation will help you stay focused and convey a clear message to the audience.
- **Determine the output.** To help decide the type of output needed, consider the availability of equipment, the size of the room where you will make the presentation, and the number of people who will be attending the presentation.
- **Show one idea per slide.** Each slide in a presentation should convey only one main idea. Too many ideas on a slide may confuse the audience and cause you to stray from the purpose of the slide.
- **Maintain a consistent design.** A consistent design and color scheme for slides in a presentation will create continuity and cohesiveness. Do not use too much color or too many images or other graphic elements.
- **Keep slides uncluttered and easy to read.** Keep slides simple to make them easy for your audience to understand. Keep words and other items, such as bullets, to a minimum.
- **Determine printing needs.** Will you be providing audience members with handouts? If so, will these handouts consist of a printing of each slide? an outline of the presentation? a printing of each slide with space for taking notes?

Activity 1.3 Opening, Navigating, and Inserting Slides; Choosing a Slide Layout

Open an existing presentation by displaying the Open backstage area and then clicking the presentation in the *Recent* option list. You can also open a presentation at the Open dialog box. Display the Open dialog box by clicking the File tab and then clicking the *Open* option. At the Open backstage area, click the *Browse* option. Navigate through slides in a presentation with buttons on the vertical scroll bar, by clicking slide thumbnails in Normal view, or by using keys on the keyboard. Insert a new slide with a specific layout by clicking the New Slide button arrow in the Slides group on the Home tab or the Insert tab and then clicking the desired layout at the drop-down list. Choose the layout that matches the type of text or object you want to insert in the slide.

What You Will Do Chris Greenbaum has asked you to add more information to the movie production meeting presentation. You will insert a new slide between the second and third slides in the presentation and another at the end of the presentation.

Tutorial Opening from a Removable Disk

Tutorial Navigating to Slides

Tutorial Choosing a Slide Layout

Tutorial Saving with the Same Name

1. Click the File tab and then click the *Open* option.
2. At the Open backstage area, click the *Browse* option.
3. In the Navigation pane of the Open dialog box, click the drive where your USB flash drive is located (such as *Removable Disk (F:)*).

   You can also display the Open dialog box without displaying the Open backstage area by pressing Ctrl + F12.
4. Double-click the *PowerPointS1* folder in the Content pane.
5. Double-click ***1-MPProdMtg.pptx*** in the Content pane.
6. With **1-MPProdMtg.pptx** open, click the Next Slide button at the bottom of the vertical scroll bar.

   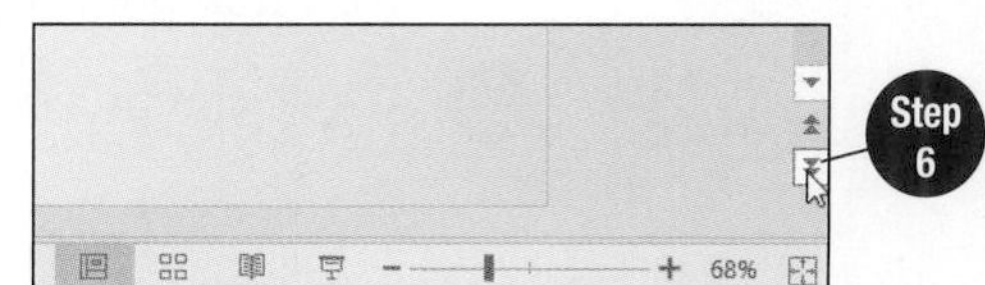

   Clicking this button displays the next slide, Slide 2, in the presentation. Notice that *Slide 2 of 4* displays at the left side of the Status bar.
7. Click the Previous Slide button above the Next Slide button to display Slide 1.

   When you click the Previous Slide button, Slide 1 displays in the slide pane and *Slide 1 of 4* displays at the left side of the Status bar.
8. Display Slide 2 in the slide pane by clicking the second slide in the slide thumbnails pane (the slide titled *Agenda*).
9. Insert a new slide between Slides 2 and 3 by clicking the New Slide button in the Slides group on the Home tab.

   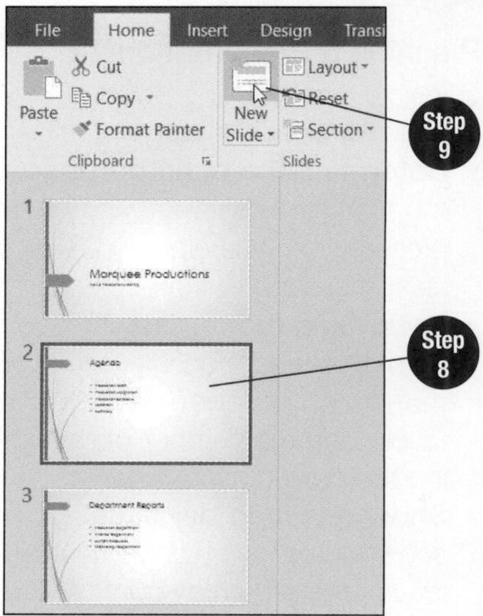

   When you select a slide in the slide thumbnails pane and then click the New Slide button, the new slide is inserted after the selected slide.

In Brief

Open Presentation from Removable Disk

1. Press Ctrl + F12.
2. In the Navigation pane of the Open dialog box, click the drive containing the removable disk.
3. Double-click folder in Content pane.
4. Double-click presentation in Content pane.

10. Click in the *Click to add title* placeholder in the slide in the slide pane and then type Production Schedule.

11. Click in the *Click to add text* placeholder in the slide and then type the bulleted text as shown at the right. Press the Enter key after typing each item except the last one.

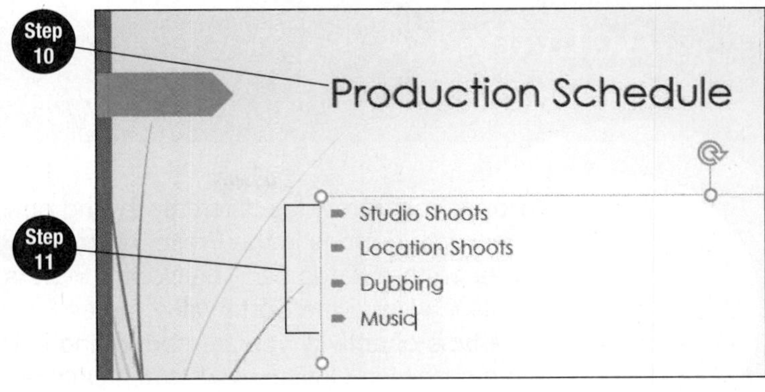

12. Click below the last thumbnail in the slide thumbnails pane. (You may need to scroll down the slide thumbnails pane to display the last slide.)

    When you click below the slide thumbnail, an orange horizontal line displays below Slide 5.

13. Click the New Slide button arrow on the Home tab and then click the *Title Slide* layout that displays in the drop-down list.

14. Click in the *Click to add title* placeholder and then type Production Leader.

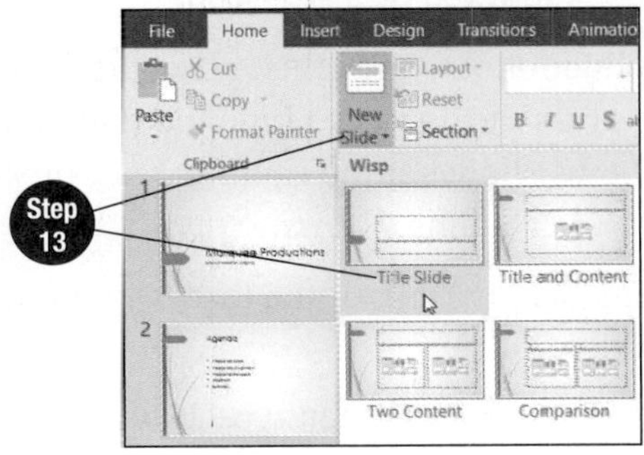

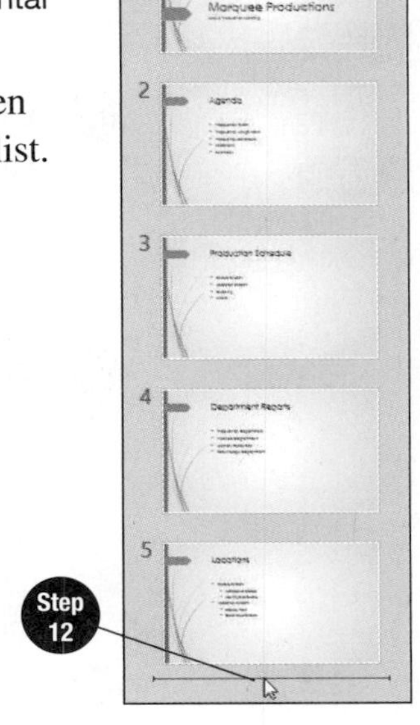

15. Click in the *Click to add subtitle* placeholder and then type Chris Greenbaum.

16. Click the Save button on the Quick Access Toolbar to save **1-MPProdMtg.pptx**.

Check Your Work Compare your work to the model answer to ensure that you have completed the activity correctly.

In Addition

Opening a Presentation from the *Recent* Option List

At the Open backstage area with the *Recent* option selected, a list of the most recently opened presentations display. The presentations are grouped into categories such as *Today*, *Yesterday*, and possibly *This Week* and *Older*. To open a presentation from the *Recent* option list, open PowerPoint to display the opening screen or display the Open backstage area with the *Recent* option selected and then click the desired presentation in the list.

Activity 1.4 Changing Views

PowerPoint provides different viewing options for a presentation. Change the presentation view with buttons in the Presentation Views group on the View tab or with buttons in the view area on the Status bar. The Normal view is the default view, and you can change the view to Outline view, Slide Sorter view, Notes Page view, or Reading view. Choose the view based on the type of activity you are performing in the presentation. Another method for entering text in a slide is in Outline view. When Outline view is active, the slide thumbnails pane changes to an outline pane for entering text. Insert speaker's notes into a presentation using the notes pane, which can be displayed by clicking the Notes button on the Status bar.

Tutorial Changing Views

Tutorial Entering Text in the Outline Pane

Tutorial Changing the Display of a Slide in the Slide Pane

What You Will Do After reviewing the movie production presentation, Chris Greenbaum has asked you to add a new slide and edit an existing slide.

1. With **1-MPProdMtg.pptx** open, click the View tab and then click the Outline View button in the Presentation Views group.

2. Click immediately right of the text *Music* in the third slide (located toward the middle of the outline pane), press the Enter key, and then press Shift + Tab.

   This moves the insertion point back a level and inserts the number *4* followed by a slide icon.

3. Type Production Assignments, press the Enter key, and then press the Tab key. Type the remaining text for Slide 4 as shown at the right. Do not press the Enter key after typing *Extras*.

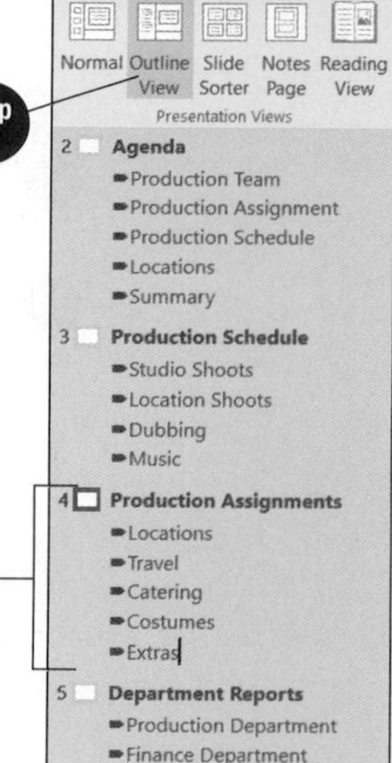

4. Click immediately right of the text *Location Shoots* in the third slide.

5. Press the Enter key and then type Editing.

   This inserts *Editing* between *Location Shoots* and *Dubbing*.

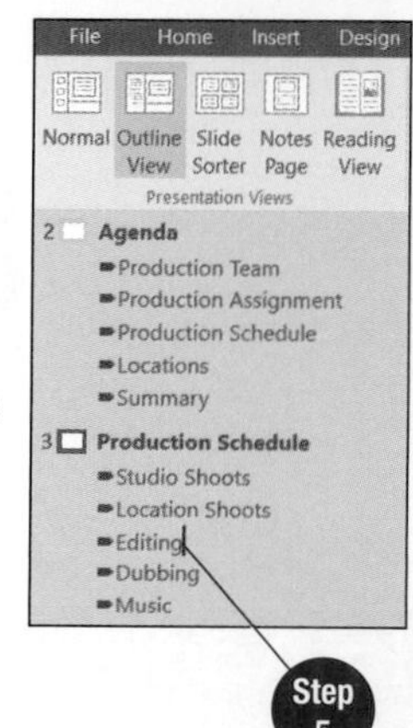

6. Make Slide 6 the active slide in the slide pane, click in the *Click to add notes* placeholder in the notes pane (if the text is not visible, click the Notes button on the Status bar to display the notes pane), and then type Camille Matsui will report on the park location.

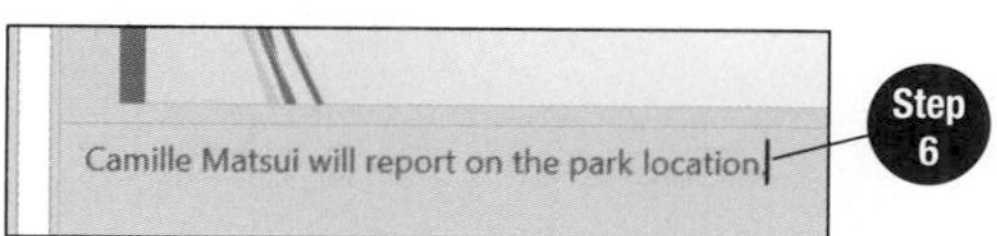

7. Display the slides in Notes Page view by clicking the Notes Page button in the Presentation Views group.

   In Notes Page view, an individual slide displays on a page with any added notes displayed below it. Notice that the note you created about Camille Matsui displays below the slide in the page.

8. Click the Previous Slide button on the vertical scroll bar until Slide 1 displays.

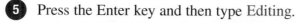

In Brief

Display in Normal View
1. Click View tab.
2. Click Normal button.

OR
Click Normal button on Status bar.

Display in Outline View
1. Click View tab.
2. Click Outline View button.

Display in Slide Sorter View
1. Click View tab.
2. Click Slide Sorter button.

OR
Click Slide Sorter button on Status bar.

Display in Notes Page View
1. Click View tab.
2. Click Notes Page button.

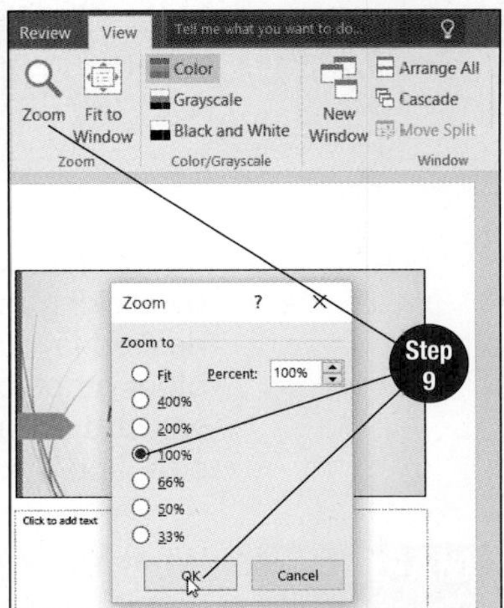

9 Increase the zoom by clicking the Zoom button in the Zoom group on the View tab, clicking *100%* at the Zoom dialog box, and then clicking OK.

10 You can also change the zoom using the Zoom slider bar. Change the zoom by positioning the mouse pointer on the Zoom slider button at the right side of the Status bar. Hold down the left mouse button, drag to the right until the zoom percentage at the right side of the Zoom slider bar displays as approximately *138%*, and then release the mouse button.

11 Click the Zoom Out button at the left side of the Zoom slider bar until *70%* displays at the right side of the slider bar.

Click the Zoom Out button to decrease the zoom display and click the Zoom In button to increase the display.

12 View all slides in the presentation as slide thumbnails by clicking the Slide Sorter button in the view area on the Status bar.

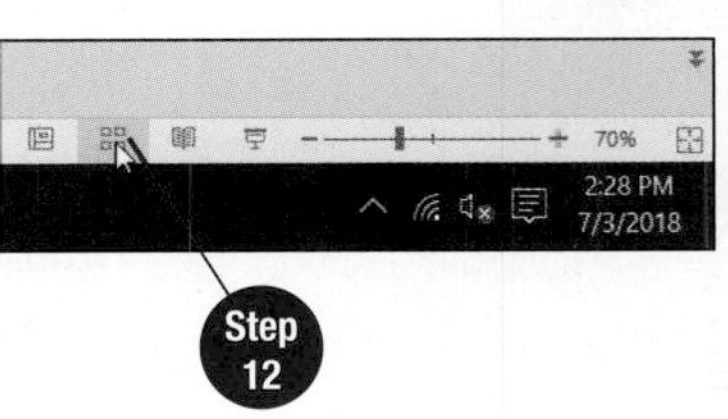

13 View the presentation in Reading view by clicking the Reading View button in the Presentation Views group.

Use Reading view to show the presentation to someone viewing the presentation on his or her own computer. You can also use Reading view to view a presentation in a window with controls that make the presentation easy to view. In Reading view, navigation buttons display in the lower right corner of the screen immediately left of the view area on the Status bar.

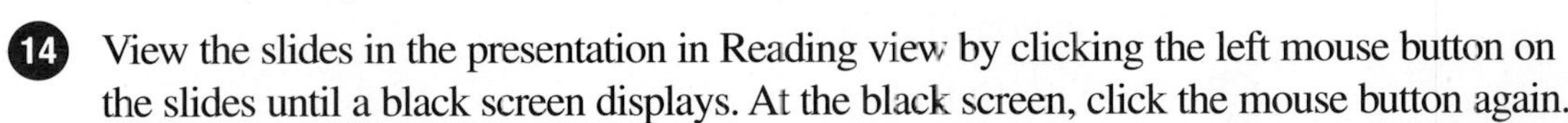

14 View the slides in the presentation in Reading view by clicking the left mouse button on the slides until a black screen displays. At the black screen, click the mouse button again.

This returns the presentation to the previous view—in this case, Slide Sorter view.

15 Return the presentation to Normal view by clicking the Normal button in the Presentation Views group.

16 If necessary, close the notes pane by clicking the Notes button on the Status bar.

17 Save **1-MPProdMtg.pptx**.

Check Your Work Compare your work to the model answer to ensure that you have completed the activity correctly.

In Addition

Navigating Using the Keyboard

You can also use the keyboard to display slides in a presentation. In Normal view, press the Down Arrow or Page Down key to display the next slide or press the Up Arrow or Page Up key to display the previous slide in the presentation. Press the Home key to display the first slide in the presentation and press the End key to display the last slide in the presentation. Navigate in Outline view and Slide Sorter view by using the arrow keys on the keyboard. Navigate in Reading view by using the Right Arrow key to move to the next slide or the Left Arrow key to move to the previous slide.

Activity 1.5 Changing the Slide Layout; Selecting and Moving a Placeholder

So far, you have created slides based on a default slide layout. Change the slide layout by clicking the Layout button in the Slides group on the Home tab and then clicking the desired layout at the drop-down list. Objects in a slide, such as text, charts, tables, and other graphic elements, are generally positioned in placeholders. Click the text or object to select the placeholder and a dashed border will surround the placeholder. You can move, size, and/or delete a selected placeholder.

What You Will Do You have decided to make a few changes to the layout of slides in the movie production presentation.

Tutorial Modifying Placeholders

Tutorial Changing Slide Layout

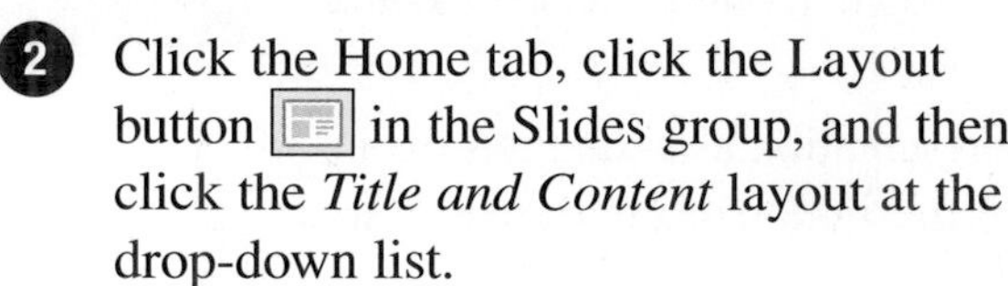

1. With **1-MPProdMtg.pptx** open, make Slide 7 active in the slide pane.
2. Click the Home tab, click the Layout button in the Slides group, and then click the *Title and Content* layout at the drop-down list.

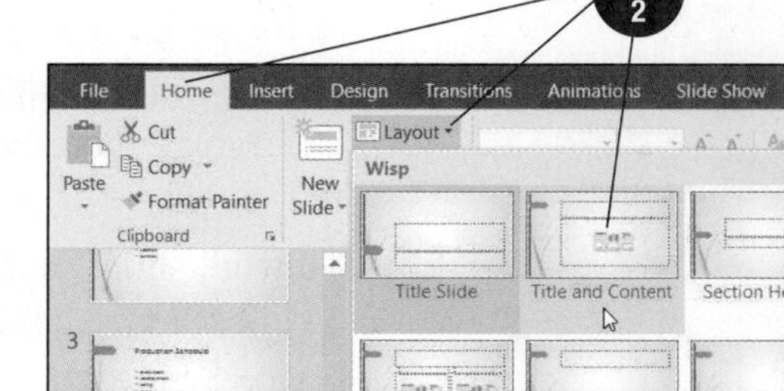

3. Click immediately right of the *r* in *Leader* (this selects the placeholder), press the Backspace key until *Leader* is deleted, and then type Team.

   Sizing handles display around the selected placeholder. Use these sizing handles to increase and/or decrease the size of the placeholder.

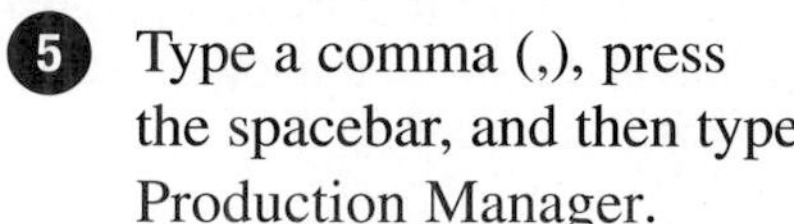

4. Click immediately right of the *m* in *Greenbaum.*
5. Type a comma (,), press the spacebar, and then type Production Manager.
6. Press the Enter key and then type the remaining names and titles shown in the slide at the right. (Do not press the Enter key after typing *Josh Hart, Locations Director*.)

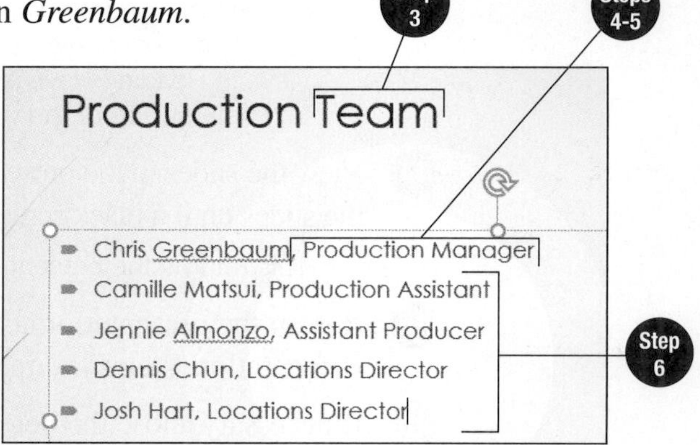

7. Click the Previous Slide button on the vertical scroll bar until Slide 4 displays.
8. Change the slide layout by clicking the Layout button in the Slides group and then clicking the *Title Slide* layout at the drop-down list.
9. Click in the title *Production Assignments.*

   This selects the placeholder.

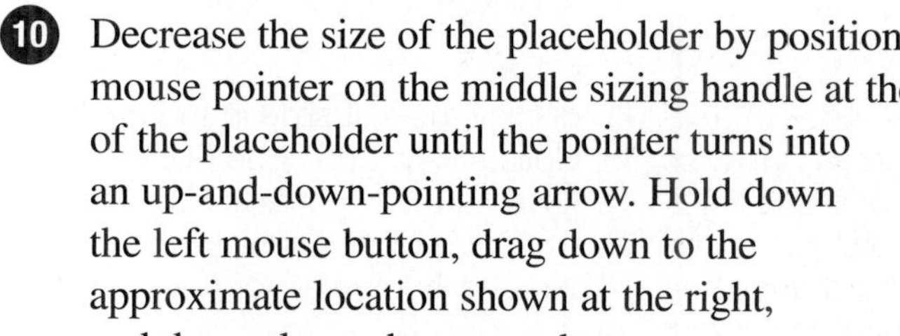

10. Decrease the size of the placeholder by positioning the mouse pointer on the middle sizing handle at the top of the placeholder until the pointer turns into an up-and-down-pointing arrow. Hold down the left mouse button, drag down to the approximate location shown at the right, and then release the mouse button.

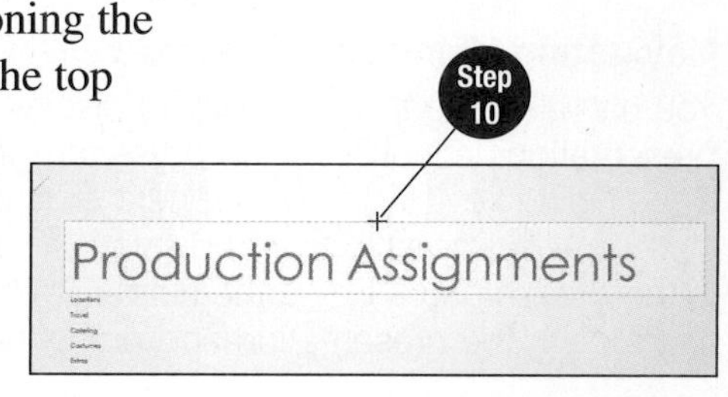

In Brief

Change Slide Layout
1. Make slide active.
2. Click Home tab.
3. Click Layout button.
4. Click layout.

Move Placeholder
1. Click inside placeholder.
2. Drag with mouse to new position.

Size Placeholder
1. Click inside placeholder.
2. Drag sizing handles to increase/decrease size.

11 Move the title placeholder so it positions the title as shown in Figure 1.2. To do this, position the mouse pointer on the placeholder border until the mouse pointer displays with a four-headed arrow attached, hold down the left mouse button, drag to the approximate location shown in the figure, and then release the mouse button.

12 Increase the size of the subtitle placeholder (and the size of the text). Begin by clicking in the word *Locations*.

This selects the placeholder containing the text.

13 Position the mouse pointer on the middle sizing handle at the top of the placeholder until the pointer turns into an up-and-down-pointing arrow. Hold down the left mouse button, drag up approximately one inch, and then release the mouse button.

Increasing the size of the placeholder automatically increases the size of the text in the placeholder. This is because, by default, PowerPoint automatically sizes the contents to fit the placeholder. Read the In Addition at the bottom of this page for information on the AutoFit Options button.

14 Move the content placeholder so it positions the text as shown in Figure 1.2. To do this, position the mouse pointer on the placeholder border until the mouse pointer displays with a four-headed arrow attached, hold down the left mouse button, drag to the approximate location shown in the figure, and then release the mouse button.

Figure 1.2 Slide 4

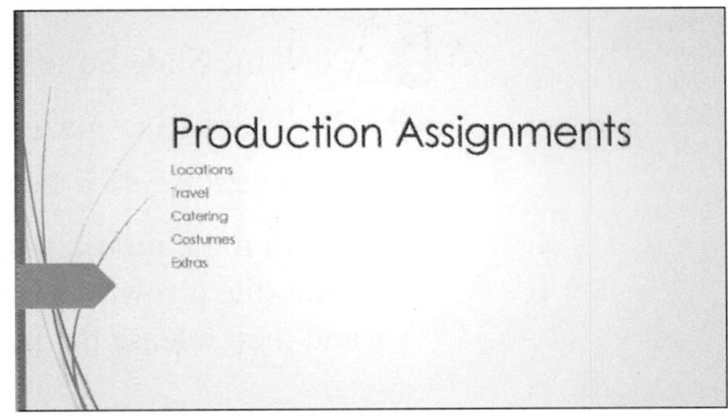

15 Click outside the placeholder to deselect it.

If you are not satisfied with the changes you make to a placeholder, click the Reset button in the Slides group on the Home tab. This resets the placeholder's position, size, and formatting to the default settings.

16 Save **1-MPProdMtg.pptx**.

Check Your Work Compare your work to the model answer to ensure that you have completed the activity correctly.

In Addition

Using the AutoFit Options Button

If you decrease the size of a placeholder so the existing text does not fit within it, PowerPoint will automatically decrease the size of the text so it fits in the placeholder. If you click anywhere in the text that has been decreased in size, an AutoFit Options button displays at the left side of the placeholder. Click the AutoFit Options button and a list of choices displays for positioning objects in the placeholder, as shown at the right. The *AutoFit Text to Placeholder* option is selected by default and tells PowerPoint to fit text within the boundaries of the placeholder. Click the middle choice, *Stop Fitting Text to This Placeholder*, and PowerPoint will not automatically fit the text or object within the placeholder. Choose the last option, *Control AutoCorrect Options*, to display the AutoCorrect dialog box with the AutoFormat As You Type tab selected. Additional options may display depending upon the placeholder and the type of data it contains.

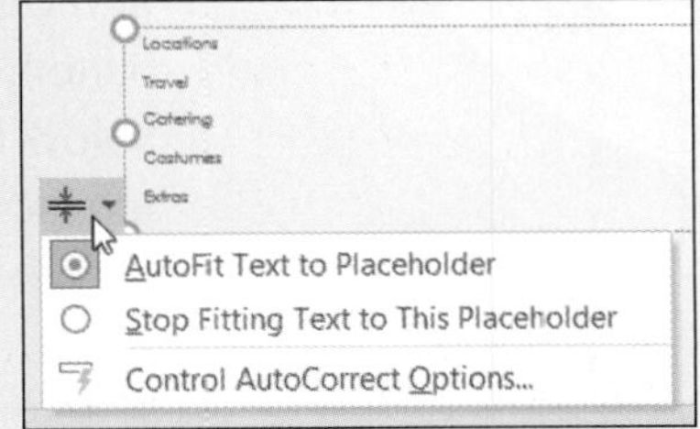

Activity 1.6 Rearranging, Deleting, and Hiding Slides

As you edit a presentation, you may need to rearrange, delete, or hide specific slides. PowerPoint provides various views for creating and managing a presentation. Manage slides in the slide thumbnails pane or in Slide Sorter view. Switch to Slide Sorter view by clicking the Slide Sorter button in the view area on the Status bar or by clicking the View tab and then clicking the Slide Sorter button in the Presentation Views group.

What You Will Do Chris Greenbaum has asked you to make some changes to the presentation, including rearranging the slides, deleting a slide, and hiding a slide.

Tutorial Rearranging Slides

Tutorial Deleting Slides

Tutorial Hiding and Unhiding Slides

1. With **1-MPProdMtg.pptx** open, click Slide 5 in the slide thumbnails pane and then press the Delete key on the keyboard.

   You can also delete a slide by right-clicking the slide in the slide thumbnails pane and then clicking *Delete Slide* at the shortcut menu.

2. Click the Slide Sorter button in the view area on the Status bar.
3. Click Slide 6 to make it active.

   A selected slide displays with an orange border.

4. Position the mouse pointer on Slide 6, hold down the left mouse button, drag the slide (the arrow pointer will display with a square attached) to the left of Slide 3, and then release the mouse button.

Step 4

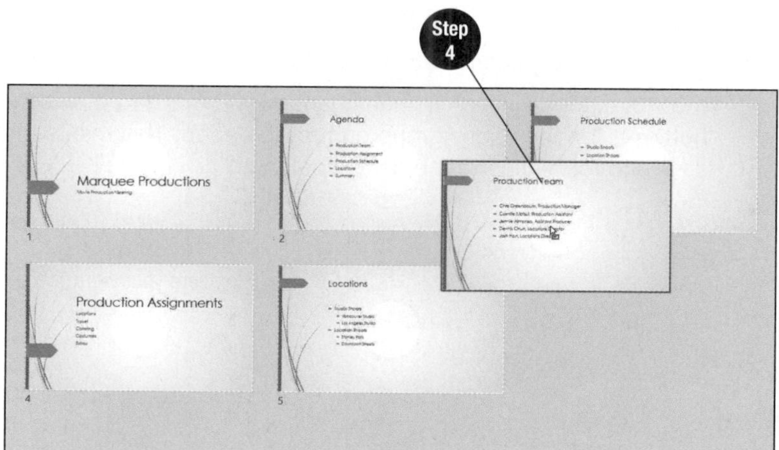

5. Click the Normal button in the view area on the Status bar.
6. Position the mouse pointer on the Slide 5 thumbnail in the slide thumbnails pane, hold down the left mouse button, drag up until the slide displays immediately below the Slide 3 thumbnail, and then release the mouse button.

Step 6

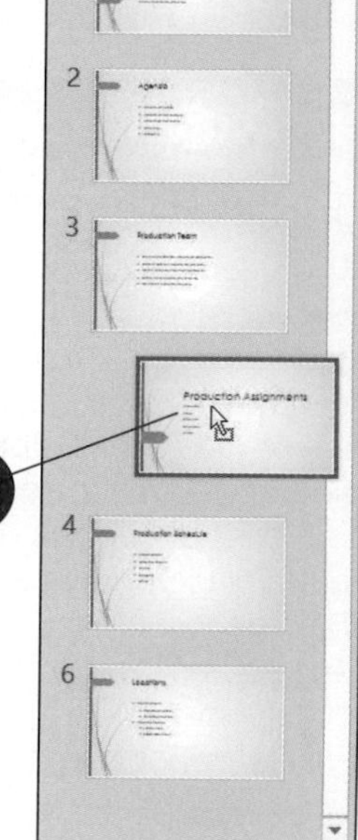

In Brief

Delete Slide
1. Right-click slide thumbnails.
2. Click *Delete Slide*.

OR
1. Click slide in slide thumbnails pane.
2. Press Delete key.

Move Slide
1. Click Slide Sorter button on Status bar.
2. Click slide.
3. Drag slide to position.

OR
1. Click slide in slide thumbnails pane.
2. Drag slide to new position.

Hide Slide
1. Click slide thumbnail.
2. Click Slide Show tab.
3. Click Hide Slide button.

7. With the Slide 4 thumbnail selected in the slide thumbnails pane (thumbnail displays with an orange border), hide the slide by clicking the Slide Show tab and then clicking the Hide Slide button in the Set Up group.

   When a slide is hidden, the slide thumbnail displays dimmed and the slide number displays with a diagonal line across the number.

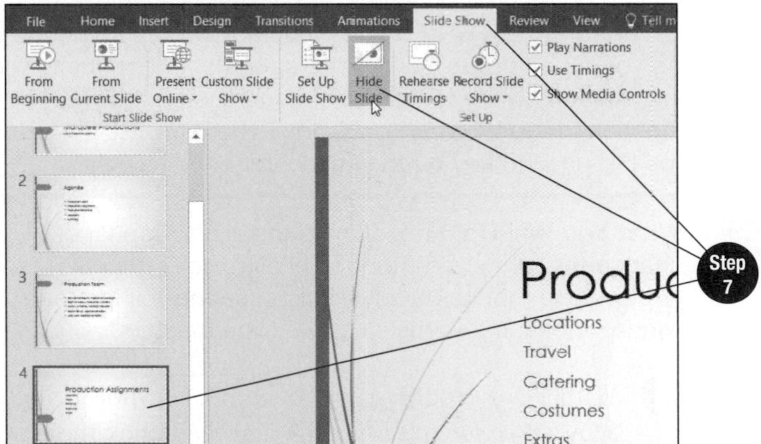

8. Run the slide show by clicking the From Beginning button in the Start Slide Show group. Click the left mouse button to advance each slide until a black screen displays. At the black screen, click the left mouse button again.
9. After running the slide show, you decide to redisplay the hidden slide. To do this, make sure the Slide 4 thumbnail is selected in the slide thumbnails pane and then click the Hide Slide button in the Set Up group.
10. Save **1-MPProdMtg.pptx**.

Check Your Work Compare your work to the model answer to ensure that you have completed the activity correctly.

In Addition

Copying Slides within a Presentation

Copying a slide within a presentation is similar to moving a slide. To copy a slide, position the arrow pointer on the desired slide and hold down the Ctrl key and the left mouse button. Drag to the location where you want the slide copied, release the left mouse button, and then release the Ctrl key. When you drag with the mouse, the mouse pointer displays with a square and a plus symbol attached.

Activity 1.7 Using the Tell Me and Help Features

PowerPoint includes the Tell Me feature, which provides information as well as guidance on how to complete a function. To use Tell Me, click in the *Tell Me* text box that displays on the ribbon to the right of the View tab and then type the function for which you want help. As you type, a drop-down list displays with options for completing the function, displaying information on the function from sources on the web, or for displaying information on the function in the Word Help window. The Word Help window can also be opened by pressing the F1 function key on the keyboard.

What You Will Do To enhance the visual appeal of Slide 1 in the presentation, you will change the font size of the subtitle *Movie Production Meeting*, using the Tell Me feature to complete the task. You will also use the Tell Me feature to access the PowerPoint Help window and locate articles about slide masters.

Tutorial
Using the Tell Me Feature

Tutorial
Using the Help Feature

1. With 1-MPProdMtg.pptx open, make Slide 1 the active slide, click in the subtitle *Movie Production Meeting*, and then click the border of the placeholder to select it.
2. Click in the *Tell Me* text box.

   The *Tell Me* text box is located on the ribbon to the right of the View tab and contains the text *Tell me what you want to do*. When you click in the text box, the last five functions entered will display in a drop-down list.

3. Type font size in the *Tell Me* text box.

   A drop-down list displays with options such as *Font Size*, *Decrease Font Size*, *Increase Font Size*, *Font Settings*, and *Font*.

4. Position the mouse pointer on the *Font Size* option at the drop-down list.

   When you position the mouse pointer on the *Font Size* option, a side menu displays.

5. At the side menu that displays, click *28*.

   The 28-point font size is applied to the selected title. The Tell Me feature guided you through the process of changing font size without you having to learn how to change font size using a button on the ribbon or an option at a dialog box.

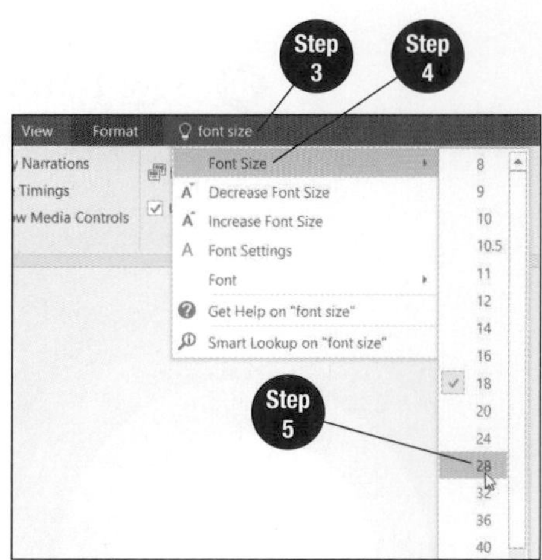

6. The Tell Me feature also includes access to the PowerPoint Help window. To display the PowerPoint Help window with information on slide masters, click in the *Tell Me* text box and then type slide master.
7. Click *Get Help on "slide master"* option at the drop-down list.

   The PowerPoint Help window opens with articles on slide masters. You can also display the Help window by pressing the F1 function key.

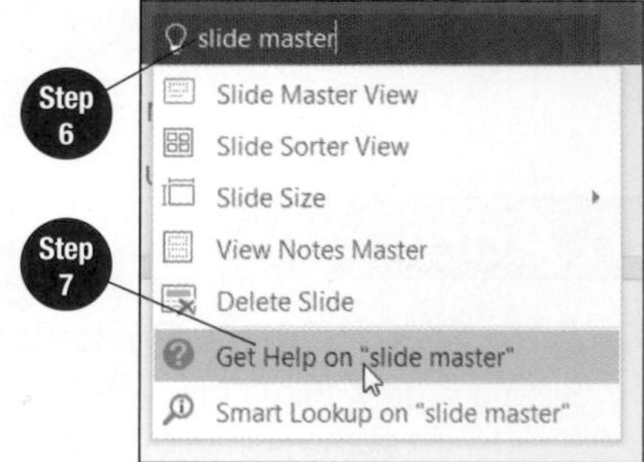

8. At the PowerPoint Help window, click the first article hyperlink that displays in the list box.

   Clicking the hyperlink opens the article in the PowerPoint Help window.

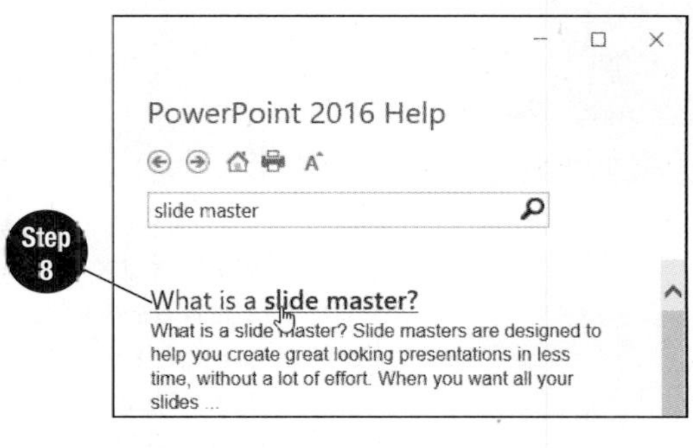

9. The PowerPoint Help window contains five buttons for navigating and managing the window. Click the Back button (contains a left-pointing arrow) in the PowerPoint Help window to display the previous window.
10. Click the Use Large Text button to increase the display of text in the window.
11. Click the Home button to return to the opening PowerPoint Help window.
12. Close the PowerPoint Help window by clicking the Close button in the upper right corner of the window.

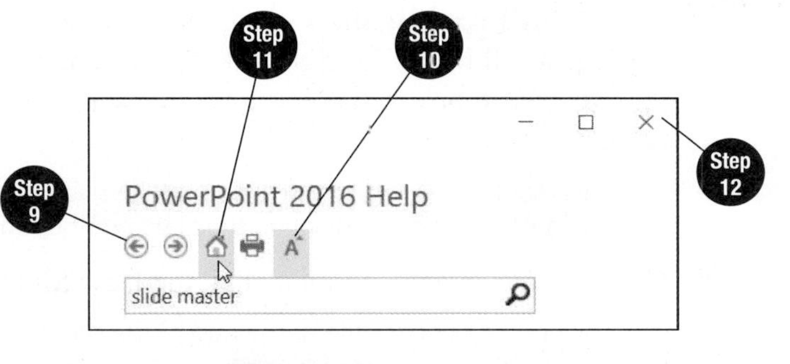

Check Your Work Compare your work to the model answer to ensure that you have completed the activity correctly.

In Addition

Accessing Smart Lookup

Using the Smart Lookup feature, you can access information on a function from a variety of sources on the web such as Wikipedia, Bing, and the Oxford Dictionary. The Tell Me feature is one way to access Smart Lookup. To use Tell Me for Smart Lookup, click in the *Tell Me* text box, type the function on which you want to display information, and then click the *Smart Lookup* option that displays in the drop-down list. Clicking the *Smart Lookup* option displays the Smart Lookup task pane at the right side of the screen with information on the function from a variety of locations on the Internet. Smart Lookup can also be accessed with the Smart Lookup button on the Review tab or by selecting text on which you want additional information, right-clicking the selected text, and then clicking *Smart Lookup* at the shortcut menu.

Getting Help on Specific Functions

Some dialog boxes and backstage areas contain a help button you can click to display the PowerPoint Help window with specific information about the functions in the dialog box or backstage area. If you hover your mouse over some buttons, the ScreenTip that displays may include a Help icon and the text *Tell me more*. Click this hyperlinked text and the PowerPoint Help window opens with information about the button feature. You can also hover the mouse pointer over a button and then press F1 to display the Word Help window with information about the button feature.

Activity 1.8 Checking Spelling; Using the Thesaurus

Use PowerPoint's spelling checker to find and correct misspelled words and duplicated words (such as *and and*). The spelling checker compares words in your slides with words in its dictionary. If a match is found, the word is passed over. If no match is found, the spelling checker stops, selects the word, and offers replacements. Use the Thesaurus to find synonyms, antonyms, and related words for a particular word. To use the Thesaurus, click the word for which you want to display synonyms and antonyms, click the Review tab, and then click the Thesaurus button in the Proofing group. This displays the Thesaurus task pane with information about the word in which the insertion point is positioned.

What You Will Do You have decided to create a new slide in the movie production presentation. Because several changes have been made to the presentation, you know that checking the spelling of all the slide text is important. Complete a spelling check of all slides and then use the Thesaurus to replace a couple of words with synonyms.

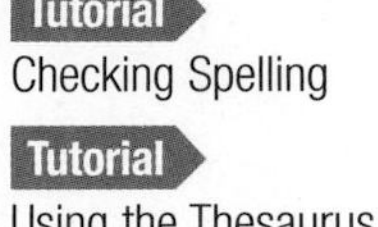

1. With **1-MPProdMtg.pptx** open, position the mouse pointer on the scroll box on the vertical scroll bar at the right side of the screen. Hold down the left mouse button, drag the scroll box to the bottom of the scroll bar, and then release the mouse button.

   This displays Slide 6 in the slide pane. As you drag the scroll box on the vertical scroll bar, a box displays indicating the slide number and slide title (if the slide contains a title).

2. Click the Home tab and then click the New Slide button in the Slides group.

   This inserts a new slide at the end of the presentation.

3. Click in the *Click to add title* placeholder and then type Summary.

4. Click in the *Click to add text* placeholder and then type the text shown in the slide at the right.

   Type the words exactly as shown. You will check the spelling in the next steps.

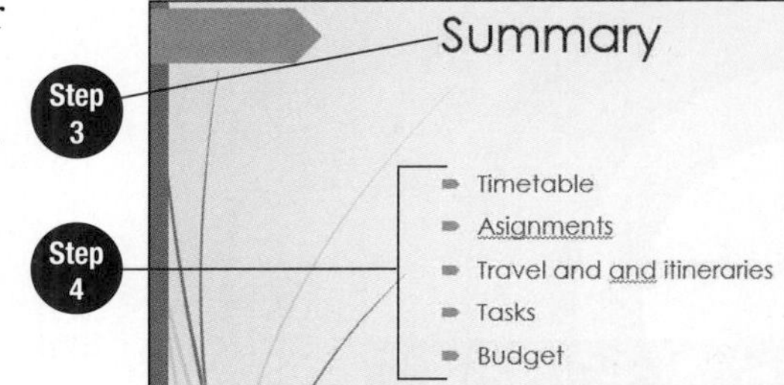

5. Complete a spelling check by moving the insertion point to the beginning of the word *Timetable*, clicking the Review tab, and then clicking the Spelling button in the Proofing group.

6. When the spelling checker selects *Asignments* in Slide 7 and displays *Assignments* in the list box in the Spelling task pane, click the Change button.

   Refer to the In Addition for a description of the Spelling task pane buttons.

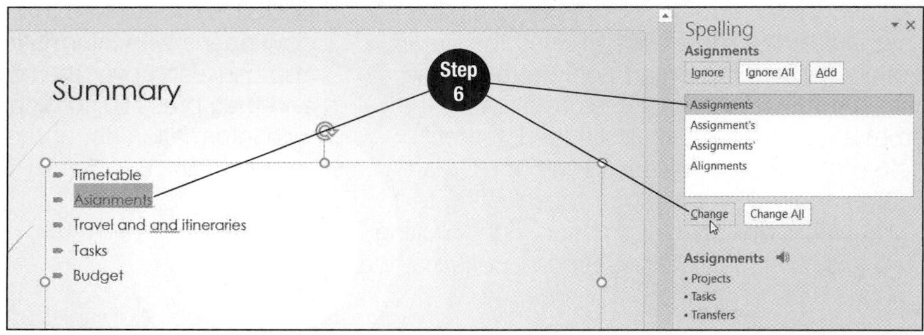

In Brief

Complete Spelling Check
1. Click Review tab.
2. Click Spelling button.
3. Change or ignore highlighted words.
4. When spelling check is completed, click OK.

Use Thesaurus
1. Click in word.
2. Click Review tab.
3. Click Thesaurus button.
4. Position mouse pointer on replacement word in Thesaurus task pane, click down-pointing arrow at right of word, click *Insert*.

7. When the spelling checker selects the second *and* in the slide, click the Delete button.
8. When the spelling checker selects *Greenbaum* in Slide 3, click the Ignore button.

   Greenbaum is a proper name and is spelled correctly. Clicking the Ignore button tells the spelling checker to leave the name as spelled.
9. When the spelling checker selects *Almonzo* in Slide 3, click the Ignore button.
10. At the message telling you that the spelling check is complete, click OK.
11. Display Slide 7 in the slide pane and then click in the word *Timetable*.
12. Look up synonyms for *Timetable* by clicking the Thesaurus button in the Proofing group.

   The Thesaurus task pane displays at the right side of the screen and contains lists of synonyms for *Timetable*. Depending on the word you are looking up, the words in the Thesaurus task pane list box may display followed by *(n.)* for *noun*, *(adj.)* for *adjective*, or *(adv.)* for *adverb*. Antonyms may display in the list of related synonyms, usually toward the end and followed by *(Antonym)*.
13. Position the mouse pointer on the word *Schedule* in the Thesaurus task pane, click the down-pointing arrow at the right of the word, and then click *Insert* at the drop-down list.

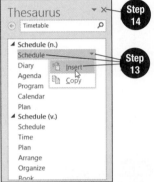

   This replaces *Timetable* with *Schedule*.
14. Close the Thesaurus task pane by clicking the Close button in the upper right corner of the task pane.
15. Right-click in the word *Tasks*, point to *Synonyms*, and then click *Responsibilities*.

   The shortcut menu offers another method for displaying synonyms for words.
16. Save **1-MPProdMtg.pptx**.

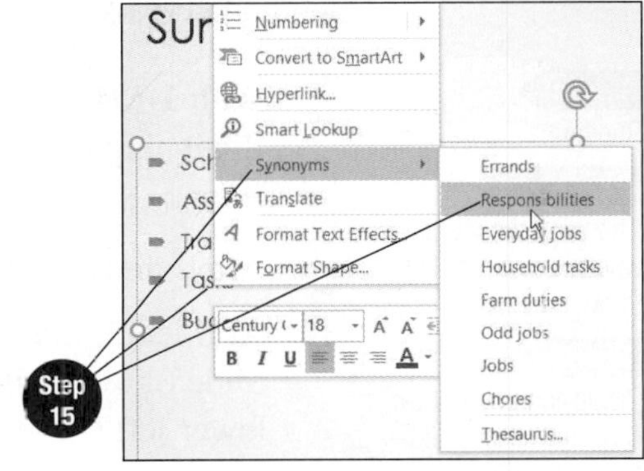

Check Your Work Compare your work to the model answer to ensure that you have completed the activity correctly.

In Addition

Using Spelling Task Pane Buttons

This table displays descriptions of the Spelling task pane buttons.

Button	Function
Ignore	skips that occurrence of the word and leaves currently selected text as written
Ignore All	skips that occurrence of the word and all other occurrences of the word in the presentation
Delete	deletes the currently selected word(s)
Change	replaces the selected word with the selected word in the suggestions list box
Change All	replaces the selected word and all other occurrences of the word in the presentation with the selected word in the suggestions list box
Add	adds the selected word to the main spelling check dictionary

Activity 1.9 Running a Slide Show; Using Ink Tools; Using the Pen Tool during a Slide Show

You can run a slide show in PowerPoint manually, advance the slides automatically, or set up a slide show to run continuously for demonstration purposes. In addition to the Start From Beginning button on the Quick Access Toolbar, you can run a slide show with the From Beginning button on the Slide Show tab or the Slide Show button on the Status bar. Run the slide show beginning with the currently active slide by clicking the From Current Slide button in the Start Slide Show group or clicking the Slide Show button in the view area. Use the mouse or keyboard to advance through the slides. You can also use buttons on the Slide Show toolbar that displays when you move the mouse pointer while running a slide show. Use the pen tool to emphasize major points or draw the attention of the audience to specific items in a slide during a presentation. To use the pen tool on a slide, run the slide show, and when the desired slide displays, move the mouse to display the Slide Show toolbar. Click the Pen button on the toolbar and then click *Pen*. Use the mouse to draw in the slide to underline, circle, or otherwise emphasize specific text. Options at the Pen button drop-down list also include a laser pointer, highlighter, and eraser. You can also write and highlight on a slide in Normal view with options on the Ink Tools Pens tab. Display this tab by clicking the Start Inking button in the Ink group on the Review tab. This feature is useful when using a pen, stylus, or finger to draw on a tablet.

What You Will Do You are now ready to run the movie production meeting slide show. You will use the mouse to perform various actions while running the slide show and use the pen tool and ink tools to emphasize points in slides.

Tutorial Running a Slide Show

Tutorial Changing the Display when Running a Slide Show

Tutorial Displaying Slide Show Help and Hiding Slides during a Slide Show

Tutorial Using the Pen Tool during a Slide Show

Tutorial Using Ink Tools

1. With **1-MPProdMtg.pptx** open, click the Slide Show tab and then click the From Beginning button in the Start Slide Show group.

   Clicking this button begins the slide show, and Slide 1 fills the entire screen.

2. After viewing Slide 1, click the left mouse button to advance to the next slide.

3. At Slide 2, move the mouse pointer until the Slide Show toolbar displays dimmed in the lower left corner of the slide and then click the Previous button (displays with a left arrow) on the toolbar to display the previous slide (Slide 1).

   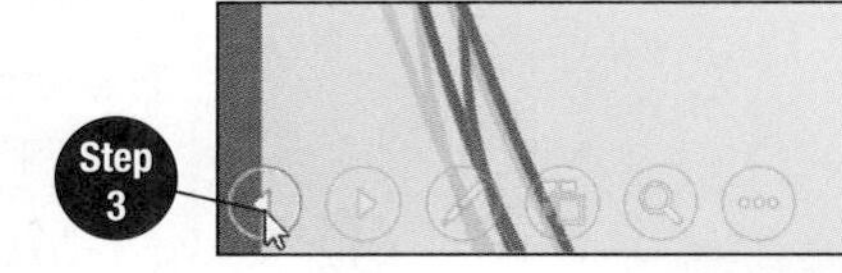

   With buttons on the Slide Show toolbar, you can display the next slide, the previous slide, or a specific slide; use the pen, laser pointer, and highlighter to emphasize text on the slide; display slide thumbnails; and zoom in on elements of a slide. You can also display the Slide Show Help dialog box, shown in Figure 1.3, which describes all the navigation options available while running a slide show. Display this dialog box by clicking the More slide show options button on the Slide Show toolbar and then clicking *Help*.

4. Click the Next button (displays with a right arrow) on the Slide Show toolbar to display the next slide (Slide 2).

5. Display the previous slide (Slide 1) by right-clicking anywhere in the slide and then clicking *Previous* at the shortcut menu.

   Right-clicking displays the shortcut menu with a variety of options including options to display the previous or next slide.

   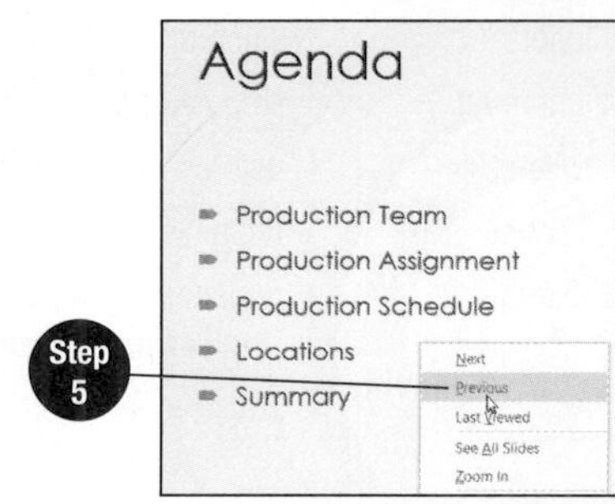

Figure 1.3 Slide Show Help Dialog Box

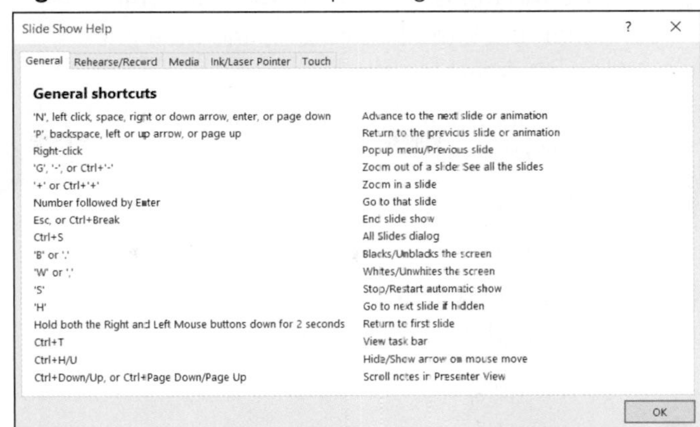

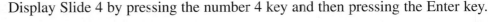

6 Display Slide 4 by pressing the number 4 key and then pressing the Enter key.

Move to any slide in a presentation by typing the slide number and then pressing the Enter key.

7 Change to a black screen by pressing the letter B key.

When you press the letter B key, the slide is removed from the screen and the screen displays black. This might be useful in a situation where you want to discuss something with your audience that is unrelated to the slide.

8 Return to Slide 4 by pressing the letter B key.

Pressing the letter B key switches between the slide and a black screen. Press the letter W key if you want to switch between the slide and a white screen.

9 Zoom in on the bulleted items in Slide 4 by clicking the Zoom into the slide button (displays as a magnifying glass) on the Slide Show toolbar, hovering the magnification area over the bulleted items, and then clicking the left mouse button.

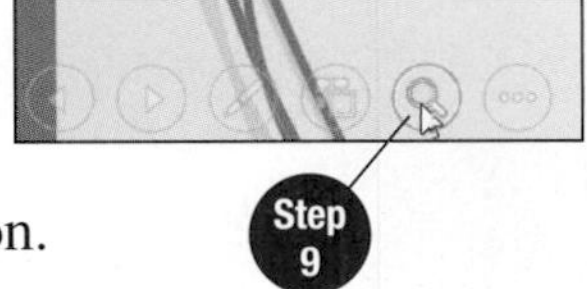

10 Right-click anywhere on the screen to display Slide 4 without magnification.

11 Display thumbnails of all the slides in the presentation while viewing the slide show by clicking the See all slides button on the Slide Show toolbar.

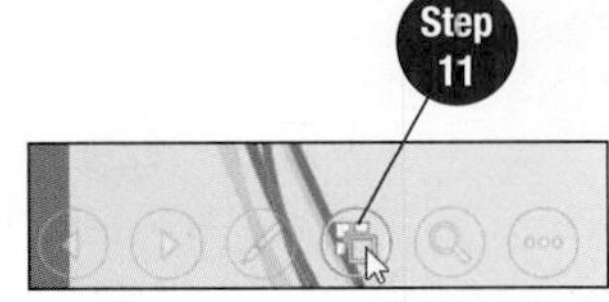

12 Click the Slide 3 thumbnail on the screen.

This displays Slide 3 in the slide show.

13 Click the left mouse button to display Slide 4. Continue clicking the left mouse button until a black screen displays. At the black screen, click the left mouse button again.

This returns the presentation to the Normal view.

14 Make Slide 1 active.

15 Display Slide 2 by clicking the Next Slide button at the bottom of the vertical scroll bar.

16 Click the From Current Slide button in the Start Slide Show group on the Slide Show tab.

Clicking this button begins the slide show with the active slide.

17 Run the slide show by clicking the left mouse button at each slide until Slide 5 is active (contains the title *Production Schedule*).

18 Move the mouse to display the Slide Show toolbar, click the Pen button, and then click *Laser Pointer*.

This turns the mouse pointer into a red, hollow, glowing circle.

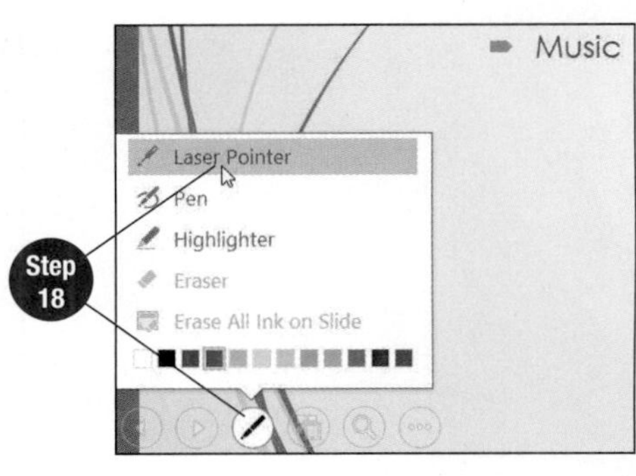

19 Practice moving the laser pointer around the screen.

20 Click the Pen button on the Slide Show toolbar and then click *Pen*.

This turns the mouse pointer into a small circle.

21 Using the mouse, draw a circle around the text *Location Shoots*.

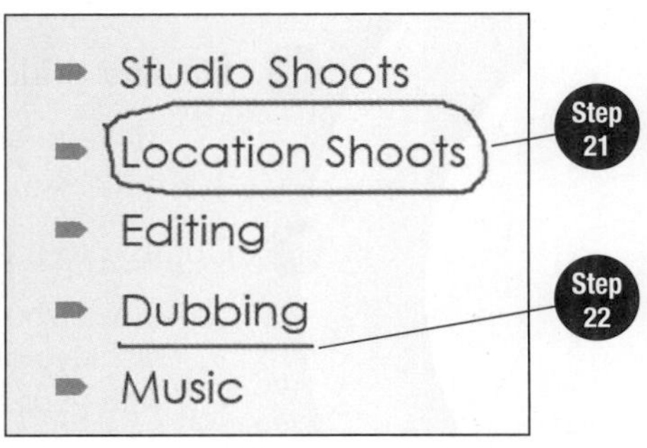

22 Using the mouse, draw a line below *Dubbing*.

23 Erase the pen markings by clicking the Pen button on the Slide Show toolbar and then clicking *Erase All Ink on Slide*.

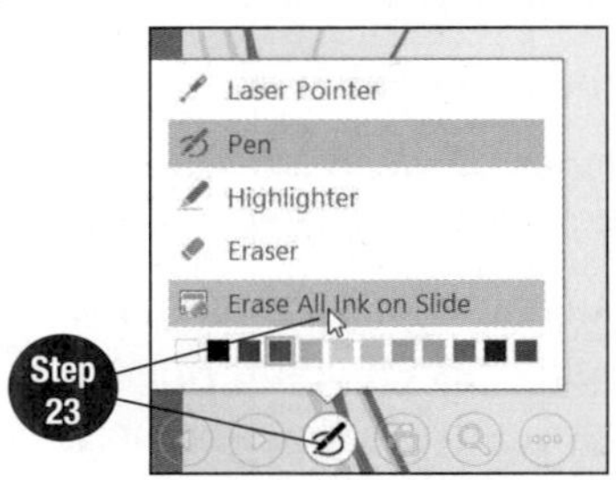

24 Change the color of the ink by clicking the Pen button and then clicking the *Blue* color (ninth color option).

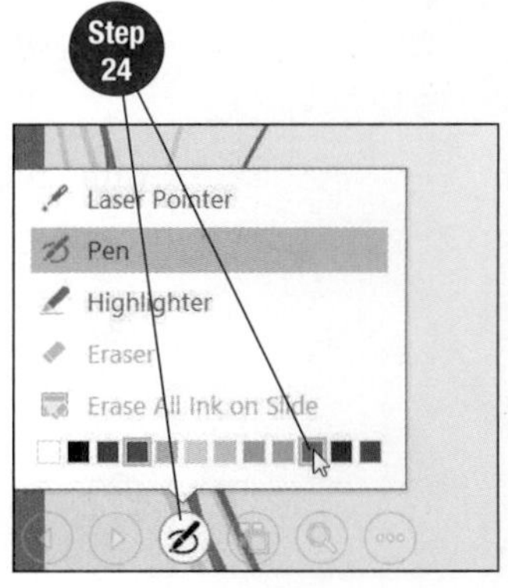

25 Draw a blue line below the word *Music*.

26 Return the mouse pointer back to an arrow by pressing the Esc key.

27 Click the left mouse button to advance to Slide 6.

28 Click the Pen button and then click *Highlighter*.

29 Using the mouse, drag through the words *Studio Shoots*.

30 Using the mouse, drag through the words *Location Shoots*.

31 Return the mouse pointer back to an arrow by pressing the Esc key.

32 Press the Esc key on the keyboard to end the slide show without viewing the remaining slides. At the message asking if you want to keep your ink annotations, click the Discard button.

In Brief

Run a Slide Show
Click Start From Beginning button on Quick Access Toolbar.
OR
1. Click Slide Show tab.
2. Click From Beginning button or From Current Slide button.

OR
Click Slide Show button on Status bar.

Use Pen Tool When Running a Slide Show
1. Run slide show.
2. Move mouse.
3. Click Pen button on Slide Show toolbar.
4. Click *Pen* option.
5. Draw in slide with pen.

Use Ink Tools
1. Click Review tab.
2. Click Start Inking button.
3. Draw or highlight on slide using pen or highlighter options.
4. Click Stop Inking button.

33 With Slide 6 displayed in Normal view, draw a circle around text to display when running a slide show. Begin by clicking the Review tab and then clicking the Start Inking button in the Ink group.

The Ink Tools Pens tab will display with options for writing or highlighting on a slide. This feature is particularly useful for tablets. The mouse pointer will display as a small circle.

34 Click the Convert to Shapes button in the Ink Art group.

35 Click the *Red Pen (0.35 mm)* option in the Pens gallery (second column, first row).

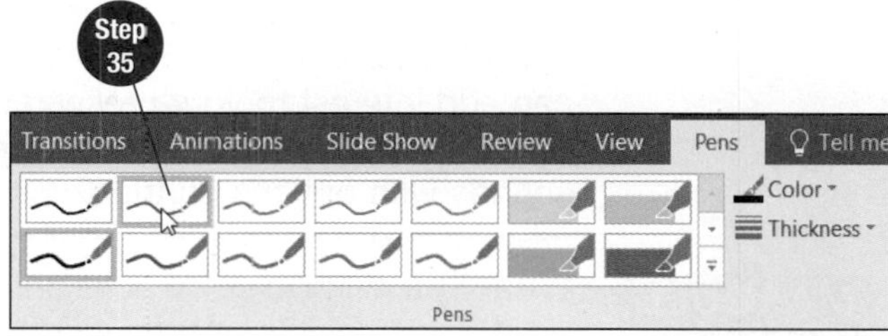

36 Using the mouse, draw a rectangle around the text *Studio Shoots*.

Notice that PowerPoint automatically converted the drawn rectangle into a more precise rectangle. If you are not satisfied with the appearance of the rectangle, click the Undo button on the Quick Access Toolbar two times, click the Pen button in the Write group, and then draw the rectangle again.

37 Click the *Aqua Highlighter (4.0 mm)* option in the Pens gallery (seventh column, first row).

38 Using the mouse, drag through the words *Los Angeles Studio*.

39 Click the Stop Inking button in the Close group to turn off the inking feature.

40 Click the Slide Show button in the view area on the Status bar.

41 Notice that the red rectangle and aqua highlighting display on the slide and then press the Esc key to return the presentation to Normal view.

42 Save **1-MPProdMtg.pptx**.

Check Your Work Compare your work to the model answer to ensure that you have completed the activity correctly.

In Addition

Hiding and Displaying the Mouse Pointer

When running a slide show, the mouse pointer is set, by default, to be hidden after three seconds of inactivity. The mouse pointer will appear again when you move the mouse. Change this default setting by clicking the More slide show options button on the Slide Show toolbar, clicking *Arrow Options*, and then clicking *Visible* if you want the mouse pointer always visible or *Hidden* if you do not want the mouse pointer to display at all as you run the slide show. The *Automatic* option is the default setting.

Viewing in Presenter View

If you are running a slide show using two monitors, you can display the presentation in Presenter view on one of the monitors. Use this view to control the slide show. For example, in Presenter view you can see your speaker notes, you have all the Slide Show toolbar options available, and you can advance slides and set slide timings. Press Alt + F5 to display the presentation in Presenter view.

Activity 1.10 Adding Transitions and Transition Sounds

You can apply a variety of transitions and transition sounds to a presentation. A transition is how one slide is removed from the screen during a slide show and the next slide is displayed. Interesting transitions such as fades, dissolves, push, cover, wipes, stripes, and bar can add interest to your presentation. You can also insert a sound that you want to play as one slide is removed from the screen and the next slide is displayed. Add transitions and sounds with options on the Transitions tab.

What You Will Do You have decided to enhance the movie production meeting presentation by adding transitions and sound to the slides.

Tutorial Adding Transitions

Tutorial Adding Sound to Slide Transitions

1. With **1-MPProdMtg.pptx** open, click Slide 1 in the slide thumbnails pane and then click the Transitions tab.
2. Click the More Transitions button in the gallery in the Transition to This Slide group.
3. Click the *Ripple* option in the *Exciting* section at the drop-down list.

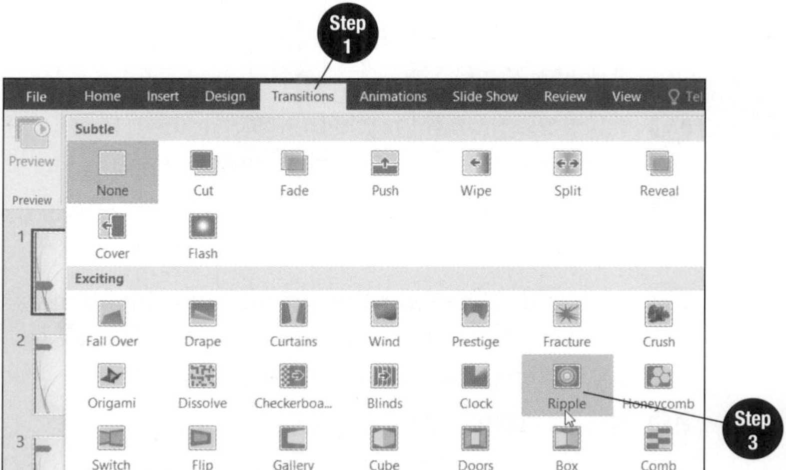

4. Click the Effect Options button in the Transition to This Slide group and then click *From Top-Left* at the drop-down list.

   The effect options change depending on the transition selected.

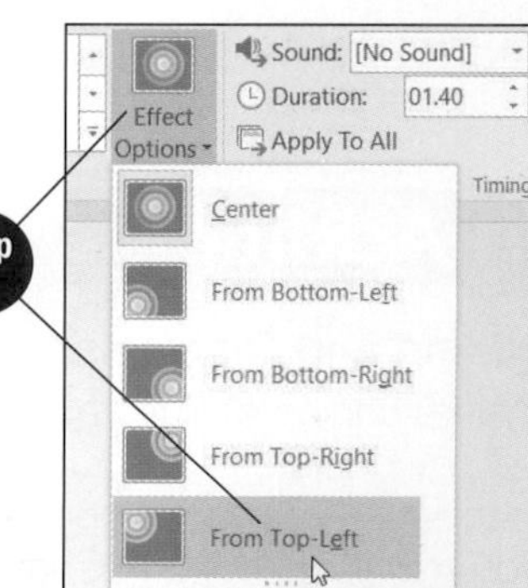

5. Click the *Sound* option box arrow in the Timing group.
6. Click the *Breeze* option at the drop-down list.

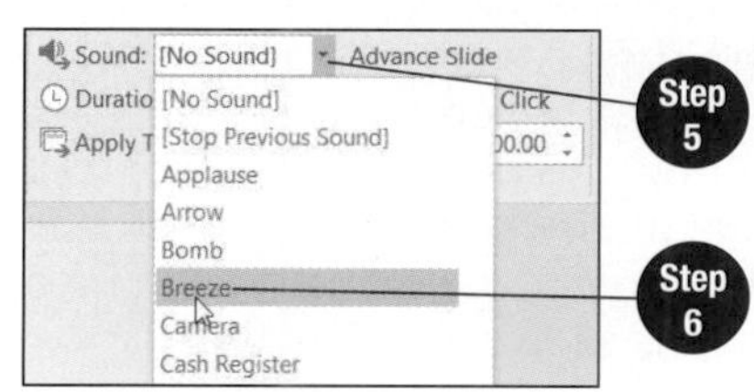

In Brief

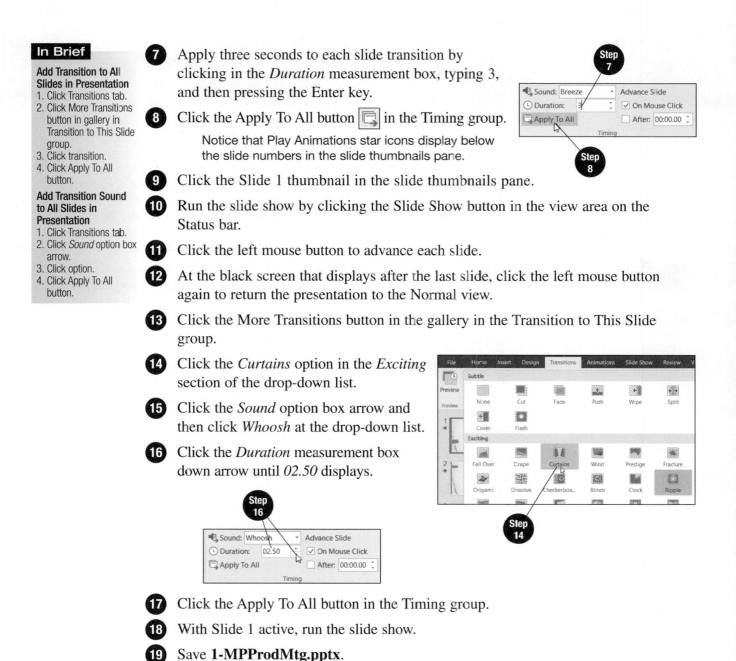

Add Transition to All Slides in Presentation
1. Click Transitions tab.
2. Click More Transitions button in gallery in Transition to This Slide group.
3. Click transition.
4. Click Apply To All button.

Add Transition Sound to All Slides in Presentation
1. Click Transitions tab.
2. Click *Sound* option box arrow.
3. Click option.
4. Click Apply To All button.

7 Apply three seconds to each slide transition by clicking in the *Duration* measurement box, typing 3, and then pressing the Enter key.

8 Click the Apply To All button in the Timing group.

Notice that Play Animations star icons display below the slide numbers in the slide thumbnails pane.

9 Click the Slide 1 thumbnail in the slide thumbnails pane.

10 Run the slide show by clicking the Slide Show button in the view area on the Status bar.

11 Click the left mouse button to advance each slide.

12 At the black screen that displays after the last slide, click the left mouse button again to return the presentation to the Normal view.

13 Click the More Transitions button in the gallery in the Transition to This Slide group.

14 Click the *Curtains* option in the *Exciting* section of the drop-down list.

15 Click the *Sound* option box arrow and then click *Whoosh* at the drop-down list.

16 Click the *Duration* measurement box down arrow until *02.50* displays.

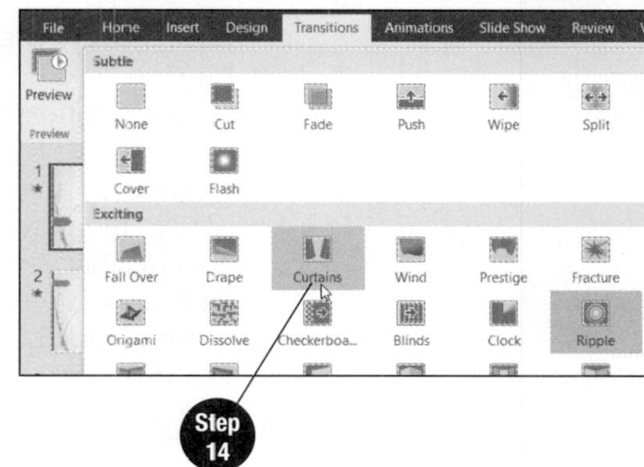

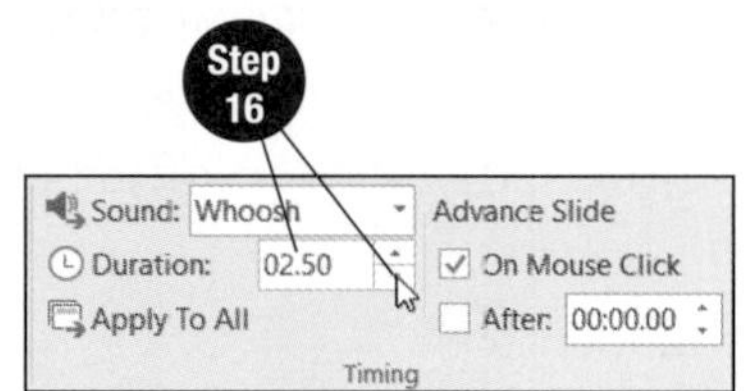

17 Click the Apply To All button in the Timing group.

18 With Slide 1 active, run the slide show.

19 Save **1-MPProdMtg.pptx**.

In Addition

Running a Slide Show Automatically

Slides in a slide show can be advanced automatically after a specific number of seconds by inserting a check mark in the *After* check box in the Timing group and removing the check mark from the *On Mouse Click* check box. Change the time in the *After* measurement box by clicking the *After* measurement box up or down arrow or by selecting the number in the measurement box and then typing the specific time. If you want the transition time to affect all slides in the presentation, click the Apply To All button. In Slide Sorter view, the transition time displays below each affected slide. Click the Slide Show button to run the slide show. The first slide displays for the specified amount of time and then the next slide automatically displays.

Activity 1.11 Previewing Slides and Printing

You can print each slide on a separate piece of paper; print each slide at the top of the page, leaving the bottom of the page for notes; print up to nine slides or a specific number of slides on a single piece of paper; or print the slide titles and topics in outline form. Before printing a presentation, consider previewing it. Choose print options and display a preview of the presentation in the Print backstage area. Display this view by clicking the File tab and then clicking the *Print* option. Click the Back button or press the Esc key to exit the backstage area without clicking an option.

What You Will Do Staff members need the movie production meeting slides printed as handouts and as an outline. You will preview and print the presentation in various formats.

1. With **1-MPProdMtg.pptx** open, display Slide 1 in the slide pane.
2. Click the File tab and then click the *Print* option.

   Slide 1 of the presentation displays at the right side of the screen as it will when printed. Use the Next Page button (right-pointing arrow) located below and to the left of the slide to view the next slide in the presentation, click the Previous Page button (left-pointing arrow) to display the previous slide in the presentation, use the Zoom slider bar to increase or decrease the size of the slide, and click the Zoom to Page button to fit the slide in the preview area in the Print backstage area. The left side of the Print backstage area displays three categories—*Print*, *Printer*, and *Settings*. Galleries display below each category name. For example, the *Printer* category has one gallery that displays the name of the currently selected printer. The *Settings* category has a number of galleries that describe how the slides will print.

3. Click the Next Page button below and to the left of the preview slide to display the next slide in the presentation.

   This displays Slide 2 in the preview area.

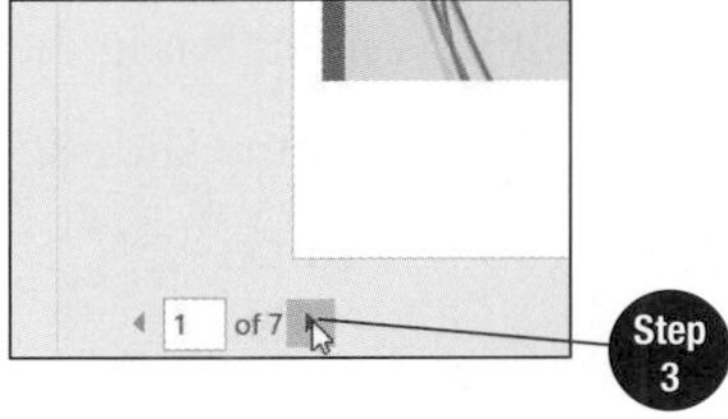

4. Click the Zoom In button [+] at the right side of the Zoom slider bar two times.

   Click the Zoom In button to increase the size of the slide or click the Zoom Out button (displays with a minus symbol) to decrease the size of the slide.

5. Click the Zoom to Page button at the right side of the Zoom slider bar.

   Click the Zoom to Page button to fit the entire slide in the viewing area in the Print backstage area.

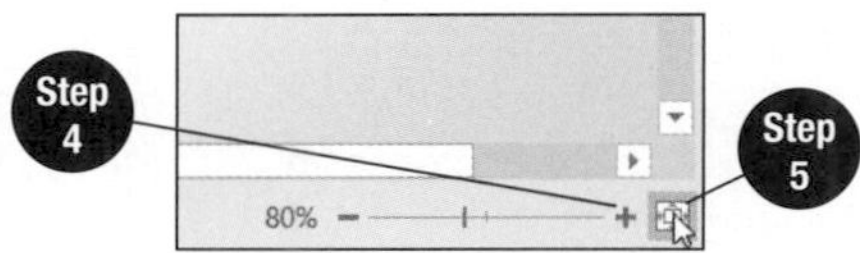

6 You decide to print the slides on two pages and you want to preview how the slides will display on the pages. To do this, click the second gallery in the *Settings* category (contains the text *Full Page Slides*) and then click *4 Slides Horizontal* in the *Handouts* section.

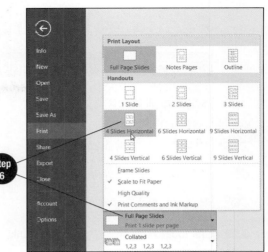

Notice how four slides display on the preview page.

7 Click the Print button at the top of the Print backstage area.

8 You want to print all slide text on one page to use as a reference during your presentation. To do this, click the File tab and then click the *Print* option.

9 At the Print backstage area, click the second gallery in the *Settings* category (contains the text *4 Slides Horizontal*) and then click *Outline* in the *Print Layout* section.

10 Click the Print button at the top of the Print backstage area.

With the *Outline* option selected, the presentation prints on one page with slide numbers, slide icons, and slide text in outline form.

11 You want to print only Slide 6. To do this, click the File tab and then click the *Print* option.

12 At the Print backstage area, click the second gallery in the *Settings* category (contains the text *Outline*) and then click *Full Page Slides* in the *Print Layout* section.

13 Click in the *Slides* text box below the first gallery in the *Settings* category, type 6, and then click the Print button.

14 Save **1-MPProdMtg.pptx**.

15 Close the presentation by clicking the File tab and then clicking the *Close* option.

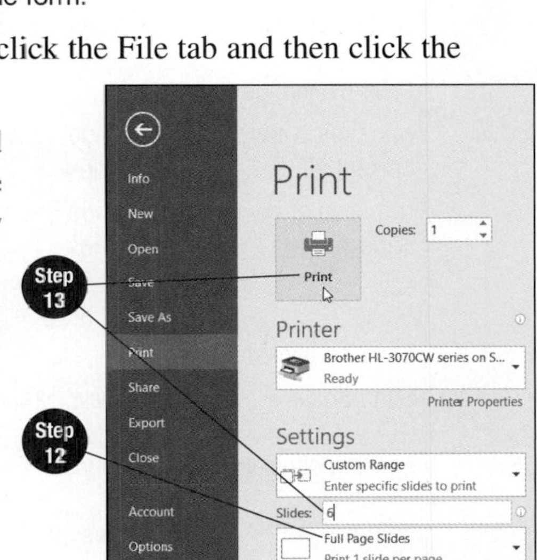

Check Your Work Compare your work to the model answer to ensure that you have completed the activity correctly.

In Addition

Using Options at the Slide Size Dialog Box

You can change orientation with options at the Slide Size dialog box, shown at the right. Display this dialog box by clicking the Design tab, clicking the Slide Size button in the Customize group, and then clicking *Customize Slide Size* at the drop-down list. With options at this dialog box you can specify how you want slides sized; page width and height; orientation for slides; and orientation for notes, handouts, and outlines.

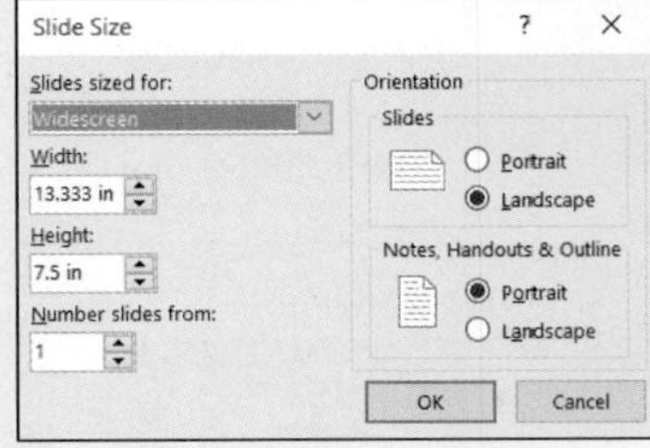

Features Summary

Feature	Ribbon Tab, Group	Button/Option	File Tab Option	Keyboard Shortcut
apply transitions and sound to all slides	Transitions, Timing			
close a presentation			*Close*	Ctrl + F4
close PowerPoint				
display Presenter view				Alt + F5
Help				F1
ink tools	Review, Ink			
layout	Home, Slides			
new slide	Home, Slides OR Insert, Slides			Ctrl + M
Normal view	View, Presentation Views			
Notes Page view	View, Presentation Views			
Open backstage area			*Open*	Ctrl + O
open blank presentation				Ctrl + N
Outline view	View, Presentation Views			
Print backstage area			*Print*	Ctrl + P
run slide show from current slide	Slide Show, Start Slide Show			Shift + F5
run slide show from Slide 1	Slide Show, Start Slide Show			F5
save			*Save*	Ctrl + S
Save As backstage area			*Save As*	
Slide Sorter view	View, Presentation Views			
spelling checker	Review, Proofing			F7
themes	Design, Themes			
Thesaurus	Review, Proofing			Shift + F7
transitions	Transitions, Transition to This Slide			
transition duration	Transitions, Timing			
transition sound	Transitions, Timing			
Zoom dialog box	View, Zoom			

Workbook Section study tools and assessment activities are available in the *Workbook* ebook. These resources are designed to help you further develop and demonstrate mastery of the skills learned in this section.

PowerPoint SECTION 2

Editing and Enhancing Slides

Data Files Before beginning section work, copy the PowerPointS2 folder to your storage medium and then make PowerPointS2 the active folder.

Skills

- Increase and decrease the indent of text
- Select, cut, copy, and paste text
- Apply font and font effects
- Find and replace fonts
- Apply formatting with Format Painter
- Change alignment and line and paragraph spacing
- Change the slide size and format design themes and slide background
- Insert, size, move, and format images
- Insert and format a screen clipping
- Insert and format a SmartArt graphic
- Apply animation to objects and text in a slide

Precheck Check your current skills to help focus your study of the skills taught in this section.

Projects Overview

Open an existing project presentation, save the presentation with a new name, and then edit and format the presentation. Open an existing annual meeting presentation for Marquee Productions and then save, edit, and format the presentation.

Open an existing presentation for the Theatre Arts Division and then save, edit, and format the presentation.

Open an existing presentation on vacation specials and then save, edit, and format the presentation.

Prepare and format a presentation on the services offered by The Waterfront Bistro.

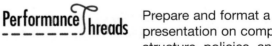

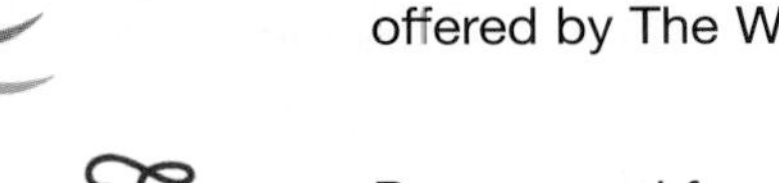

Prepare and format a presentation on company structure, policies, and benefits.

Prepare and format a presentation for a planning meeting of the distribution department.

If you are a SNAP user, launch the Precheck and Tutorials from your Assignments page.

Model Answers Preview the model answers for an overview of the projects you will complete in the section activities.

Activity 2.1 Increasing and Decreasing Indent; Cutting, Copying, and Pasting Text

Text that is formatted as a bulleted list in a slide can have multiple levels. Click the Decrease List Level button in the Paragraph group on the Home tab or press Shift + Tab to promote text to the previous level. Click the Increase List Level button or press the Tab key to demote text to the next level. You can also promote text levels (decrease the text indent) and/or demote text levels (increase text indent) in the slide in Outline view. Select text in a slide and then delete the text from the slide, cut text from one location and paste it into another, or copy and paste the text. Use buttons in the Clipboard group on the Home tab to cut, copy, and paste text.

What You Will Do Chris Greenbaum, production manager for Marquee Productions, has prepared a documentary project presentation and has asked you to edit the presentation by increasing and decreasing text levels and selecting, deleting, moving, copying, and pasting text in slides.

Tutorial Increasing and Decreasing Indent

Tutorial Selecting Text

Tutorial Cutting, Copying, and Pasting Text

1. Open **MPProj.pptx** from the PowerPointS2 folder on your storage medium and then save the presentation with the name **2-MPProj.pptx**.
2. Display Slide 5 in the slide pane.
3. You decide to promote the names below *Script Authors* so that they display as second-level bullets. To do this, position the mouse pointer immediately left of the *D* in *Dana*, click the left mouse button, and then click the Decrease List Level button in the Paragraph group on the Home tab.

   Clicking the Decrease List Level button will promote text to the previous tab position, while clicking the Increase List Level button will demote text to the next tab position.
4. Position the insertion point immediately left of the *K* in *Karl* in Slide 5 and then promote the text to the previous level by pressing Shift + Tab.
5. Demote two of the names below *Script Consultants*. Begin by clicking immediately left of the *J* in *Jaime* and then clicking the Increase List Level button in the Paragraph group on the Home tab.
6. Position the insertion point immediately left of the *G* in *Genaro* and then press the Tab key.
7. Display Slide 6 in the slide pane.

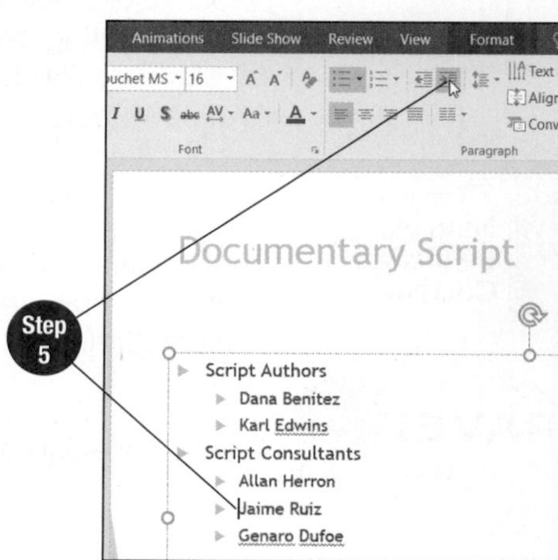

In Brief

Decrease Text Level Indent
Click Decrease List Level button or press Shift + Tab.

Increase Text Level Indent
Click Increase List Level button or press Tab.

Cut and Paste Text
1. Select text.
2. Click Cut button.
3. Position insertion point.
4. Click Paste button.

Copy and Paste Text
1. Select text.
2. Click Copy button.
3. Position insertion point.
4. Click Paste button

8 Position the mouse pointer on the bullet that displays before *Script Rewriting* until the mouse pointer turns into a four-headed arrow and then click the left mouse button.

This selects the text *Script Rewriting* and displays the Mini toolbar, which provides easy access to formatting options and buttons. Refer to the In Addition for additional information on selecting text.

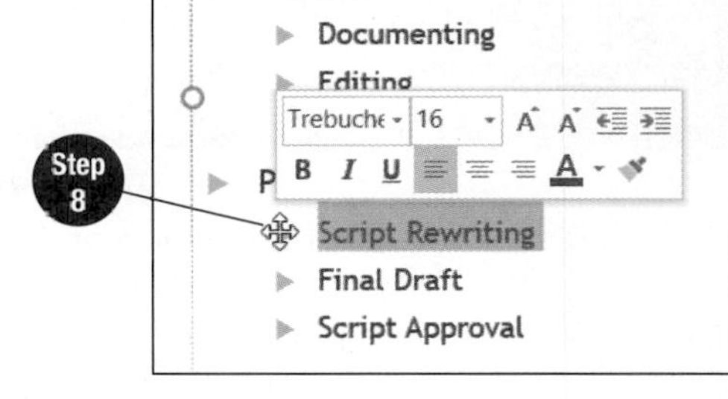

9 Press the Delete key.

This deletes the selected text.

10 Display Slide 5 in the slide pane.

11 Position the mouse pointer on the bullet that displays before *Genaro Dufoe* until the mouse pointer turns into a four-headed arrow and then click the left mouse button.

12 Click the Cut button in the Clipboard group on the Home tab.

The keyboard shortcut to cut text is Ctrl + X.

13 Position the mouse pointer immediately left of the *A* in *Allan Herron*, click the left mouse button, and then click the Paste button in the Clipboard group.

The keyboard shortcut to paste text is Ctrl + V.

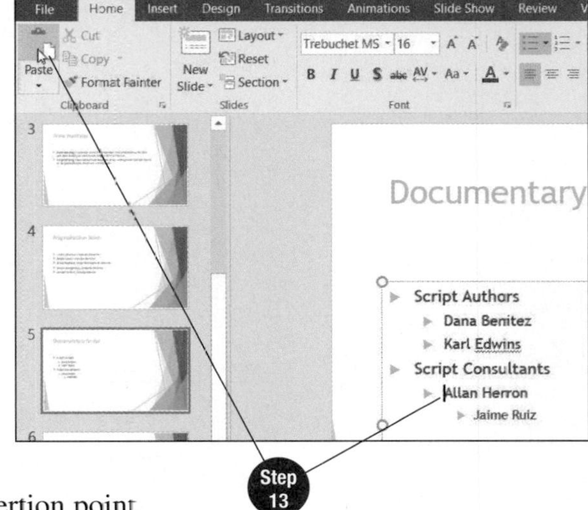

14 Using the mouse, drag to select the text *Script Authors* and then click the Copy button in the Clipboard group.

The keyboard shortcut to copy text is Ctrl + C.

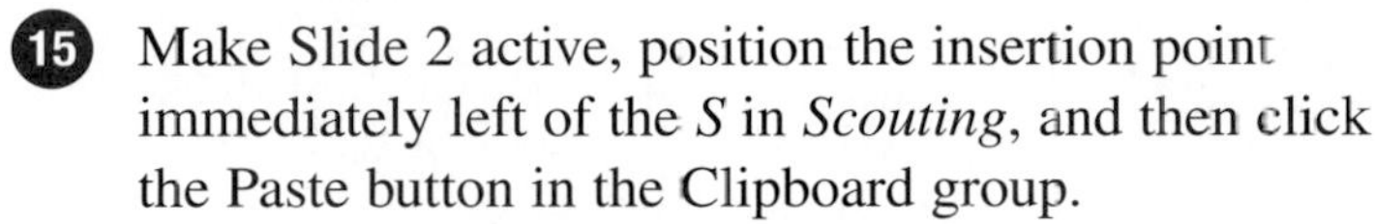

15 Make Slide 2 active, position the insertion point immediately left of the *S* in *Scouting*, and then click the Paste button in the Clipboard group.

If *Script Authors* and *Scouting* display on the same line, press the Enter key.

16 Save **2-MPProj.pptx**.

Check Your Work Compare your work to the model answer to ensure that you have completed the activity correctly.

In Addition

Selecting Text

To select	Perform this action
entire word	Double-click word.
entire paragraph	Triple-click anywhere in paragraph.
text mouse pointer passes through	Click and drag with mouse.
all text in selected object box	Click Select button in Editing group and then click Select All; or press Ctrl + A.

Activity 2.2 Applying Font Formatting and Font Effects

The Font group on the Home tab contains two rows of options and buttons. The top row contains options and buttons for changing the font and font size and a button for clearing formatting. The bottom row contains buttons for applying font effects such as bold, italics, underlining, text shadow, strikethrough, and character spacing, as well as buttons for changing the case and/or font color of selected text.

What You Will Do Certain text elements on slides in the documentary project presentation need to be highlighted to make them stand out. You decide to apply font effects to and change the font size of specific text.

Applying Font Formatting

1. With **2-MPProj.pptx** open, display Slide 1 in the slide pane.
2. Select the title *Marquee Productions* and then click the Italic button *I* in the Font group on the Home tab.

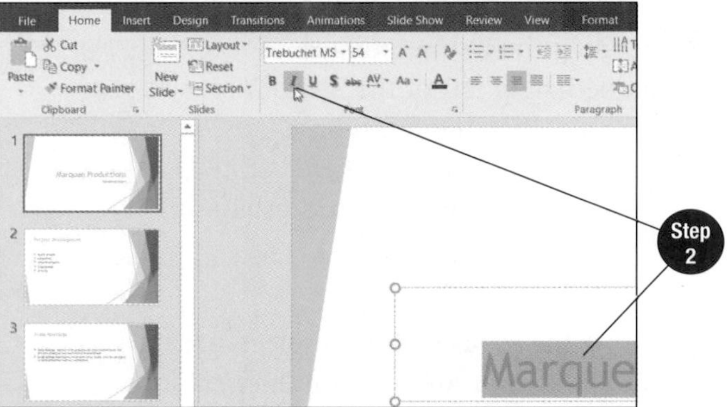

3. Select the subtitle *Documentary Project*, click the Increase Font Size button A, and then click the Bold button **B** in the Font group.

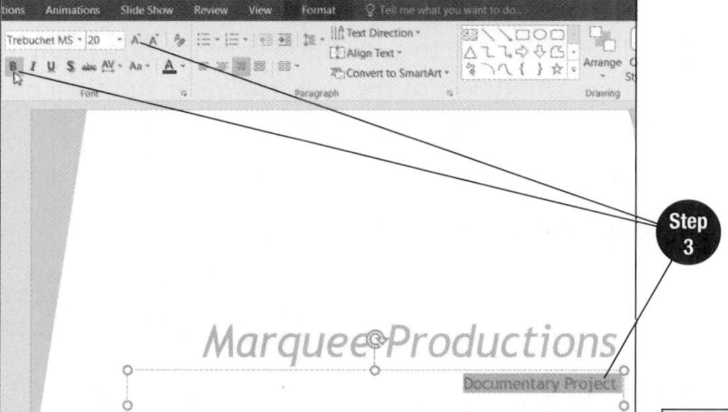

4. Make Slide 6 active in the slide pane, select the text *Phase 1*, and then click the Underline button U in the Font group.
5. Select and then underline the text *Phase 2*.
6. Select and then underline the text *Phase 3*.
7. Make Slide 1 active.

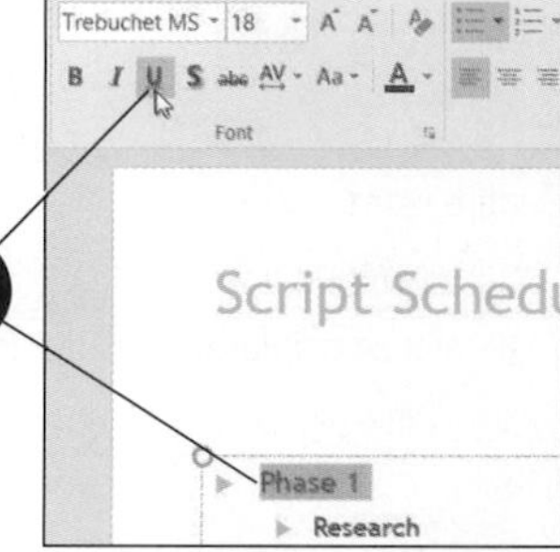

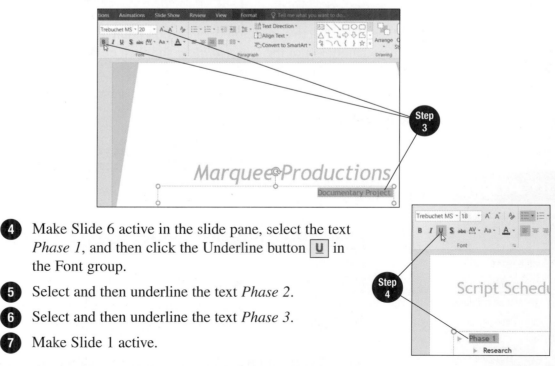

In Brief

Apply Font Effects with Font Group
1. Select text.
2. Click appropriate button in Font group.

8 Select the title *Marquee Productions*, click the *Font* option box arrow in the Font group, scroll down the drop-down gallery (fonts display in alphabetical order), and then click *Cambria*.

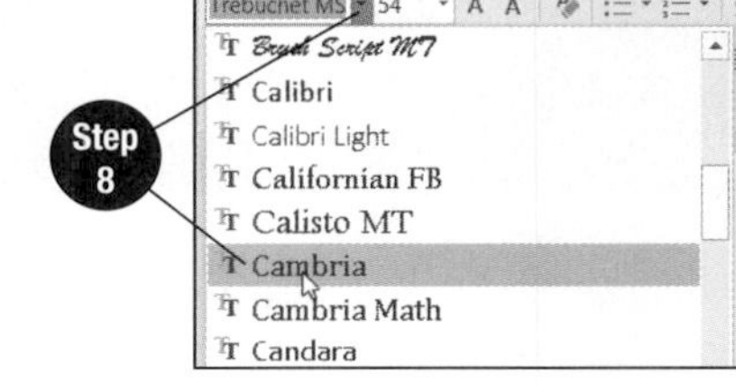

9 Select the subtitle *Documentary Project*, click the *Font* option box arrow, and then click *Cambria* at the drop-down gallery.

The drop-down gallery displays the most recently used fonts toward the top of the gallery.

10 Make Slide 6 active, select the text *Phase 1*, click the Underline button to remove underlining, and then click the Bold button to apply bold formatting.

11 With *Phase 1* still selected, click *Trebuchet MS* in the *Font* option box, type cam, and then press the Enter key.

An alternative method for selecting a font is to type the first few letters of the font name in the *Font* option box until the entire font name displays and then press the Enter key.

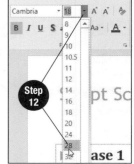

12 Click the *Font Size* option box arrow and then click *28*.

13 Select the text *Phase 2*, remove the underlining, apply bold formatting, change the font to Cambria, and then change the font size to 28 points.

14 Select the text *Phase 3*, remove the underlining, apply bold formatting, change the font to Cambria, and then change the font size to 28 points.

15 Print Slides 1 and 6. Begin by clicking the File tab and then clicking the *Print* option.

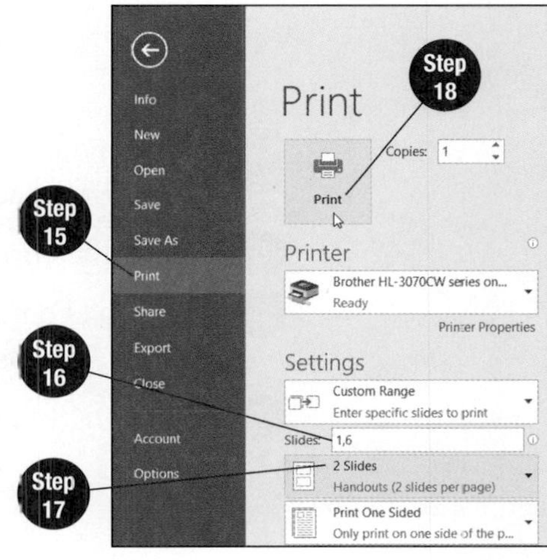

16 At the Print backstage area, click in the *Slides* text box (located below the first gallery in the *Settings* category) and then type 1,6.

17 Click the second gallery in the *Settings* category (contains the text *Full Page Slides*) and then click *2 Slides* in the *Handouts* section of the drop-down list.

18 Click the Print button.

The two slides print on the same page.

19 Save **2-MPProj.pptx**.

Check Your Work Compare your work to the model answer to ensure that you have completed the activity correctly.

In Addition

Choosing Fonts

A typeface is a set of characters with a common design and shape. PowerPoint refers to a typeface as a *font*. Fonts can be decorative or plain and are either monospaced or proportional. A monospaced font allots the same amount of horizontal space for each character, while a proportional font allots a different amount of space for each character. Proportional fonts are divided into two main categories: serif and sans serif. A serif is a small line at the end of a character stroke. Consider using a serif font for text-intensive slides, because the serifs can help move the reader's eyes across the text. Use a sans serif font for titles, subtitles, headings, and short lines of text.

Activity 2.3 Applying Font Formatting at the Font Dialog Box; Replacing Fonts

In addition to options and buttons in the Font group on the Home tab, you can apply font formatting with options at the Font dialog box. Use options at this dialog box to change the font, as well as its style and size; change the font color; and apply formatting effects such as underline, strikethrough, superscript, subscript, small caps, and all caps. If you decide to change the font for all slides in a presentation, use the Replace Font dialog box to replace all occurrences of a specific font in the presentation.

What You Will Do You are still not satisfied with the fonts in the documentary project presentation, so you decide to change the font for the title and subtitle and replace the Verdana font on the remaining slides.

Tutorial Applying Font Formatting at the Font Dialog Box

Tutorial Replacing Fonts

1. With **2-MPProj.pptx** open, make Slide 1 active.
2. Select the title *Marquee Productions.*
3. Display the Font dialog box by clicking the Font group dialog box launcher on the Home tab.

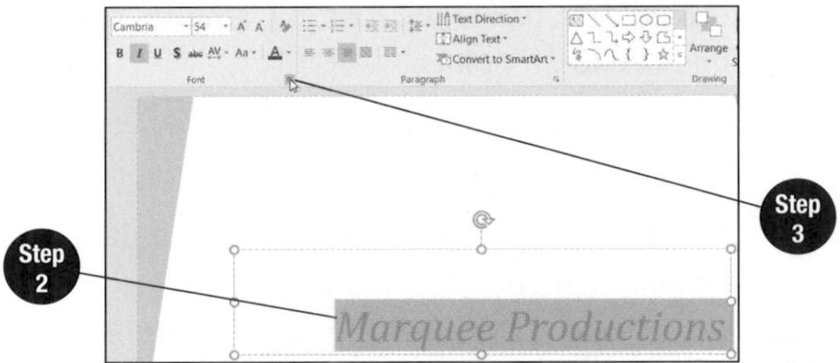

4. At the Font dialog box, click the *Latin text font* option box arrow and then click *Candara* at the drop-down list.
5. Select the current measurement in the *Size* measurement box and then type 60.
6. Click the Font color button in the *All text* section and then click the *Blue, Accent 2, Darker 25%* option (sixth column, fifth row in the *Theme Colors* section).
7. Click OK to close the Font dialog box.

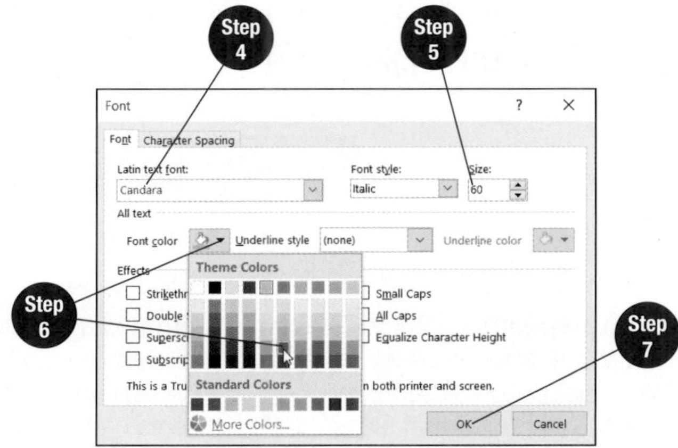

8. Select the subtitle *Documentary Project.*
9. Click the Font group dialog box launcher.

In Brief

Change Font at Font Dialog Box
1. Select text.
2. Click Font group dialog box launcher.
3. Click options at Font dialog box.
4. Click OK.

Change All Occurrences of Font
1. Click Replace button arrow.
2. Click *Replace Fonts.*
3. Make sure appropriate font displays in *Replace* text box.
4. Press Tab.
5. Click *With* option box arrow.
6. Click new font.
7. Click Replace button.
8. Click Close button.

10. At the Font dialog box, click the *Latin text font* option box arrow and then click *Candara* at the drop-down list.

11. Click the *Font style* option box arrow and then click *Bold Italic* at the drop-down list.

12. Select the current measurement in the *Size* measurement box and then type 30.

13. Click the Font color button in the *All text* section and then click the *Turquoise, Accent 1* color option (fifth colomn, first row in the *Theme Colors* section).

14. Click OK to close the Font dialog box.

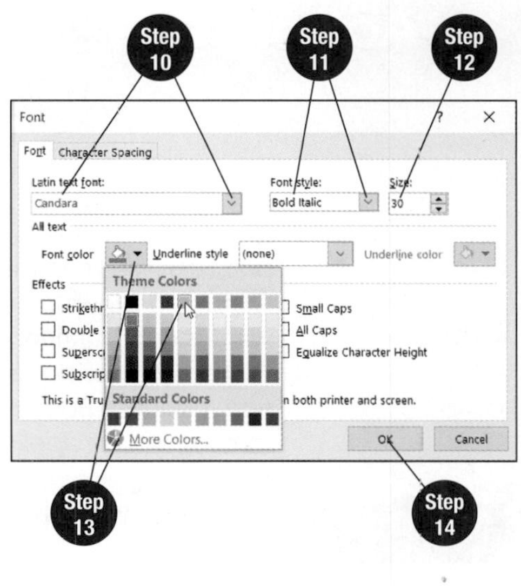

15. Make Slide 2 active.

16. You decide to replace all occurrences of the Trebuchet MS font in the presentation with the Cambria font. To begin, click the Replace button arrow in the Editing group on the Home tab and then click *Replace Fonts* at the drop-down list.

17. At the Replace Font dialog box, click the *Replace* option box arrow and then click *Trebuchet MS* at the drop-down list.

18. Click the *With* option box arrow, scroll down the drop-down list to display Cambria, and then click *Cambria* at the drop-down list.

19. Click the Replace button and then click the Close button.

20. Save **2-MPProj.pptx**.

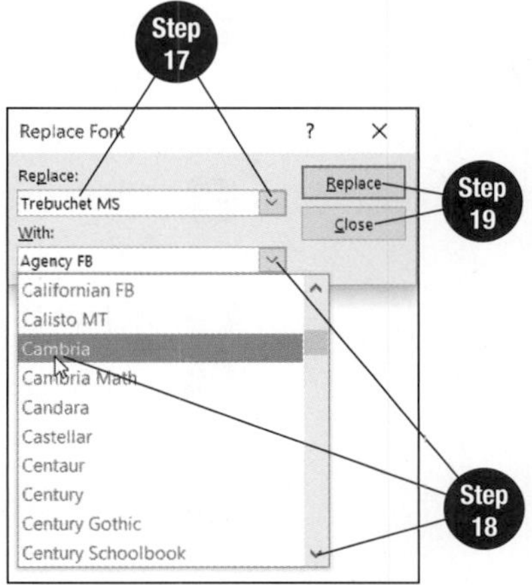

Check Your Work Compare your work to the model answer to ensure that you have completed the activity correctly.

In Addition

Choosing Fonts

Choose a font for a presentation based on the tone and message you want the presentation to convey. For example, choose a more serious font such as Constantia or Cambria for a conservative audience and choose a less formal font such as Comic Sans MS, Lucida Handwriting, or Mistral for a more informal or lighthearted audience. For text-intensive slides, choose a serif font such as Cambria, Constantia, Garamond, or Bookman Old Style. For titles, subtitles, headings, and short text items, consider a sans serif font such as Calibri, Candara, Arial, or Trebuchet MS. Use no more than two or three different fonts in each presentation. To ensure text readability in a slide, choose a font color that contrasts with the slide background.

Activity 2.4 Formatting with Format Painter

Use the Format Painter feature to apply the same formatting in more than one location in a slide or slides. To use the Format Painter, apply formatting to text, position the insertion point anywhere in the formatted text, and then double-click the Format Painter button in the Clipboard group on the Home tab. Using the mouse, select the additional text to which you want the formatting applied. After applying the formatting in the desired locations, click the Format Painter button to deactivate it. If you only need to apply formatting in one other location, click the Format Painter button just once. The first time you click or select text, the formatting will be applied and the Format Painter button will be deactivated.

What You Will Do Improve the appearance of slides in the documentary project presentation by applying a font and then using the Format Painter to apply the formatting to other text.

Formatting with Format Painter

1. With **2-MPProj.pptx** open, make sure Slide 2 is active.
2. Select the title *Project Development.*
3. Click the Font group dialog box launcher.
4. At the Font dialog box, click in the *Latin text font* option box, type can, and then press the Tab key.

   As you type letters, fonts that match the letters display in the list box.
5. Click the *Font style* option box arrow and then click *Bold Italic* at the drop-down list.
6. Select the current measurement in the *Size* measurement box and then type 40.
7. Click the Font color button in the *All text* section and then click the *Blue, Accent 2, Darker 25%* color option (sixth column, fifth row in the *Theme Colors* section).
8. Click OK to close the Font dialog box.

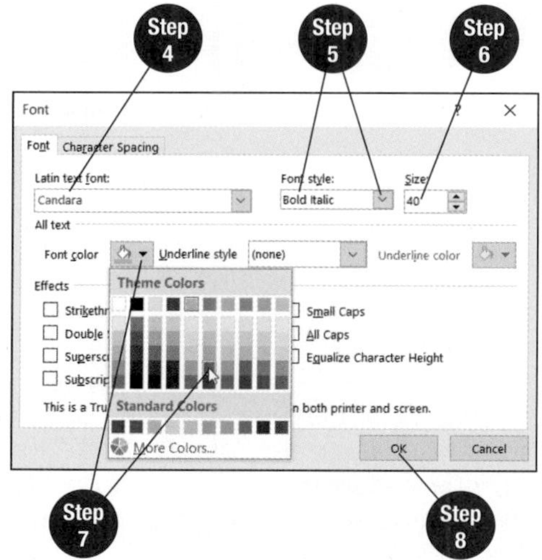

9. Deselect the text by clicking in the slide in the slide pane.

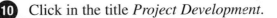

In Brief

Format with Format Painter
1. Click in formatted text.
2. Double-click Format Painter button.
3. Click in or select text to be formatted
4. Click Format Painter button.

10. Click in the title *Project Development.*
11. Double-click the Format Painter button in the Clipboard group on the Home tab.

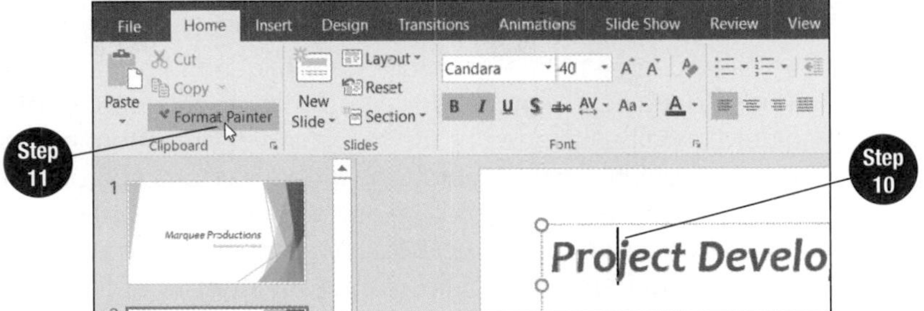

12. Click the Next Slide button to display Slide 3.
13. Triple-click *Team Meetings* to select the title.

    The mouse pointer displays with a paintbrush attached. This indicates that the Format Painter is active. You can also apply the formatting by clicking individual words in the title, but doing so will not format the spaces within titles that consist of more than one word. If the paintbrush is no longer attached to the mouse pointer, Format Painter has been turned off. Turn it back on by clicking in a slide title with the desired formatting and then double-clicking the Format Painter button.

14. Click the Next Slide button to display Slide 4.
15. Using the mouse, select the title *Preproduction Team.*
16. Apply formatting to the titles in the remaining three slides.
17. When formatting has been applied to all slide titles, click the Format Painter button in the Clipboard group on the Home tab.

    Clicking the Format Painter button turns off the feature.

18. Save **2-MPProj.pptx**.

Check Your Work Compare your work to the model answer to ensure that you have completed the activity correctly.

In Addition

Choosing a Custom Color

Click the Font color button at the Font dialog box and a palette of color choices displays. Click the *More Colors* option and the Colors dialog box displays with the Standard tab selected, showing a honeycomb of color options. Click the Custom tab and the dialog box displays as shown at the right. Use options on this tab to mix your own color. Click the desired color in the *Colors* palette or enter the values for the color in the *Red*, *Green*, and *Blue* text boxes. Adjust the luminosity of the current color by dragging the slider at the right side of the color palette.

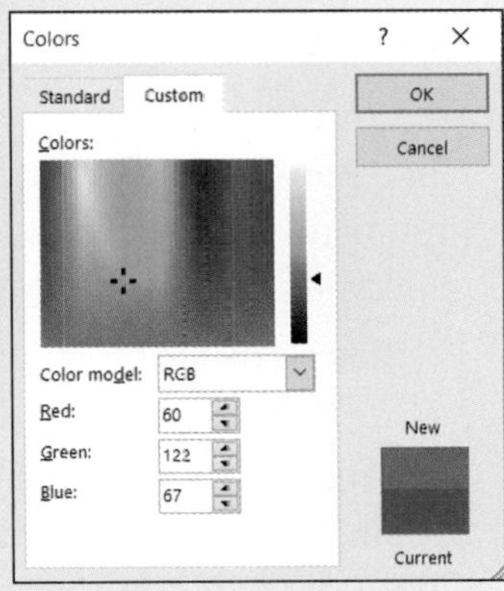

Activity 2.5 Changing Alignment and Line and Paragraph Spacing

The slide design theme generally determines the horizontal and vertical alignment of text in placeholders. Text may be left-aligned, center-aligned, right-aligned, or justified in a placeholder as well as aligned at the top, middle, or bottom of the placeholder. Change alignment for specific text with buttons in the Paragraph group on the Home tab or with options from the Align Text button drop-down gallery. Use options at the Line Spacing button drop-down gallery or the *Line Spacing* option at the Paragraph dialog box to change line spacing. The Paragraph dialog box also contains options for changing text alignment and indentation as well as spacing before and after text.

What You Will Do Change the alignment and improve the appearance of specific text in slides by adjusting the vertical alignment and paragraph spacing of text.

Tutorial
Changing Alignment

Tutorial
Changing Line Spacing

Tutorial
Changing Paragraph Spacing

1. With **2-MPProj.pptx** open, make Slide 1 active.
2. Click in the text *Marquee Productions* and then click the Center button in the Paragraph group on the Home tab.

   You can also change text alignment with the keyboard shortcuts shown in Table 2.1.

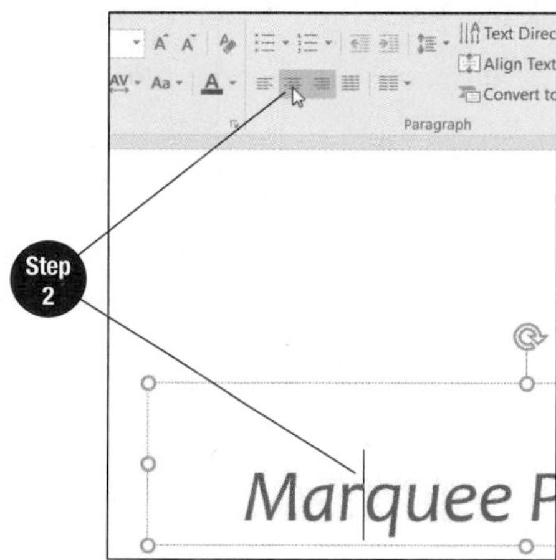

3. Click in the text *Documentary Project* and then click the Center button.
4. Make Slide 3 active (contains the title *Team Meetings*), click in the bulleted text, and then press Ctrl + A to select all of the bulleted text.

   Ctrl + A is the keyboard shortcut for selecting all text in a placeholder.

5. Justify the text by clicking the Justify button in the Paragraph group.
6. Click the Align Text button in the Paragraph group and then click *Middle* at the drop-down gallery.

   This aligns the bulleted text vertically in the middle of the placeholder.

7. With the bulleted text still selected, click the Line Spacing button and then click *Line Spacing Options* at the drop-down gallery.

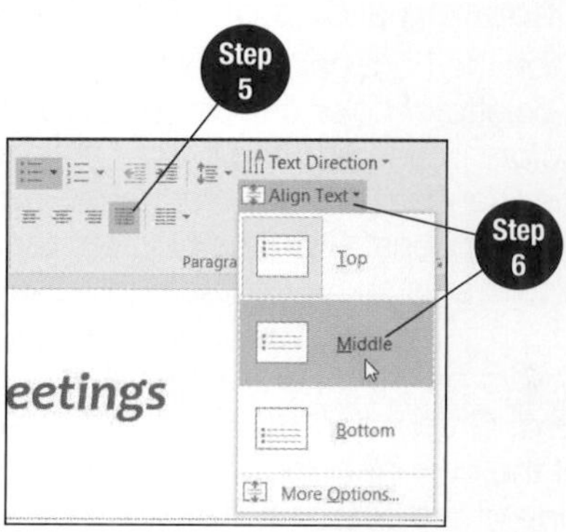

In Brief

Change Horizontal Text Alignment
1. Select text or click in paragraph.
2. Click alignment button in Paragraph group.

Change Vertical Text Alignment
1. Click Align Text button.
2. Click alignment.

Change Line Spacing
1. Click Line Spacing button.
2. Click spacing.

OR
1. Click Line Spacing button.
2. Click *Line Spacing Options*.
3. At Paragraph dialog box, specify spacing.
4. Click OK.

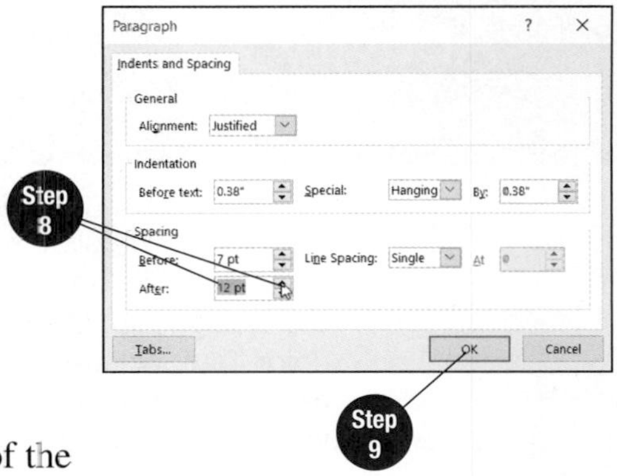

8. At the Paragraph dialog box, click the *After* measurement box up arrow two times.

   This inserts *12 pt* in the *After* measurement box.

9. Click OK to close the dialog box.
10. Make Slide 4 active (contains the title *Preproduction Team*).
11. Click in the bulleted text and then select all of the bulleted text by clicking the Select button in the Editing group on the Home tab and then clicking *Select All* at the drop-down list. 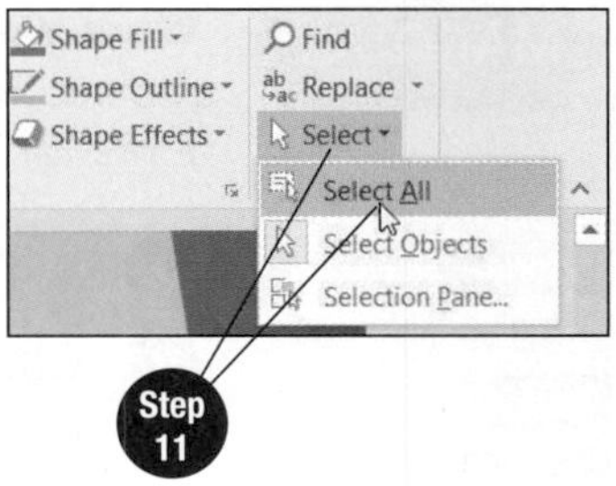
12. Click the Line Spacing button and then click *1.5* at the drop-down gallery.
13. Make Slide 7 active (contains the title *Preproduction Assignments*).
14. Click in the bulleted text and then press Ctrl + A.
15. Click the Line Spacing button in the Paragraph group and then click *Line Spacing Options* at the drop-down gallery.
16. At the Paragraph dialog box, click the *After* measurement box up arrow two times.

    This inserts *12 pt* in the *After* measurement box.

17. Click OK to close the dialog box.
18. Print only Slide 1 of the presentation as a handout.
19. Save **2-MPProj.pptx**.

Table 2.1 Alignment Keyboard Shortcuts

Alignment	Keyboard Shortcut
left	Ctrl + L
center	Ctrl + E
right	Ctrl + R
justify	Ctrl + J

Check Your Work Compare your work to the model answer to ensure that you have completed the activity correctly.

In Addition

Inserting a New Line

When creating bulleted text in a slide, pressing the Enter key causes the insertion point to move to the next line, inserting another bullet. Situations may occur wherein you want to create a blank line between bulleted items without creating another bullet. One method for doing this is to use the New Line command, Shift + Enter. Pressing Shift + Enter inserts a new line that is considered part of the previous paragraph.

Activity 2.6 Changing Slide Size and Design Themes; Formatting Slide Background

By default, the slide size in PowerPoint 2016 is Widescreen (16:9), but you can change the slide size with options in the Slide Size button drop-down list in the Customize group on the Design tab. Change the design theme applied to slides in a presentation or change the color, font, or effects of a theme with options on the Design tab. Format the slide background with options in the Format Background task pane. Display this task pane by clicking the Format Background button in the Customize group on the Design tab.

What You Will Do You are not pleased with the design theme for the documentary project presentation and decide to apply a different theme and then change the colors and fonts for the theme.

Tutorial Changing Slide Size

Tutorial Changing and Modifying Design Themes

Tutorial Formatting the Slide Background

1. With **2-MPProj.pptx** open, click the Design tab.
2. Click the Slide Size button in the Customize group and then click *Standard (4:3)* at the drop-down list.

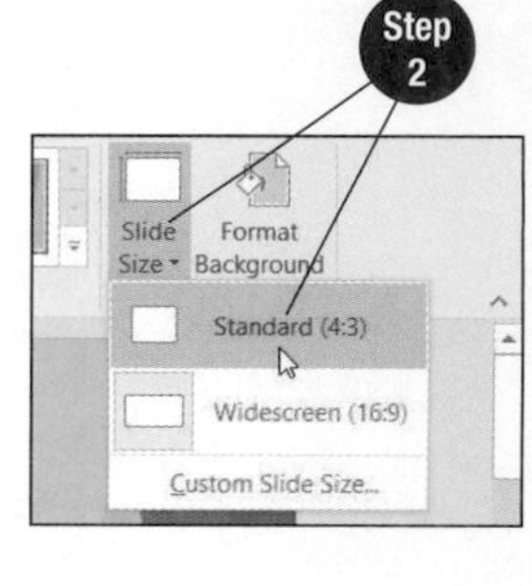

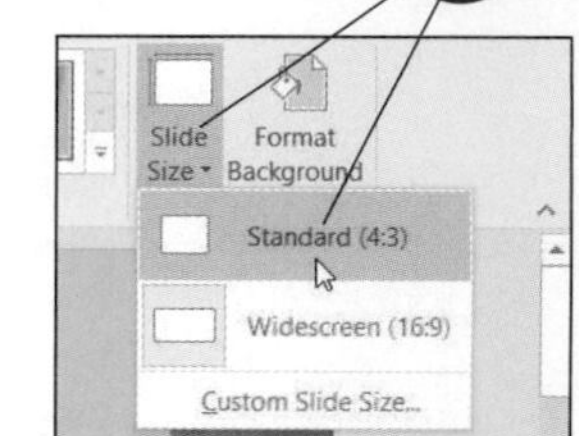

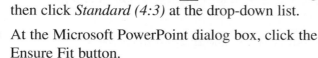

3. At the Microsoft PowerPoint dialog box, click the Ensure Fit button.

   Click the Ensure Fit button to scale down the contents of the slide to fit on the new slide. Click the Maximize button to maximize the size of the content on the new slide.

4. Run the slide show beginning with Slide 1 and notice any changes to the layout of the slides.
5. Click the Slide Size button and then click *Custom Slide Size* at the drop-down list.
6. At the Slide Size dialog box, click the *Slide sized for* option box arrow and then click *Widescreen* at the drop-down list.
7. Click OK.
8. Click the More Themes button in the Themes group.
9. Click *Dividend* at the drop-down gallery.
10. Click the More Variants button in the Variants group.
11. Click *Colors*, and then click *Yellow Orange* at the side menu.
12. Make Slide 2 active.

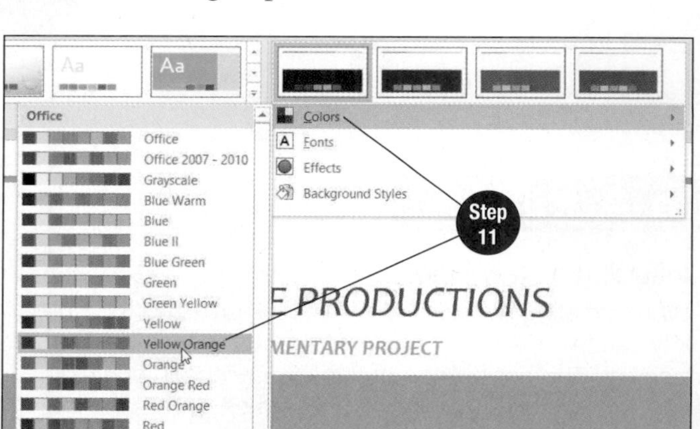

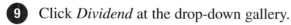

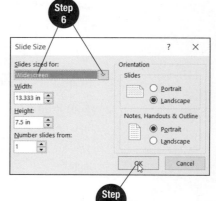

In Brief

Change Slide Size
1. Click Design tab.
2. Click Slide Size button.
3. Click slide size.

Change Design Theme
1. Click Design tab.
2. Click More Themes button.
3. Click theme.

Change Theme Colors
1. Click Design tab.
2. Click More Variants button.
3. Point to *Colors*.
4. Click option.

Change Theme Fonts
1. Click Design tab.
2. Click More Variants button.
3. Point to *Fonts*.
4. Click option at side menu.

Format Slide Background
1. Click Design tab.
2. Click Format Background button.
3. Make changes in task pane.

13 Click the More Variants button in the Variants group.

14 Click *Fonts*, scroll down the side menu, and then click *Cambria*.

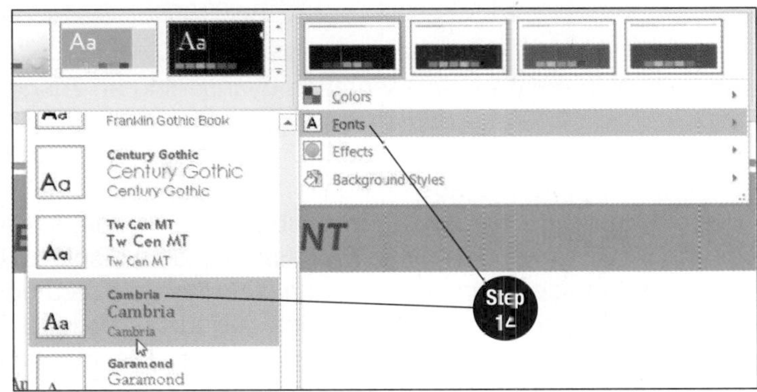

15 Apply a background style by clicking the More Variants button in the Variants group, pointing to *Background Styles*, and then clicking *Style 9* at the side menu (first column, third row).

16 Run the slide show beginning with Slide 1.

17 Customize the background by clicking the Format Background button in the Customize group on the Design tab.

This displays the Format Background task pane with a number of options for customizing slide backgrounds.

18 At the Format Background task pane, if necessary, click *Fill* to display fill options.

19 Click the *Solid fill* option, click the Color button, and then click the *Light Yellow, Background 2* color option (third column, first row in the *Theme Colors* section).

20 Click the Apply to All button toward the bottom of the task pane.

21 Close the task pane by clicking the close button in the upper right corner.

22 Save **2-MPProj.pptx** and then print Slide 1 of the presentation.

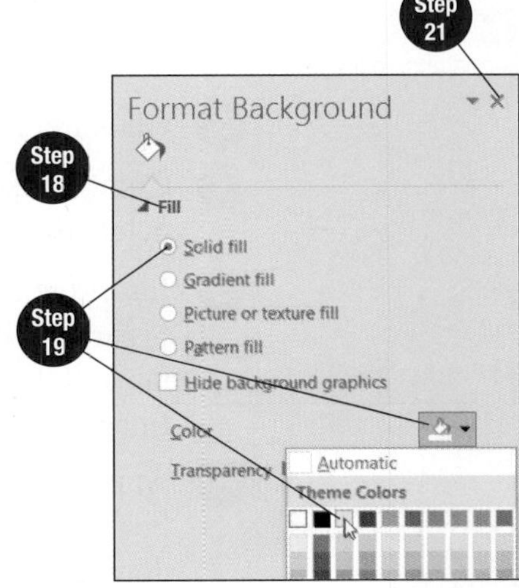

Check Your Work Compare your work to the model answer to ensure that you have completed the activity correctly.

In Addition

Inserting an Image as a Slide Background

Insert an image as the background of an entire slide by clicking the Design tab and then clicking the Format Background button in the Customize group. At the Format Background task pane, click *Fill* to display fill options, and then click the *Picture or texture fill* option. Click the File button in the *Insert picture from* section, navigate to the folder containing the image, and then double-click the image. The image will automatically be inserted as the current slide's background.

Activity 2.7 Inserting, Sizing, Moving, and Formatting an Image

Add visual interest to a presentation by inserting an image such as a logo, picture, or clip art in a slide. Insert an image from a drive or folder with the Insert Picture dialog box. Display the Insert Picture dialog box by clicking the Pictures button on the Insert tab or clicking the picture image in the content placeholder. At this dialog box, navigate to the desired drive or folder and then double-click the image. Click the Online Pictures button on the Insert tab and the Insert Pictures window displays. Use options in this window to search for images using Bing. At the window, type a category in the search text box to the right of the *Bing Image Search* option and then press the Enter key. In the list of images that displays, double-click the desired image. The image is inserted in the slide and the Picture Tools Format tab is selected. Use buttons on the Picture Tools Format tab to recolor the image, apply a picture style, arrange the image in the slide, and size the image. You can also size an image using the sizing handles that display around the selected image and move the image using the mouse.

What You Will Do Chris Greenbaum has asked you to insert the company logo on the first slide of the presentation and insert and format an image on a new slide at the end of the presentation.

Tutorial
Inserting, Sizing, and Moving an Image

Tutorial
Formatting an Image

1. With **2-MPProj.pptx** open, make sure Slide 1 is active.
2. Click in the title *Marquee Productions*, click the title placeholder border (border turns into a solid line when selected), and then press the Delete key.

   The title text will be deleted but the placeholder will not.

3. Click the title placeholder border again and then press the Delete key.
4. Complete steps similar to those in Steps 2 and 3 to delete the subtitle text and placeholder.
5. Insert the company logo in the slide as shown in Figure 2.1 on the next page. To begin, click the Insert tab and then click the Pictures button in the Images group.

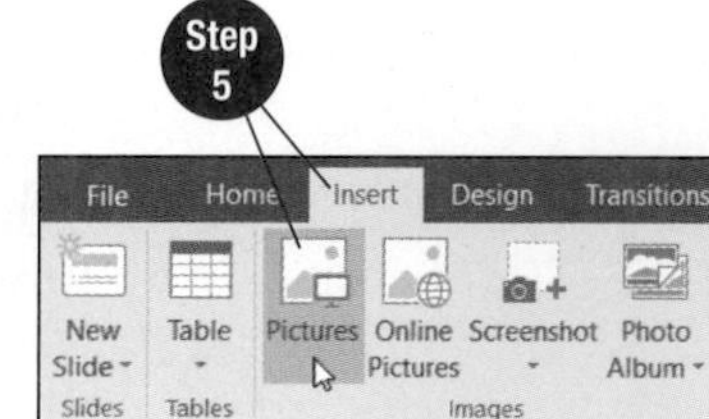

6. At the Insert Picture dialog box, navigate to the PowerPointS2 folder on your storage medium and then double-click ***MPLogo.jpg***.

   The image is inserted in the slide, selection handles display around the image, and the Picture Tools Format tab is selected.

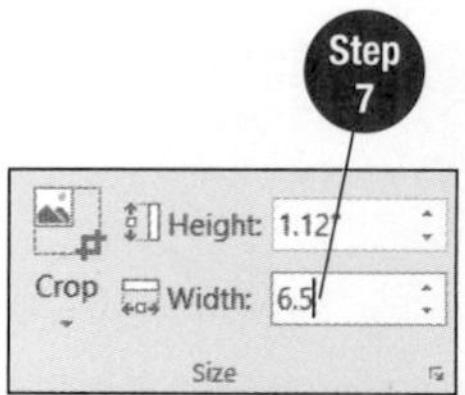

7. Increase the size of the logo by clicking in the *Shape Width* measurement box in the Size group, typing 6.5, and then pressing the Enter key.

   When you change the width of the logo, the height automatically adjusts to maintain the proportions of the logo. You can also size an image using the sizing handles that display around the selected image. Use the middle sizing handles to change the width of an image. Use the top and bottom handles to change the height, and use the corner sizing handles to adjust both the width and height of the image at the same time.

8 Move the logo so it is positioned as shown in Figure 2.1. To do this, position the mouse pointer on the image until the pointer displays with a four-headed arrow attached, click and hold down the left mouse button, drag the image to the position shown in the figure, and then release the mouse button.

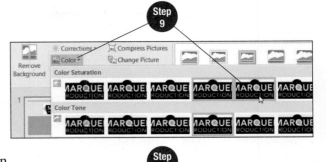

9 With the image selected, click the Color button in the Adjust group and then click the *Saturation 200%* option (fifth option in the *Color Saturation* section).

10 Click the Corrections button in the Adjust group and then click the *Brightness: +20% Contrast: -40%* option (fourth column, first row in the *Brightness/Contrast* section).

11 Click the *Drop Shadow Rectangle* option in the Picture Styles gallery (fourth option).

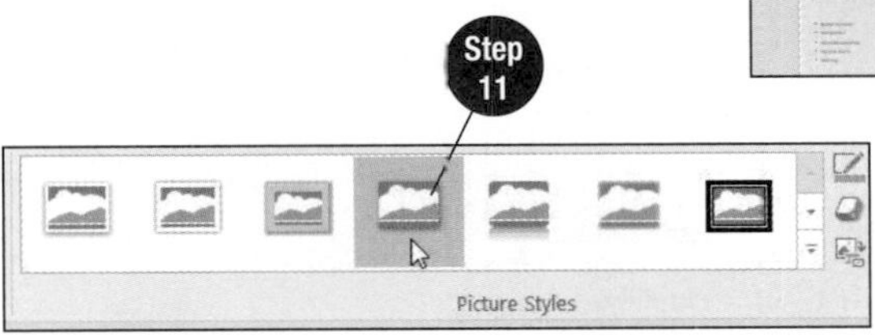

12 Click the Picture Effects button in the Picture Styles group, point to *Glow*, and then click the *Orange, 5 pt glow, Accent color 1* option (first column, first row in the *Glow Variations* section).

13 Click outside the logo to deselect it.

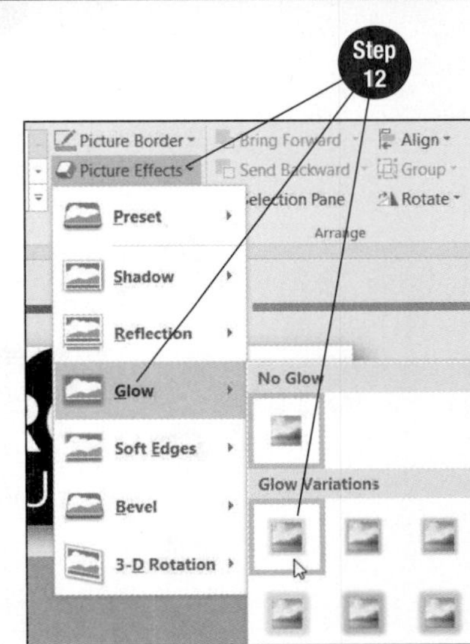

Figure 2.1 Slide 1

14 Make Slide 7 active.

15 Insert a new slide by clicking the New Slide button in the Slides group on the Home tab.

16 Click in the *CLICK TO ADD TITLE* placeholder and then type Travel Arrangements.

17 Click in the *Click to add text* placeholder and then type the bulleted text shown in Figure 2.2.

18 Click the Insert tab and then click the Online Pictures button in the Images group.

19 At the Insert Pictures window, click in the search text box at the right of *Bing Image Search*, type airport, symbol, and then press the Enter key.

20 Double-click the image shown below.

If the image is not available, insert the **Airport.png** image from the PS2 folder on your storage medium.

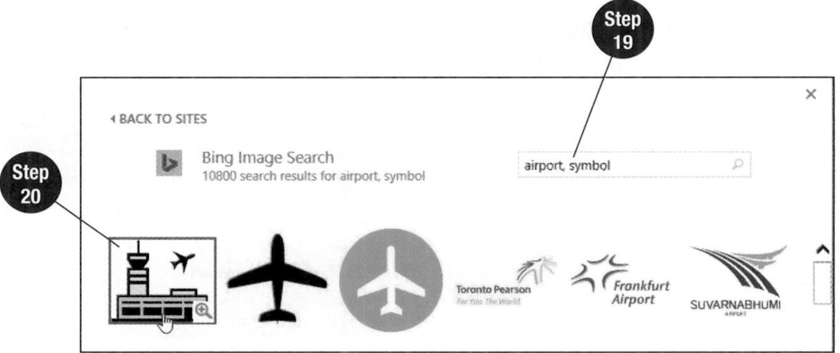

21 Click in the *Shape Height* measurement box in the Size group on the Picture Tools Format tab, type 3.5, and then press the Enter key.

When you change the height measurement, the width measurement changes automatically to maintain the proportions of the image.

22 Using the mouse, drag the image so it is positioned as shown in Figure 2.2.

23 Click the Color button in the Adjust group on the Picture Tools Format tab and then click the *Brown, Accent color 2 Light* option (third column, third row in the *Recolor* section).

24 Click the Corrections button in the Adjust group and then click the *Brightness: 0% (Normal) Contrast: +40%* option (third column, fifth row in the *Brightness/Contrast* section).

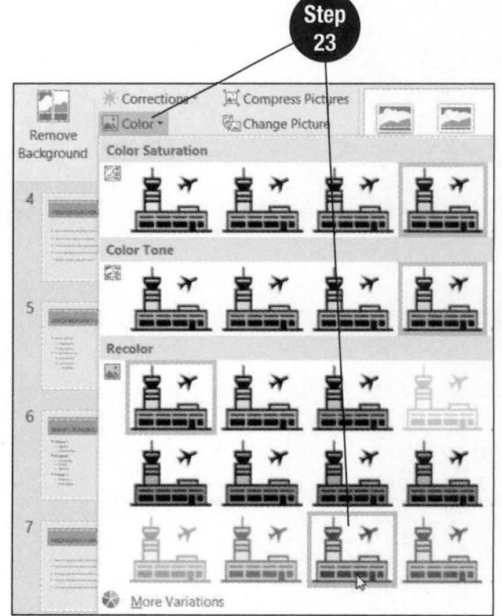

In Brief

Insert Image
1. Click Insert tab.
2. Click Pictures button.
3. At Insert Picture dialog box, navigate to folder.
4. Double-click image file.

Insert Online Image
1. Click Insert tab.
2. Click Online Pictures button.
3. At Insert Pictures window, type category, press Enter.
4. Double-click image.

25 Click the Picture Effects button in the Picture Styles group, point to *Shadow*, and then click the *Offset Diagonal Top Right* option (first column, third row in the *Outer* section).

26 Click the Rotate button in the Arrange group and then click *Flip Horizontal* at the drop-down gallery.

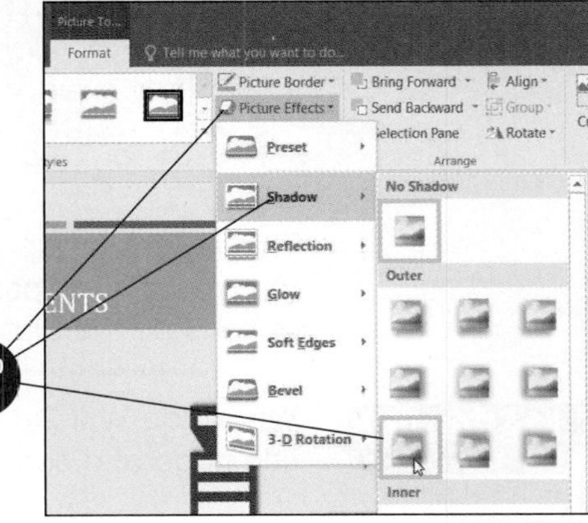

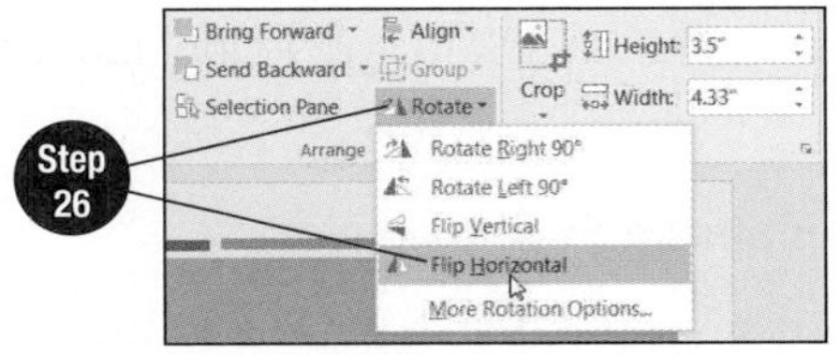

27 Make Slide 7 active and then click the Home tab.

28 Click in the title *PREPRODUCTION ASSIGNMENTS* and then click the Format Painter button in the Clipboard group.

29 Make Slide 8 active and then select the entire title *TRAVEL ARRANGEMENTS*.

This applies 40-point Candara bold italic formatting in a brown accent color.

30 Save **2-MPProj.pptx**.

Figure 2.2 Slide 8

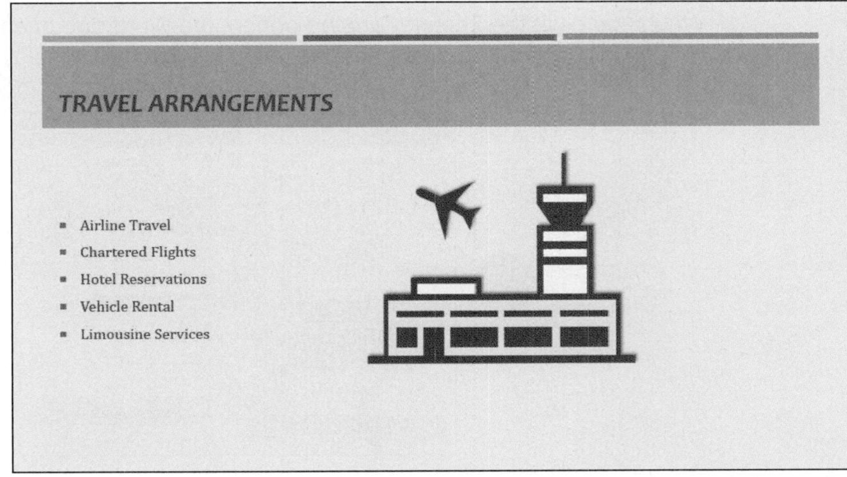

Check Your Work Compare your work to the model answer to ensure that you have completed the activity correctly.

In Addition

Formatting with Buttons on the Picture Tools Format Tab

Format images in a slide with buttons and options on the Picture Tools Format tab. Use buttons in the Adjust group to adjust the brightness and contrast of the image; change the image color or change to a different image; reset the image to its original size, position, and color; and compress the image. (Compress an image to reduce the resolution or discard extra information to save room on a hard drive or to reduce download time.) Use buttons in the Picture Styles group to apply a predesigned style, insert a picture border, or apply a picture effect. The Arrange group contains buttons for positioning the image and aligning and rotating the image. Use options in the Size group to crop the image and specify the height and width of the image.

Activity 2.8 Inserting and Formatting a Screen Clipping

The Images group on the Insert tab contains the Screenshot button, which you can use to capture all or part of the contents of a screen as an image. Format a screenshot with options on the Picture Tools Format tab.

What You Will Do Chris Greenbaum has asked you to include a screen clipping of the title page of a script document in a slide.

Tutorial
Inserting and Formatting Screenshot and Screen Clipping Images

1. With **2-MPProj.pptx** open, make Slide 6 active.
2. Insert a screenshot image from a Word document into the slide. Begin by opening Word and then opening **MPScript.docx**.

   Make sure 2-MPProj.pptx and MPScript.docx are the only open files.
3. Click the Zoom Out button at the left side of the Zoom slider bar until *40%* displays at the right side of the slider bar.
4. Click the button on the taskbar representing the PowerPoint presentation **2-MPProj.pptx**.
5. Click the Insert tab, click the Screenshot button in the Images group, and then click *Screen Clipping* at the drop-down list.

   When you click the *Screen Clipping* option, the Word document will automatically display in a dimmed manner and the insertion point will display as crosshairs.

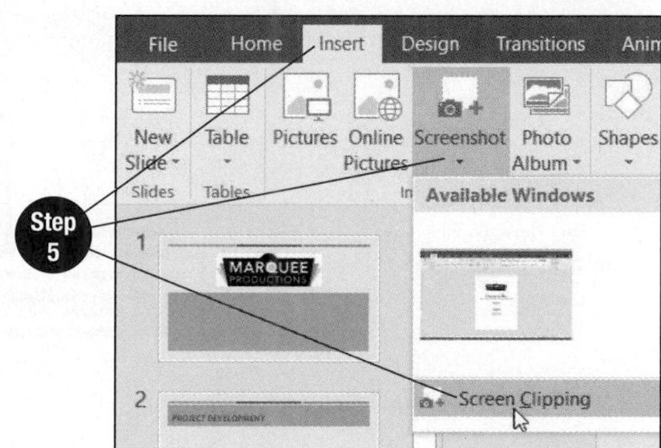

6. With the Word document displayed in a dimmed manner, position the crosshairs in the top left corner of the Word document and then drag down and to the right to select the entire document.

   Once you have created a screenshot of the Word document, the image will automatically be inserted into Slide 6 of 2-MPProj.pptx.
7. With the screenshot selected, click in the *Shape Height* measurement box in the Size group on the Picture Tools Format tab, type 5, and then press the Enter key.

In Brief

Insert Screenshot
1. Click Insert tab.
2. Click Screenshot button.
3. Click *Screen Clipping*.
4. Select image or text.

8 Click the Picture Border button arrow in the Picture Styles group and then click the *Orange, Accent 1* option at the drop-down list (fifth column, first row in the *Theme Colors* section).

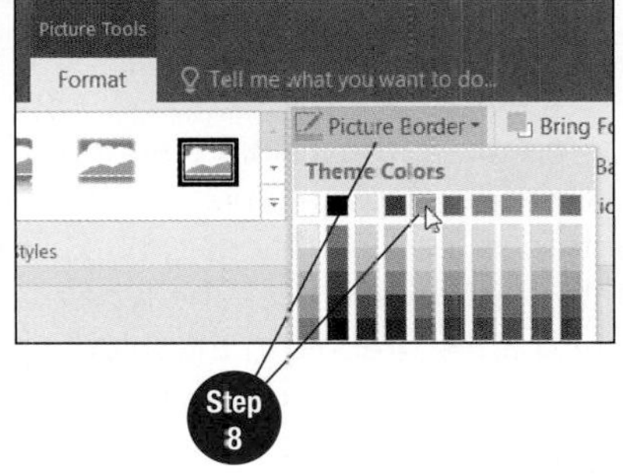

9 Position the screenshot in the slide as shown in Figure 2.3.

10 Click the Word button on the taskbar, close the document, and then close Word.

If a message displays asking if you want to save changes made in the document, click the Don't Save button.

11 Save **2-MPProj.pptx**.

Figure 2.3 Slide 6

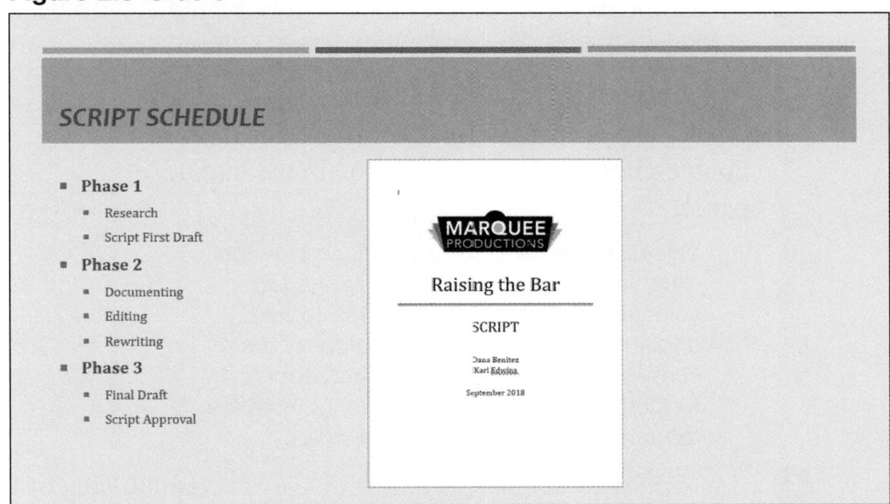

SCRIPT SCHEDULE
Phase 1
Research
Script First Draft
Phase 2
Documenting
Editing
Rewriting
Phase 3
Final Draft
Script Approval
MARQUEE
PRODUCTIONS
Raising the Bar
SCRIPT
September 2018

Check Your Work Compare your work to the model answer to ensure that you have completed the activity correctly.

In Addition

Inserting a Screenshot

If you want to capture the entire screen, open the desired file, click the Insert tab, click the Screenshot button in the Images group, and then click the screen thumbnail at the drop-down list. The currently active file does not display as a thumbnail at the drop-down list—only any other files that you have open.

Activity 2.9 Inserting and Formatting SmartArt

Use the SmartArt feature to create a variety of graphic diagrams, including process, cycle, relationship, matrix, and pyramid diagrams. You can also use SmartArt to visually illustrate hierarchical data. To display a menu of SmartArt choices, click the Insert tab and then click the SmartArt button in the Illustrations group. This displays the Choose a SmartArt Graphic dialog box. At this dialog box, click the type of organization chart or graphic in the left panel and then double-click the graphic in the middle panel. This inserts the chart or graphic in the slide. Some SmartArt graphics are designed to include text. Type text in a graphic shape by selecting the shape and then typing text in the shape. Use buttons on the SmartArt Tools Design tab and the SmartArt Tools Format tab to customize a graphic.

What You Will Do Chris Greenbaum has asked you to create a slide containing an organizational chart that illustrates the hierarchy of the people involved in production and a slide containing a SmartArt graphic of travel expenses.

Tutorial Inserting, Sizing, and Moving SmartArt

Tutorial Formatting SmartArt

1. With **2-MPProj.pptx** open, make Slide 2 active and then click the New Slide button in the Slides group on the Insert tab.
2. Create the organizational chart shown in Figure 2.4. To begin, click the Insert tab and then click the SmartArt button in the Illustrations group.
3. At the Choose a SmartArt Graphic dialog box, click *Hierarchy* in the left panel and then double-click the *Hierarchy* option in the middle panel.

   This displays the organizational chart in the slide with the SmartArt Tools Design tab selected. Use buttons on this tab to add additional boxes, change the order of the shapes, choose a different layout, apply formatting with a SmartArt style, or reset the formatting of the organizational chart.

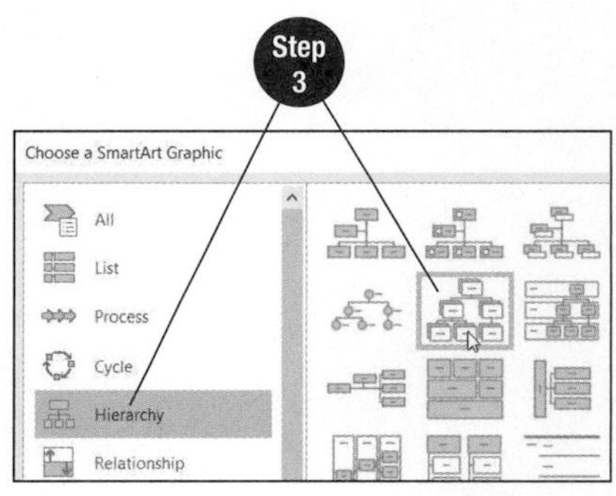

4. If a *Type your text here* window displays at the left side of the organizational chart, close it by clicking the Text Pane button in the Create Graphic group.

   You can also close the window by clicking the Close button in the upper right corner of the window.
5. Delete one of the boxes in the organizational chart. Begin by clicking the border of the second text box from the top at the left side of the chart.

   Make sure *[Text]* displays in the box.
6. Press the Delete key.
7. With the second box from the top at the right side selected, click the Add Shape button in the Create Graphic group.

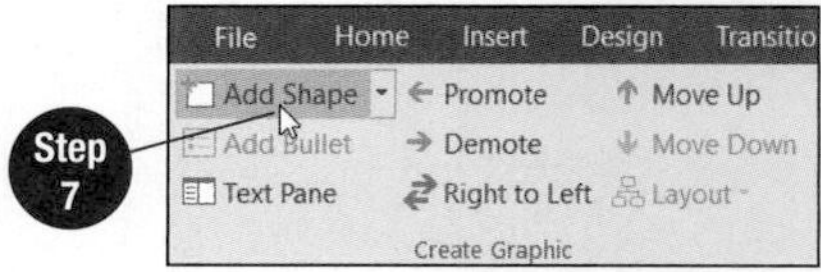

   This inserts a box to the right of the selected box. Your organizational chart should contain the same boxes shown in Figure 2.4. (The new box does not contain a *[Text]* placeholder, but you can still type text in the box.)

8 Click the *[Text]* placeholder in the top box, type Chris Greenbaum, press the Enter key, and then type Production Manager. Click in each of the remaining boxes and type the text as shown in Figure 2.4.

9 Click the Change Colors button in the SmartArt Styles group on the SmartArt Tools Design tab and then click the *Colorful Range - Accent Colors 4 to 5* option (fourth option in the *Colorful* section).

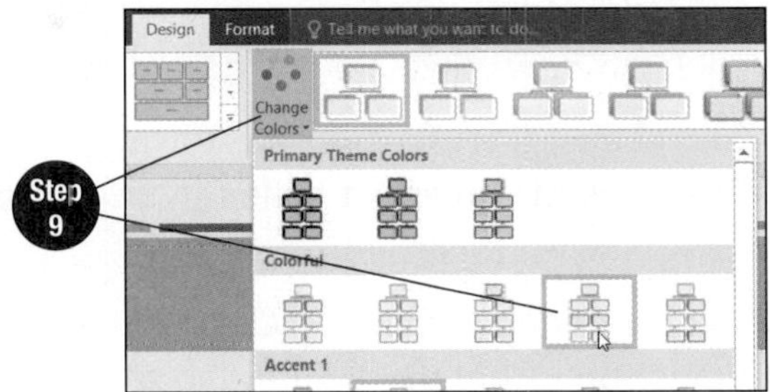

10 Click the More SmartArt Styles button at the right side of the gallery in the SmartArt Styles group.

11 Click the *Inset* option at the drop-down gallery (second column, first row in the *3-D* section).

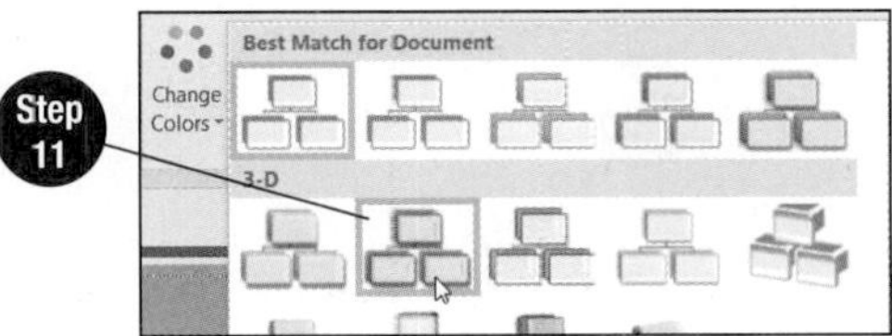

12 Click the SmartArt Tools Format tab.

13 Click inside the SmartArt graphic border but outside any shape.

14 Click in the *Shape Height* measurement box in the Size group, type 5, click in the *Shape Width* measurement box, type 10, and then press the Enter key.

15 Move the graphic so it is positioned in the slide as shown in Figure 2.4. Do this by positioning the mouse pointer on the graphic border until the pointer displays with a four-headed arrow attached, clicking and holding down the left mouse button, dragging the graphic to the desired location, and then releasing the mouse button.

Figure 2.4 Organizational Chart

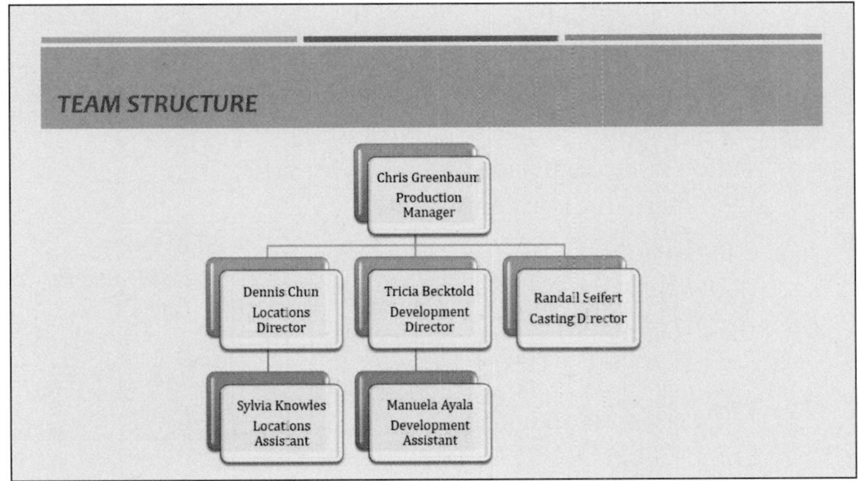

16 Click in the *CLICK TO ADD TITLE* placeholder and then type Team Structure.

17 Make Slide 2 active, click in the title *Project Development*, click the Home tab, and then click the Format Painter button in the Clipboard group.

18 Make Slide 3 active and then select the entire title *Team Structure*.

19 Make Slide 9 active.

20 Click the New Slide button arrow in the Slides group on the Home tab and then click the *Blank* layout at the drop-down list.

21 Create the SmartArt graphic shown in Figure 2.5. To begin, click the Insert tab and then click the SmartArt button in the Illustrations group.

22 At the Choose a SmartArt Graphic dialog box, click *Relationship* in the left panel and then double-click the *Converging Radial* option. (This option may be the first option from the right in the sixth row or the first option from the left in the seventh row.)

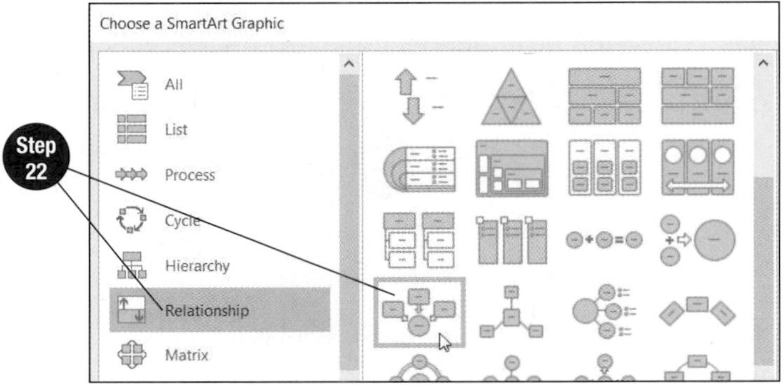

23 If necessary, close the *Type your text here* window by clicking the Close button in the upper right corner of the window.

24 Click the Add Shape button in the Create Graphic group.

25 Click in each of the shapes and insert the text shown in Figure 2.5.

26 Click the Change Colors button in the SmartArt Styles group and then click the *Colorful - Accent Colors* option (first option in the *Colorful* section).

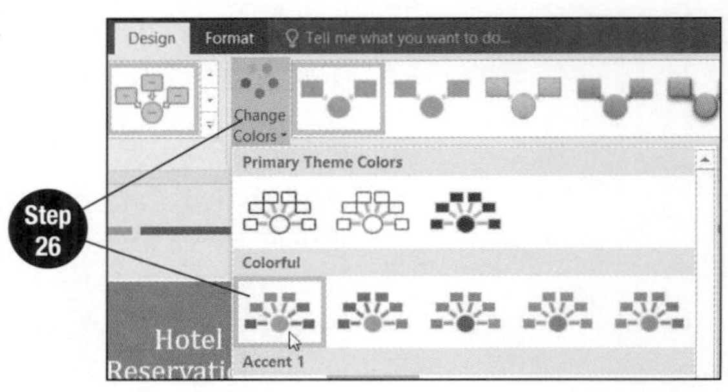

27 Click the More SmartArt Styles button at the right side of the gallery in the SmartArt Styles group.

28 Click the *Cartoon* option at the drop-down gallery (third column, first row in the *3-D* section).

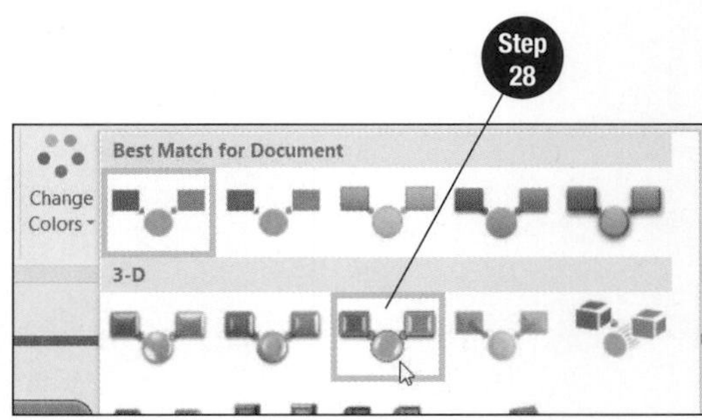

In Brief

Create Organizational Chart
1. Click Insert tab.
2. Click SmartArt button.
3. Click *Hierarchy.*
4. Double-click organizational chart.

Create SmartArt Graphic
1. Click Insert tab.
2. Click SmartArt button.
3. Click category in left panel.
4. Double-click graphic.

29 Click the SmartArt Tools Format tab.

30 Click inside the SmartArt graphic border but outside any shape.

This deselects the shapes but keeps the graphic selected.

31 Click the More WordArt button at the right side of the gallery in the WordArt Styles group and then click the *Fill - White, Outline - Accent 1, Glow - Accent 1* option (fourth column, second row).

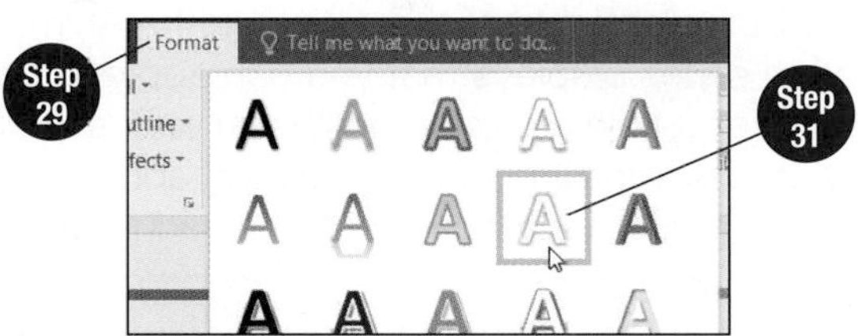

32 Click in the *Shape Width* measurement box in the Size group, type 9.5, and then press the Enter key.

33 Click the Align button in the Arrange group and then click *Align Center* at the drop-down list.

34 Save **2-MPProj.pptx**

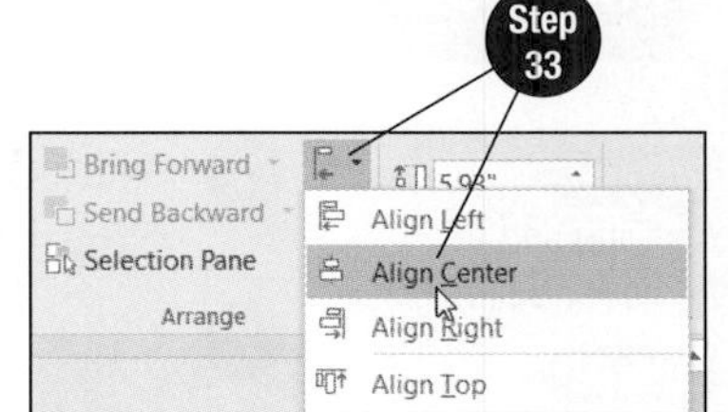

Figure 2.5 SmartArt Graphic

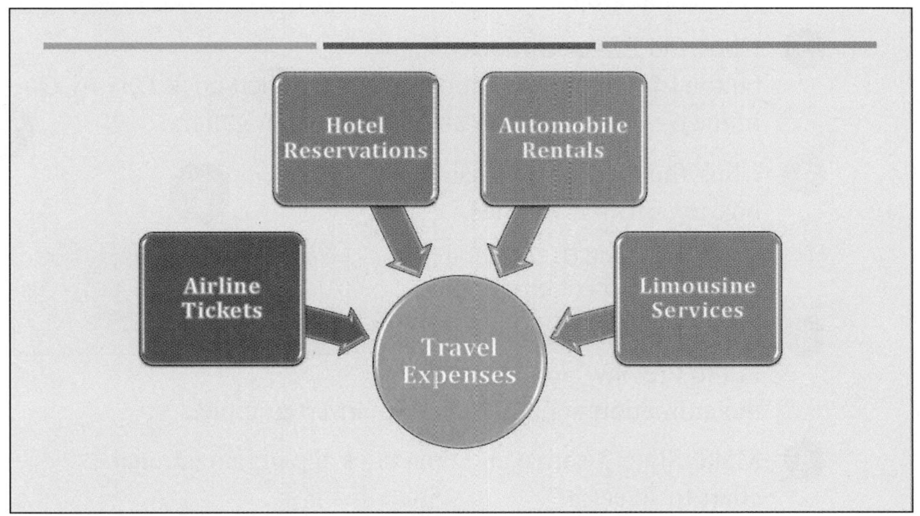

Check Your Work Compare your work to the model answer to ensure that you have completed the activity correctly.

In Addition

Inserting Text in the Text Pane

Enter text in a SmartArt shape by clicking in the shape and then typing the text. You can also insert text in a SmartArt shape by typing text in SmartArt's text pane. Display the text pane by clicking the Text Pane button in the Create Graphic group on the SmartArt Tools Design tab.

Activity 2.10 Applying Animation to Objects and Text

Animate individual objects and text in a slide with options on the Animations tab. Click the Animations tab and the tab displays with a variety of animation styles and options for customizing and applying times to animations in a presentation. Click the More Animations button at the right side of the gallery in the Animation group and a drop-down gallery of animation styles displays that you can apply to objects and text as they enter a slide, exit a slide, and/or follow a motion path. You can also apply animations to emphasize objects in a slide. If you want the same animation applied to other objects in a presentation, use the Animation Painter button in the Advanced Animation group on the Animations tab.

What You Will Do To finalize the presentation, Chris Greenbaum has asked you to apply animation to objects and text in the presentation.

Tutorial
Applying and Removing Animations

Tutorial
Modifying Animations

1. With **2-MPProj.pptx** open, make sure Slide 10 is active and the SmartArt graphic is selected.

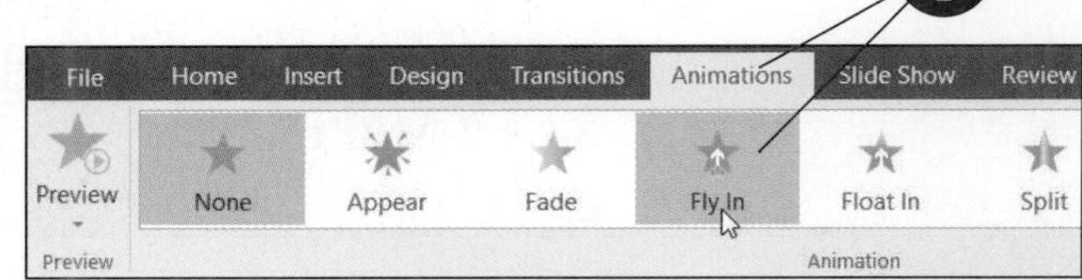

2. Click the Animations tab and then click the *Fly In* option in the Animation gallery in the Animation group.
3. Click the Effect Options button in the Animation group and then click *One by One* in the *Sequence* section at the drop-down gallery.

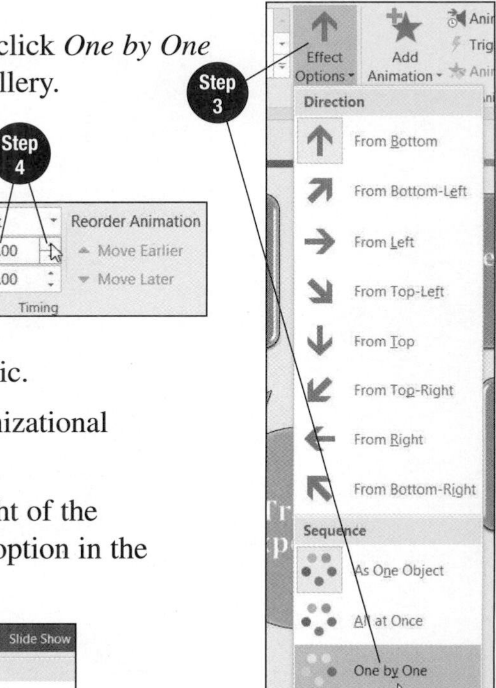

4. Click the *Duration* measurement box up arrow two times.

   This inserts *01.00* in the measurement box.

Step 4
Start: On Click
Duration: 01.00
Delay: 00.00
Reorder Animation
Move Earlier
Move Later
Timing

5. Click the Preview button in the Preview group to view the animation applied to the SmartArt graphic.
6. Make Slide 3 active and then click the organizational chart to select it.
7. Click the More Animations button at the right of the Animation gallery and then click the *Zoom* option in the *Entrance* section at the drop-down gallery.

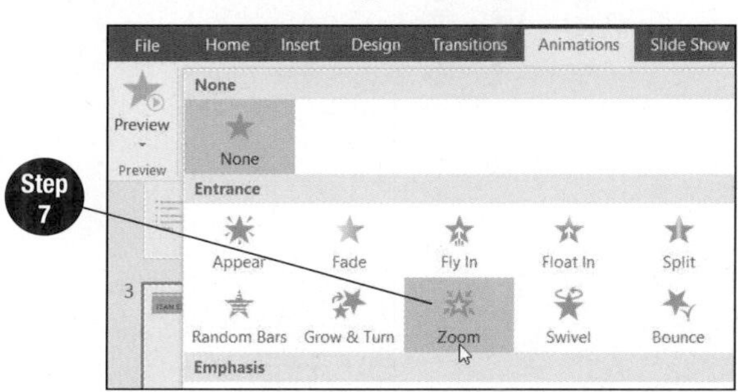

8. Click the Effect Options button in the Animation group and then click *One by One* in the *Sequence* section at the drop-down gallery.

In Brief

Apply Animation to Object
1. Click object.
2. Click Animations tab.
3. Click animation option.

9 Click Slide 2 to make it active and then click in the bulleted text to select the placeholder.

10 Click the *Fly In* option in the gallery in the Animation group.

Applying this animation creates a *build* for the bulleted items. A build displays important points in a slide one point at a time and is useful for keeping the audience's attention focused on the point being presented rather than reading ahead.

11 Click the *Duration* measurement box up arrow in the Timing group two times.

This inserts *01.00* in the measurement box.

12 Apply the same animation to the bulleted text in Slides 4 through 9. To begin, click in the bulleted text to select the placeholder and then double-click the Animation Painter button in the Advanced Animation group.

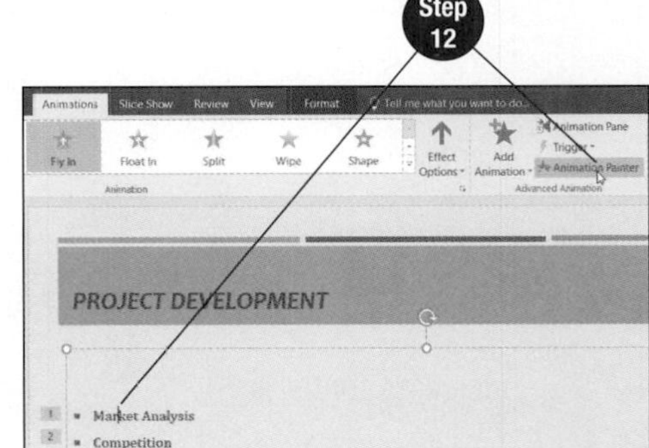

13 Make Slide 4 active and then click in the bulleted text. (This selects the placeholder and applies the Fly In animation and the duration time.)

14 Make Slide 5 active and then click in the bulleted text.

15 Make Slide 6 active and then click in the bulleted text. Repeat this action for Slides 7–9.

16 Click the Animation Painter button to turn off the feature.

17 Make Slide 1 active and then run the slide show. Click the mouse button to advance slides and to display the individual organizational chart boxes, bulleted items, and SmartArt graphic boxes.

18 Print the presentation as handouts with six slides displayed horizontally on one page. To do this, click the File tab and then click the *Print* option.

19 At the Print backstage area, click the second gallery (contains the text *Full Page Slides*) in the *Settings* category and then click *6 Slides Horizontal* at the drop-down list.

20 Click the Print button.

21 Save and then close **2-MPProj.pptx**.

Check Your Work Compare your work to the model answer to ensure that you have completed the activity correctly.

In Addition

Applying Custom Animation

Apply custom animation to selected objects in a slide by clicking the Animation Pane button in the Advanced Animation group on the Animations tab. This displays the Animation task pane at the right side of the screen. Use options in this task pane to control the order in which objects appear on a slide, choose animation direction and speed, and specify how objects will appear in the slide.

Features Summary

Feature	Ribbon Tab, Group	Button	Keyboard Shortcut
align left	Home, Paragraph		Ctrl + L
align right	Home, Paragraph		Ctrl + R
align vertically	Home, Paragraph		
animation effect options	Animations, Animation		
bold	Home, Font	B	Ctrl + B
center	Home, Paragraph		Ctrl + E
copy selected text	Home, Clipboard		Ctrl + C
cut selected text	Home, Clipboard		Ctrl + X
decrease font size	Home, Font	A	Ctrl + Shift + <
decrease list level	Home, Paragraph		Shift + Tab
font	Home, Font		
font color	Home, Font	A	
Font dialog box	Home, Font		Ctrl + Shift + F
font size	Home, Font		
format background	Design, Customize		
Format Painter	Home, Clipboard		
increase font size	Home, Font	A	Ctrl + Shift + >
increase list level	Home, Paragraph		Tab
insert image	Insert, Images		
insert online image	Insert, Images		
insert screenshot	Insert, Images		
insert SmartArt	Insert, Illustrations		
italic	Home, Font	I	Ctrl + I
justify	Home, Paragraph		Ctrl + J
line spacing	Home, Paragraph		
paste selected text	Home, Clipboard		Ctrl + V
preview animation	Animations, Preview		
slide size	Design, Customize		
underline	Home, Font	U	Ctrl + U

Workbook Section study tools and assessment activities are available in the *Workbook* ebook. These resources are designed to help you further develop and demonstrate mastery of the skills learned in this section.

PowerPoint SECTION 3

Customizing a Presentation

Skills

Data Files Before beginning section work, copy the PowerPointS3 folder to your storage medium and then make PowerPointS3 the active folder.

- Copy and paste items using the Clipboard task pane
- Find and replace text
- Insert and format WordArt
- Draw and customize objects
- Display gridlines
- Insert a text box
- Copy and rotate shapes
- Create and format a table
- Insert action buttons
- Insert a hyperlink
- Format with a slide master
- Insert headers and footers
- Add audio and video
- Set and rehearse timings for a slide show

Precheck Check your current skills to help focus your study of the skills taught in this section.

Projects Overview

Add visual appeal to a presentation on filming in Toronto by inserting WordArt, shapes, text boxes, and a table. Improve a presentation on a biography project by inserting WordArt, shapes, text boxes, an image, a logo, and a footer. Update a presentation on the annual meeting by applying a design theme, theme colors, and theme fonts and formatting using a slide master. Prepare and format a project schedule presentation.

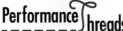

Performance Threads Format a presentation on costume designs for Marquee Productions and add visual appeal by inserting a logo, WordArt, shapes, text boxes, a table, and a footer.

Add a video clip and audio file to a presentation on eco-tour adventures. Format a presentation about a vacation cruise and add visual appeal by inserting a logo and audio clip, setting and rehearsing timings, and setting up the slide show to run continuously. Enhance a presentation on tours in Australia and New Zealand by inserting WordArt, a footer, and an audio clip; setting and rehearsing timings; and setting up the slide show to run continuously. Prepare a presentation on a Moroccan tour.

If you are a SNAP user, launch the Precheck and Tutorials from your Assignments page.

Model Answers Preview the model answers for an overview of the projects you will complete in the section activities.

Activity 3.1 Using the Clipboard Task Pane

Using the Clipboard task pane, you can collect up to 24 different items and then paste them in various locations in slides. To display the Clipboard task pane, click the Clipboard group task pane launcher in the Clipboard group on the Home tab. The Clipboard task pane displays at the left side of the screen. Select text or an object you want to copy and then click the Copy button in the Clipboard group. Continue selecting text or items and clicking the Copy button. To paste an item into a slide in a presentation, position the insertion point in the desired location and then click the item in the Clipboard task pane. (If the copied item is text, the first 50 characters display in the Clipboard task pane.) After inserting all items into the presentation, click the Clear All button to remove any remaining items from the Clipboard task pane.

What You Will Do In preparation for a meeting about the Toronto location shoot, you will open the Toronto presentation and then copy and paste multiple items into the appropriate slides.

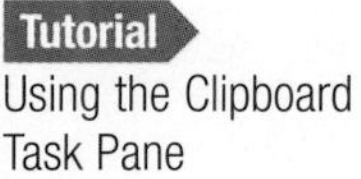

Using the Clipboard Task Pane

1. Open **MPToronto.pptx** and then save it with the name **3-MPToronto**.
2. Display the Clipboard task pane by clicking the Clipboard group task pane launcher. If items display in the Clipboard task pane, click the Clear All button in the upper right corner of the task pane.
3. Make Slide 2 active and then select the name *Chris Greenbaum*. (Do not include the space after the name.)
4. With *Chris Greenbaum* selected, click the Copy button in the Clipboard group.

   When you click the Copy button, the name *Chris Greenbaum* is inserted as an item in the Clipboard task pane.

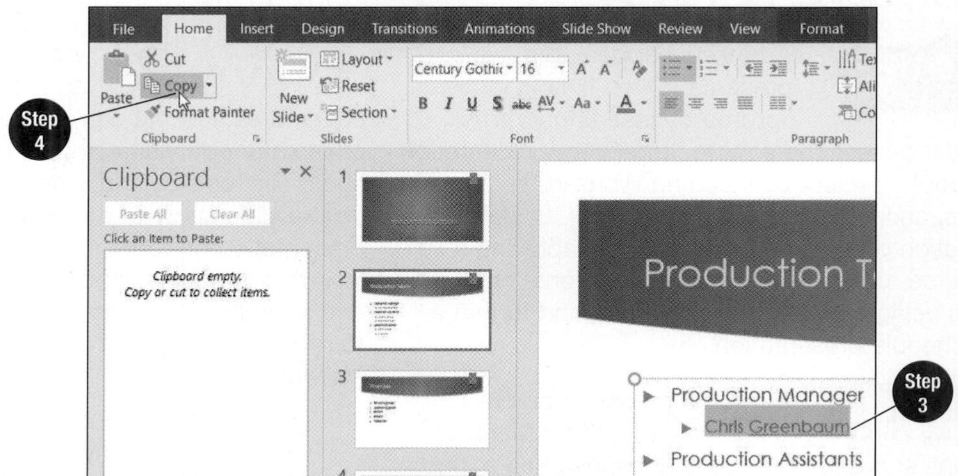

5. Select the name *Camille Matsui* (do not include the space after the name) and then click the Copy button. Select the name *Dennis Chun* (without the space after) and then click the Copy button. Select the name *Josh Hart* (without the space after) and then click the Copy button.
6. Make Slide 3 active, position the insertion point immediately to the right of *Location Expenses*, press the Enter key, and then press the Tab key.

In Brief

Use Clipboard Task Pane

1. Click Clipboard group task pane launcher.
2. Select text, click Copy button.
3. Continue selecting text and clicking Copy button.
4. Position insertion point.
5. Click item in Clipboard task pane.
6. Insert additional items.
7. Click Clear All button.
8. Close Clipboard task pane.

7. Click *Chris Greenbaum* in the Clipboard task pane.

8. Position the insertion point immediately right of *Production*, press the Enter key, press the Tab key, and then click *Camille Matsui* in the Clipboard task pane.
9. Make Slide 4 active, position the insertion point immediately right of *Royal Ontario Museum*, press the Enter key, press the Tab key, and then click *Dennis Chun* in the Clipboard task pane.
10. Position the insertion point immediately right of *Island Airport*, press the Enter key, press the Tab key, and then click *Dennis Chun* in the Clipboard task pane.
11. Position the insertion point immediately right of *King Street*, press the Enter key, press the Tab key, and then click *Josh Hart* in the Clipboard task pane.
12. Click the Clear All button in the Clipboard task pane and then click the Close button ☒ in the upper right corner of the task pane.

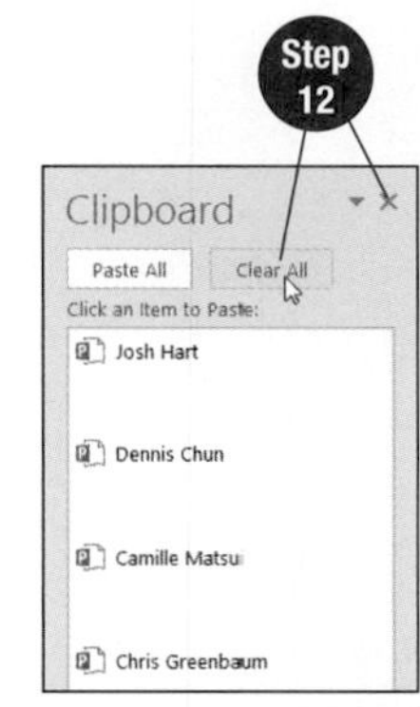

13. Make Slide 1 active and then insert the **MPLogo.jpg** file. To begin, click the Insert tab and then click the Pictures button in the Images group. Make the PowerPointS3 folder active and then double-click ***MPLogo.jpg***.
14. Size and move the logo so it better fills the slide.
15. Save **3-MPToronto.pptx**.

Check Your Work Compare your work to the model answer to ensure that you have completed the activity correctly.

In Addition

Using Clipboard Task Pane Options

Click the Options button at the bottom of the Clipboard task pane and a drop-down list displays with five options, as shown at the right. Click to insert a check mark before those options you want active. For example, you can choose to display the Clipboard task pane automatically when you cut or copy text, cut and copy text without displaying the Clipboard task pane, display the Clipboard task pane by pressing Ctrl + C twice, display the Office Clipboard icon on the taskbar when the Clipboard is active, and display the item message near the taskbar when copying items to the Clipboard.

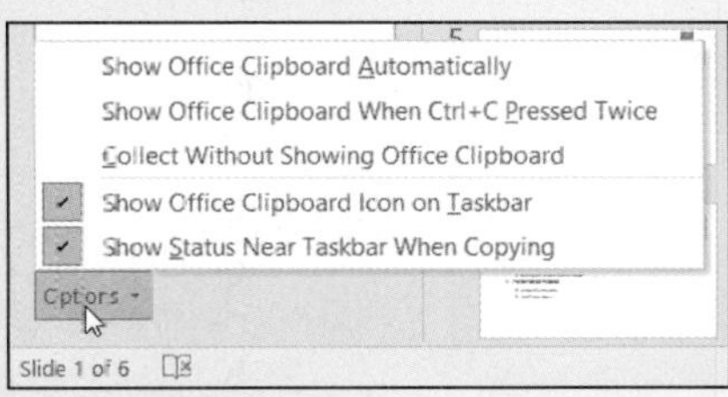

Activity 3.2 Finding and Replacing Text

Use the Find and Replace feature to search for specific text or formatting in slides in a presentation and replace it with other text or formatting. Display the Find dialog box if you want to find something specific in a presentation. Display the Replace dialog box if you want to find something in a presentation and replace it with another item.

What You Will Do A couple of people have been replaced on the Toronto location shoot. Use the Replace feature to find names and replace them with new names in the Toronto presentation.

Tutorial
Finding and Replacing Text

1. With **3-MPToronto.pptx** open, make sure Slide 1 is active.
2. Camille Matsui has been replaced by Jennie Almonzo. Begin the find and replace by clicking the Replace button in the Editing group on the Home tab.

   This displays the Replace dialog box with the insertion point positioned in the *Find what* text box.

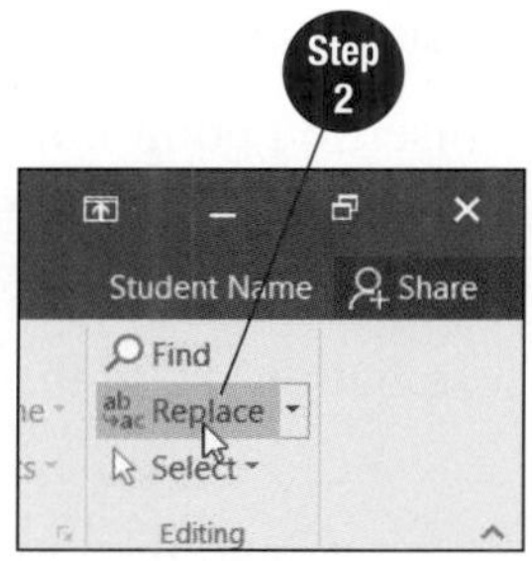

3. Type Camille Matsui in the *Find what* text box.
4. Press the Tab key and then type Jennie Almonzo in the *Replace with* text box.
5. Click the Replace All button.

   Clicking the Replace All button replaces all occurrences of the *Find what* text in the presentation. If you want control over which occurrences are replaced in a presentation, click the Find Next button to move to the next occurrence of the text. Click the Replace button if you want to replace the text, or click the Find Next button if you want to leave the text as written and move to the next occurrence.

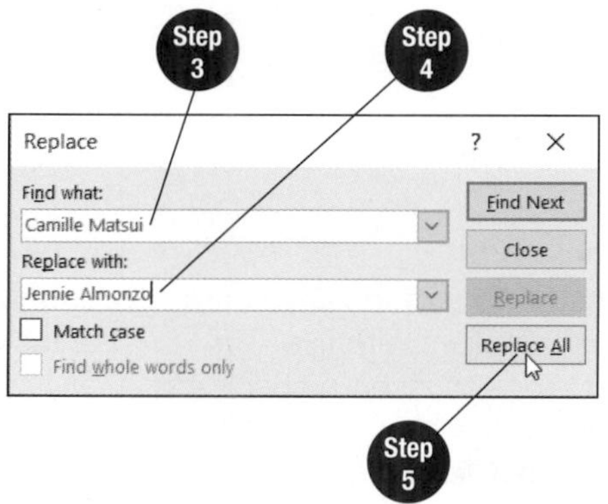

6. At the message telling you that two replacements were made, click OK.

   The Replace dialog box remains on the screen.

In Brief

Find and Replace Text
1. Click Replace button.
2. At Replace dialog box, type find text.
3. Press Tab and then type replace text.
4. Click Replace All button.
5. Click Close button.

7. Josh Hart had to leave the project and is being replaced by Jaime Ruiz. At the Replace dialog box, type Josh Hart in the *Find what* text box.

   When you begin typing the name *Josh Hart*, the previous name, *Camille Matsui*, is deleted.

8. Press the Tab key, type Jaime Ruiz in the *Replace with* text box, and then click the Replace All button.

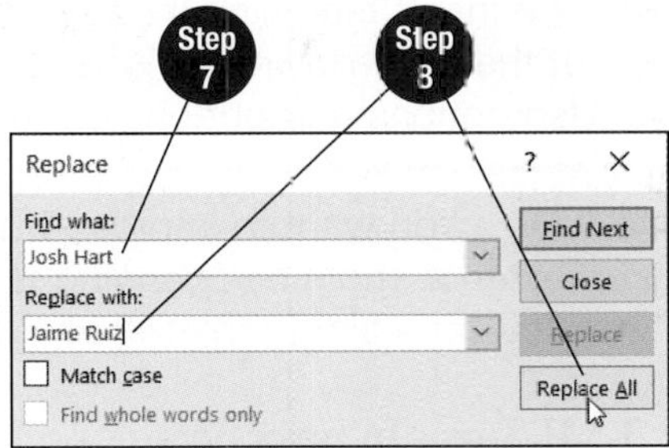

9. At the message telling you that two replacements were made, click OK.

   The Replace dialog box remains on the screen.

10. The title *Manager* has been changed to *Director*. At the Replace dialog box, type Manager in the *Find what* text box.

11. Press the Tab key, type Director in the *Replace with* text box, and then click the Replace All button.

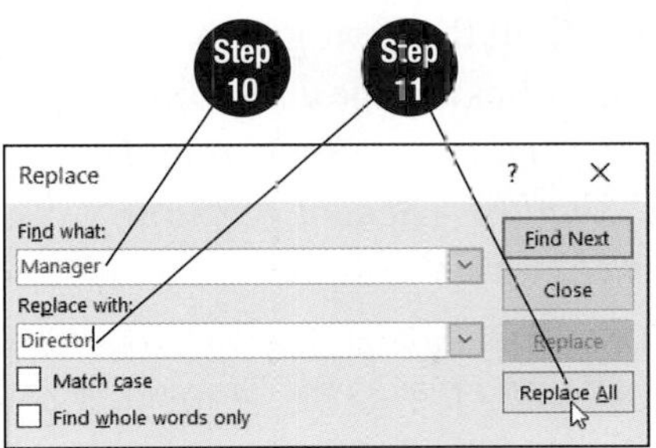

12. At the message telling you that one replacement was made, click OK.

13. Close the Replace dialog box by clicking the Close button in the upper right corner of the dialog box.

14. Save **3-MPToronto.pptx**.

Check Your Work Compare your work to the model answer to ensure that you have completed the activity correctly.

In Addition

Using Replace Dialog Box Options

The Replace dialog box, shown at the right, contains two options for completing a find and replace. Choose the *Match case* option if you want to exactly match the case of the find text. For example, if you look for *Company*, PowerPoint will stop at *Company* but not *company* or *COMPANY*. Choose the *Find whole words only* option if you want to find a whole word, not a part of a word. For example, if you search for *his* and do not select *Find whole words only*, PowerPoint will stop at *this*, *his*tory, *chis*el, and so on.

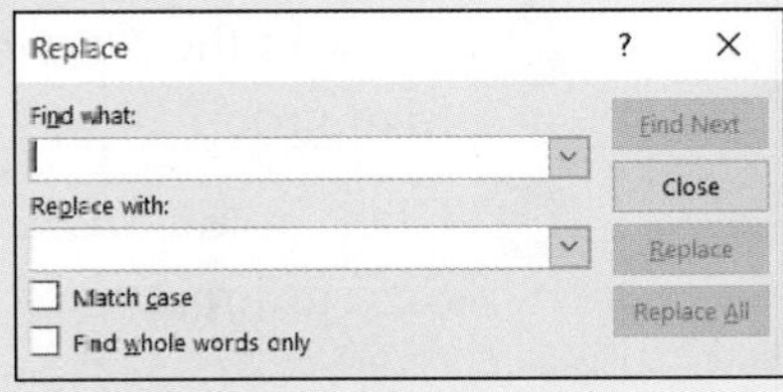

Activity 3.3 Inserting and Formatting WordArt

Use the WordArt feature to create text with special formatting that makes it stand out. You can format WordArt in a variety of ways, including conforming it to a shape. To insert WordArt, click the Insert tab, click the WordArt button in the Text group, and then click a WordArt style at the drop-down list. When WordArt is selected, the Drawing Tools Format tab displays. Use options and buttons on this tab to modify and customize WordArt.

What You Will Do You want to improve the appearance of the slide containing information on exterior shots by changing text to WordArt. You also want to insert a new slide with the title of the film formatted as WordArt.

Tutorial
Inserting and Formatting WordArt

1. With **3-MPToronto.pptx** open, make sure Slide 1 is active.
2. Click the New Slide button arrow in the Slides group on the Home tab and then click the *Blank* layout (first column, third row).

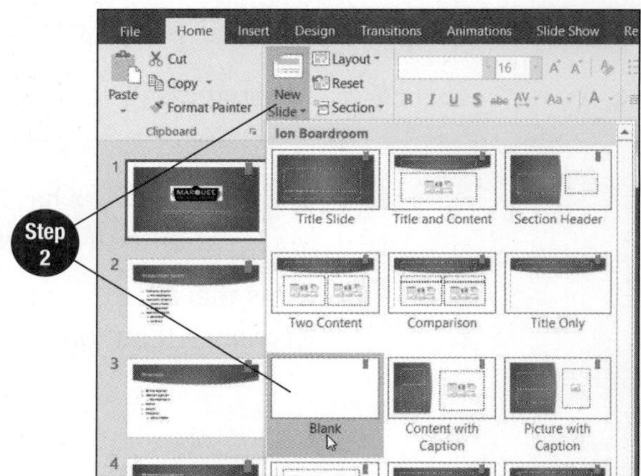

3. Insert WordArt by clicking the Insert tab, clicking the WordArt button in the Text group, and then clicking the *Fill - Tan, Accent 1, Outline - Background 1, Hard Shadow - Accent 1* option (third column, third row).

   This inserts a text box with *Your text here* inside and makes the Drawing Tools Format tab active.

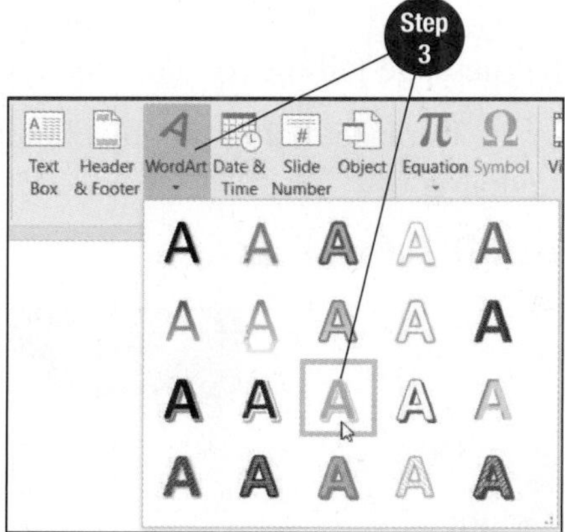

4. Type Ring of Roses.
5. Click in the *Shape Height* measurement box in the Size group, type 4, and then press the Enter key.
6. Click in the *Shape Width* measurement box in the Size group, type 9, and then press the Enter key.

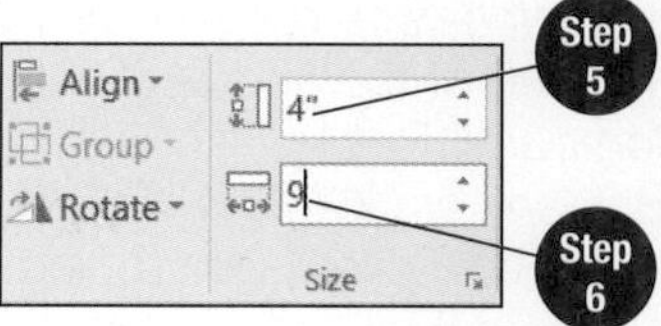

In Brief

Insert WordArt
1. Click Insert tab.
2. Click WordArt button.
3. Click WordArt option.
4. Type WordArt text.
5. Apply formatting

7. Click the Text Effects button in the WordArt Styles group, point to *Transform* at the drop-down list, scroll down the side menu, and then click *Deflate* (second column, sixth row in the *Warp* section).

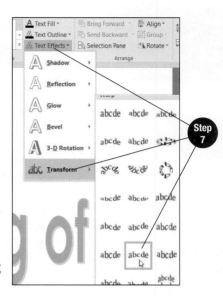

8. Click the border of the WordArt (border will display as a solid line), click the Text Outline button arrow, and then click the *Orange, Accent 1* color option at the drop-down gallery (fifth column, first row in *Theme Colors* section).

9. Position the WordArt in the middle of the slide as shown in Figure 3.1 by clicking the Align button in the Arrange group and then clicking *Distribute Horizontally* at the drop-down list. Click the Align button again and then click *Distribute Vertically* at the drop-down list.

10. Make Slide 4 active and then insert the **DollarSymbol.png** from the PowerPointS3 folder. You determine the size, position, and color of the image.

11. Save **3-MPToronto.pptx**.

Figure 3.1 Slide 2

Check Your Work Compare your work to the model answer to ensure that you have completed the activity correctly.

In Addition

Using the Drawing Tools Format Tab

When WordArt is selected in a slide, the Drawing Tools Format tab displays as shown below. You can draw a shape or text box with buttons in the Insert Shapes group. Apply a style, fill, outline, and/or effects to the WordArt text box with options in the Shape Styles group. Change the style of the WordArt text with options in the WordArt Styles group, specify the layering of the WordArt text with options in the Arrange group, and identify the height and width of the WordArt text box with measurement boxes in the Size group.

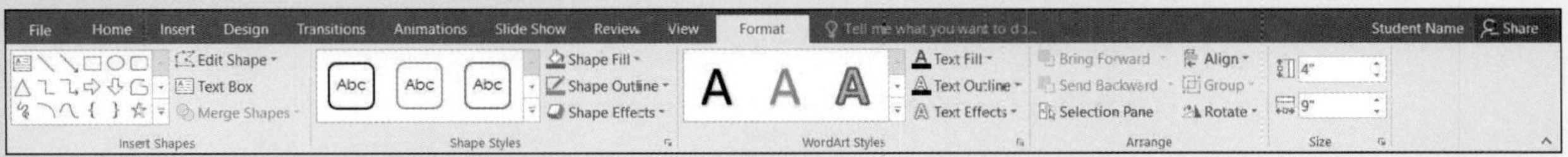

Activity 3.4 Drawing and Customizing Shapes

Use the shape options in the Drawing group on the Home tab or the Shapes button on the Insert tab to draw shapes in a slide, including lines, rectangles, basic shapes, block arrows, equation shapes, flowchart shapes, stars, banners, and callout shapes. Click a shape and the mouse pointer displays as crosshairs (plus sign). Click in the slide to insert the shape or position the crosshairs where you want the image to begin, click and hold down the left mouse button, drag to create the shape, and then release the mouse button. This inserts the shape in the slide and also displays the Drawing Tools Format tab. Use buttons on this tab to change the shape, apply a style to the shape, arrange the shape, and change the size of the shape. You can type text directly into a shape or you can use the Text Box button in the Text group on the Insert tab to draw a text box inside a shape and then type text in the box. The Drawing Tools Format tab also provides a Text Box button you can use to draw a text box in a slide.

What You Will Do You will create a new slide for the Toronto site presentation that includes the Toronto office address inside a shape.

Tutorial
Inserting, Sizing, and Positioning Shapes

Tutorial
Formatting Shapes

1. With **3-MPToronto.pptx** open, make Slide 2 active.
2. Click the New Slide button in the Slides group on the Home tab. (Make sure the slide layout is *Blank*.)
3. Click the More Shapes button in the Drawing group on the Home tab.
4. Click *Horizontal Scroll* at the drop-down list (sixth column, bottom row in the *Stars and Banners* section).
5. Position the mouse pointer in the slide, click and hold down the left mouse button, drag to create the shape as shown below, and then release the mouse button.

   If you are not satisfied with the size and shape of the image, press the Delete key to remove the image, select the desired shape, and then draw the image again.

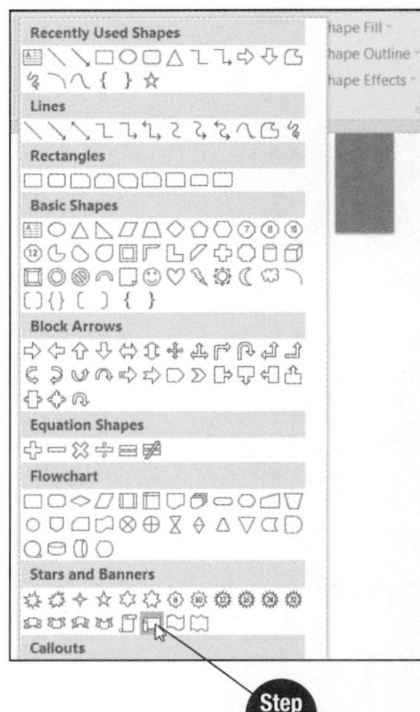

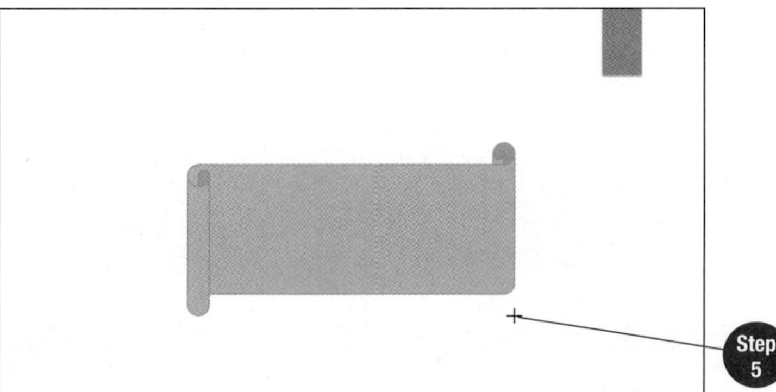

In Brief

Draw Shape
1. Click Home tab.
2. Click More Shapes button in gallery in Drawing group.
3. Click shape.
4. Click or drag in slide to draw shape.

OR
1. Click Insert tab.
2. Click Shapes button.
3. Click shape.
4. Click or drag in slide to draw shape.

6. With the image selected, click the Drawing Tools Format tab and then change the shape style by clicking the More Shape Styles button in the Shape Styles group and then clicking the *Subtle Effect - Green, Accent 6* option at the drop-down gallery (seventh column, fourth row in the Theme Styles section).
7. Click the Shape Effects button in the Shape Styles group, point to *Glow*, and then click the *Orange, 18 pt glow, Accent color 1* option (first column, fourth row in the *Glow Variations* section).

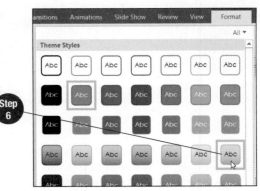

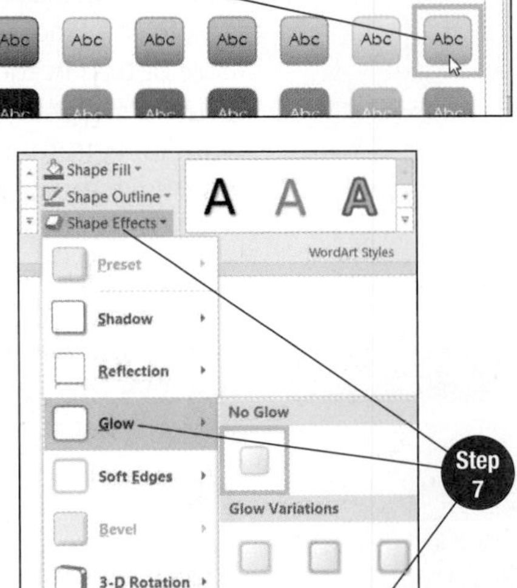

8. Click the Home tab.
9. Click the *Font Size* option box arrow and then click *24* at the drop-down gallery.
10. Click the Bold button in the Font group.
11. Click the Font Color button in the Font group and then click the *Orange, Accent 1, Darker 25%* color option (fifth column, fifth row in the *Theme Colors* section).
12. If the paragraph alignment is not set to center, click the Center button in the Paragraph group.
13. Type the following text in the text box:

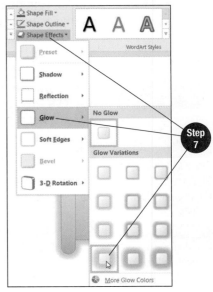

MARQUEE PRODUCTIONS
Toronto Office
905 Bathurst Street
Toronto, ON M4P 4E5

14. Distribute the shape horizontally and vertically on the slide using options in the Arrange button drop-down list in the Drawing group on the Home tab.
15. Save **3-MPToronto.pptx**.

Check Your Work Compare your work to the model answer to ensure that you have completed the activity correctly.

In Addition

Displaying the Selection Task Pane

If you want to select an object or multiple objects in a slide, consider turning on the display of the Selection task pane. Turn on the display of this task pane by clicking the Selection Pane button in the Arrange group on the Drawing Tools Format tab. Select an object by clicking the object name in the Selection task pane (see example at right). Select multiple objects by holding down the Ctrl key as you click objects. Click the button that displays at the right side of the object name to turn on/off the display of the object.

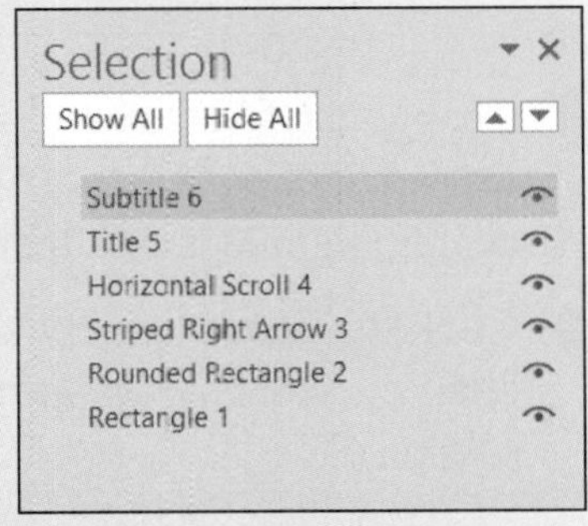

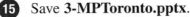

Activity 3.5 Displaying Gridlines; Inserting a Text Box; Copying and Rotating Shapes

To help position elements such as shapes and images on a slide, consider displaying gridlines. Gridlines are intersecting horizontal and vertical dashed lines that display on the slide in the slide pane. Display gridlines by clicking the View tab and then clicking the *Gridlines* check box in the Show group to insert a check mark. Create a text box in a slide by clicking the Text Box button in the Text group on the Insert tab. Click or drag in the slide to create the text box. Draw a shape in a slide and the selected shape displays with sizing handles and a rotation handle. Rotate a shape with the rotation handle or with the Rotate button in the Arrange group on the Drawing Tools Format tab. If you draw more than one object in a slide, you can select multiple objects at once so you can work with them as if they were a single object. You can format, size, move, flip, and/or rotate selected objects as a single unit.

What You Will Do You need to create a new slide for the Toronto presentation that displays the date for the last day of filming in Toronto. To highlight this important information, you will insert an arrow shape and then copy and rotate the shape.

Tutorial Displaying Rulers, Gridlines, and Guides; Copying and Rotating Shapes

Tutorial Inserting and Formatting Text Boxes

1. With **3-MPToronto.pptx** open, make Slide 8 active and then click the Insert tab.
2. Click the New Slide button arrow and then click *Title Only* at the drop-down list.
3. Click in the *Click to add title* placeholder and then type Last Day of Filming.
4. Turn on the display of gridlines by clicking the View tab and then clicking the *Gridlines* check box in the Show group to insert a check mark.
5. Click the Insert tab and then click the Text Box button in the Text group.
6. Position the mouse pointer in the slide and then draw a text box similar to what you see below. Use the gridlines to help you position the mouse when drawing the text box.

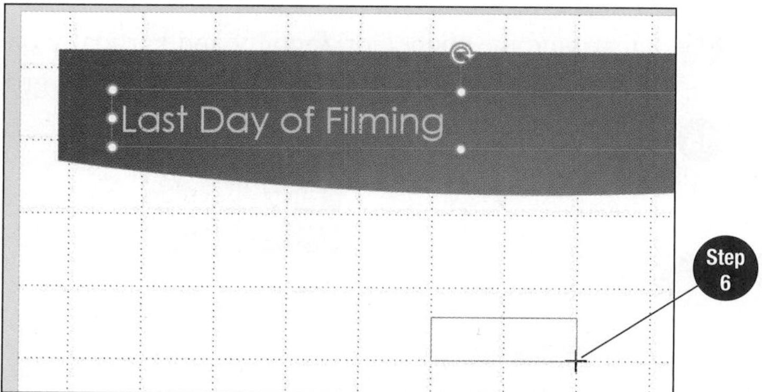

7. Change the font size to 24 points, apply bold formatting, apply the Orange, Accent 1, Darker 25% font color (fifth column, fifth row in *Theme Colors* section), change to center alignment, and then type August 28. Click outside the text box to deselect it.
8. Click the Insert tab, click the Shapes button in the Illustrations group, and then click the *Notched Right Arrow* shape (sixth column, second row in the *Block Arrows* section).

In Brief

Display Gridlines
1. Click View tab.
2. Click *Gridlines* check box.

Insert Text Box
1. Click Insert tab.
2. Click Text Box button.
3. Click in slide or drag to create text box.

9. Position the mouse pointer at the left side of the slide, click and hold down the left mouse button, drag to create the arrow shape as shown at the right, and then release the mouse button.

   Use the gridlines to help position the arrow.

10. With the arrow shape selected, copy the arrow by positioning the mouse pointer inside the shape until the mouse pointer displays with a four-headed arrow attached. Press and hold down the Ctrl key and then click and hold down the left mouse button. Drag the arrow to the right side of the date, release the left mouse button, and then release the Ctrl key.

11. Click the Drawing Tools Format tab and then flip the copied arrow by clicking the Rotate button in the Arrange group and then clicking *Flip Horizontal* at the drop-down list.

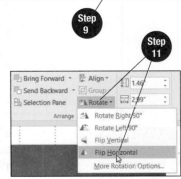

12. Using the mouse pointer, draw a border around the three objects.

    When you release the mouse button, the three objects are selected.

13. With the Drawing Tools Format tab active, center-align the three grouped objects by clicking the Align button in the Arrange group and then clicking *Align Middle* at the drop-down list.

14. With the three objects still selected, horizontally distribute them by clicking the Align button and then clicking *Distribute Horizontally* at the drop-down list.

15. Turn off the display of gridlines by clicking the View tab and then clicking the *Gridlines* check box to remove the check mark.

16. Click outside the objects to deselect them.

17. Save **3-MPToronto.pptx**.

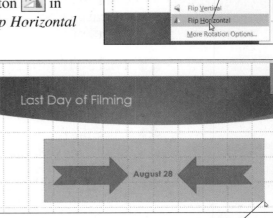

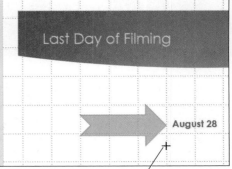

Check Your Work Compare your work to the model answer to ensure that you have completed the activity correctly.

In Addition

Rotating Objects

Use the rotation handle that displays near a selected object to rotate the object. Position the mouse pointer on the rotation handle until the pointer displays as a circular arrow, as shown at the right. Click and hold down the left mouse button, drag in the desired direction, and then release the mouse button.

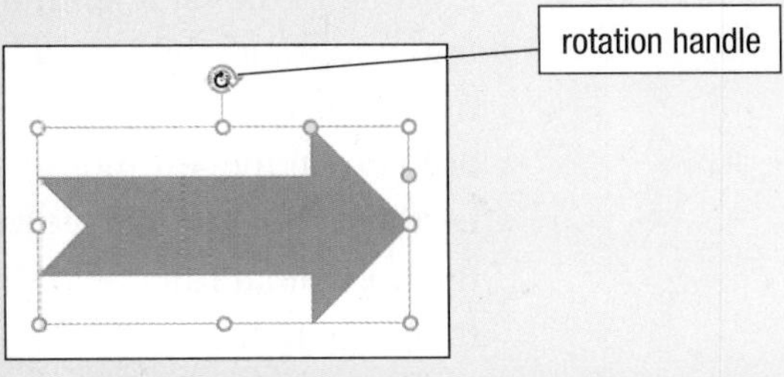

Activity 3.6 Creating and Formatting a Table

PowerPoint includes a Table feature you can use for displaying columns and rows of data. Insert a table in a slide with the Table button on the Insert tab or with the Insert Table button in a content placeholder. When you insert a table in a slide, the Table Tools Design tab is selected. Use buttons on this tab to enhance the appearance of the table. With options in the Table Styles group, apply predesigned colors and border lines to a table. Maintain further control over the predesigned style formatting applied to columns and rows with options in the Table Style Options group. Apply additional design formatting to cells in a table with the Shading and Borders buttons in the Table Styles group. Draw a table or draw additional rows and/or columns in a table with options in the Draw Borders group. Click the Table Tools Layout tab and display options and buttons for inserting and deleting columns and rows; changing cell size, alignment, direction, and margins; changing the table size; and arranging the table in the slide.

What You Will Do After reviewing the slides, you decide to include additional information on the location timeline. To do this, you will insert a new slide and then create a table with specific dates.

Tutorial Creating a Table

Tutorial Changing the Table Design

Tutorial Changing the Table Layout

1. With **3-MPToronto.pptx** open, make Slide 8 active and then click the Insert tab.
2. Click the New Slide button arrow and then click the *Title and Content* layout at the drop-down list.
3. Click the *Click to add title* placeholder in the new slide and then type Timeline.
4. Click the Insert Table button in the content placeholder.
5. At the Insert Table dialog box, press the Delete key and then type 2 in the *Number of columns* measurement box.
6. Press the Tab key and then type 9 in the *Number of rows* measurement box.
7. Click OK to close the Insert Table dialog box.
8. Turn on the display of the horizontal and vertical rulers. To do this, click the View tab and then click the *Ruler* check box in the Show group to insert a check mark.
9. Column 1 needs to be widened to accommodate the project tasks. To do this, position the mouse pointer on the middle gridline in the table until the pointer turns into a left-and-right-pointing arrow with two short lines in the middle. Click and hold down the left mouse button, drag to approximately the 6-inch mark on the horizontal ruler, and then release the mouse button.

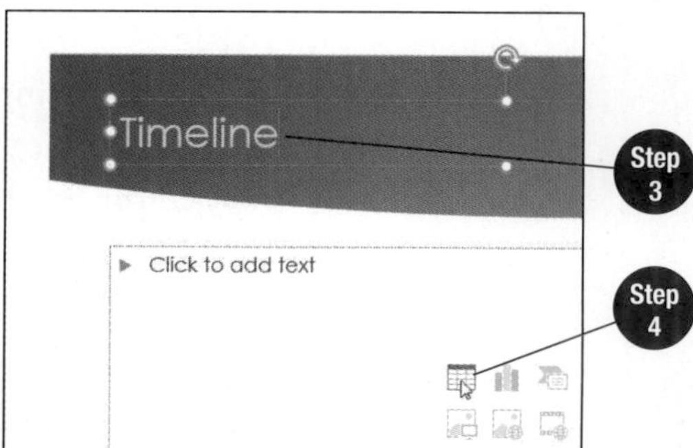

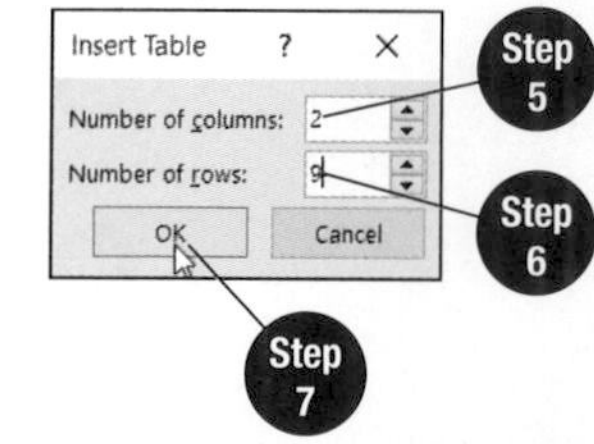

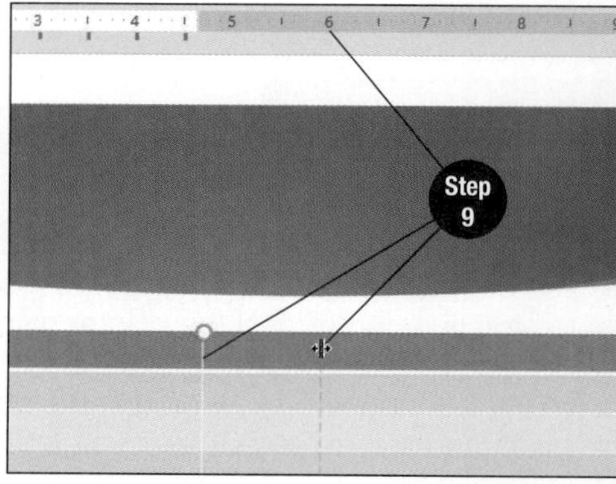

In Brief

Create Table
1. Click Insert Table button in content placeholder.
2. At Insert Table dialog box, type number of columns and rows.
3. Click OK.

10. Starting with the insertion point positioned in the first cell, type all of the text shown in Figure 3.2. Press the Tab key to move the insertion point to the next cell. Press Shift + Tab to move the insertion point to the previous cell.
11. Click the More Table Styles button in the gallery in the Table Styles group on the Table Tools Design tab.
12. Click the *Medium Style 1 - Accent 1* option in the drop-down gallery (second column, first row in the *Medium* section).
13. Click the Table Tools Layout tab.
14. Select the first row in the table by positioning the mouse pointer at the left side of the first row in the table until the pointer turns into a black, right-pointing arrow and then clicking the left mouse button.
15. Click the Center button in the Alignment group.
16. Click in the *Height* measurement box in the Table Size group, type 4, and then press the Enter key.
17. Distribute the table horizontally on the slide.
18. Save **3-MPToronto.pptx**.

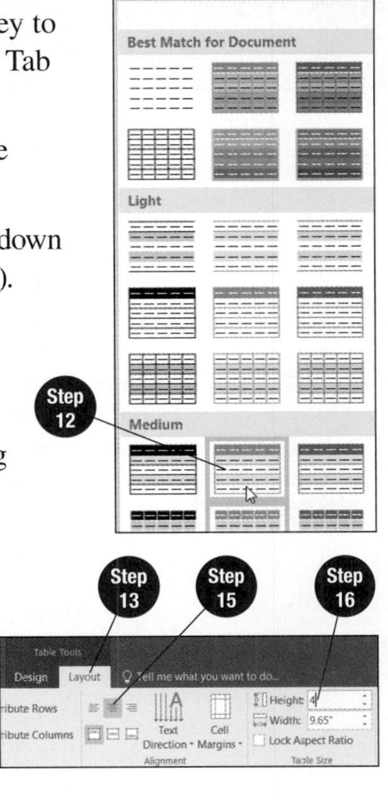

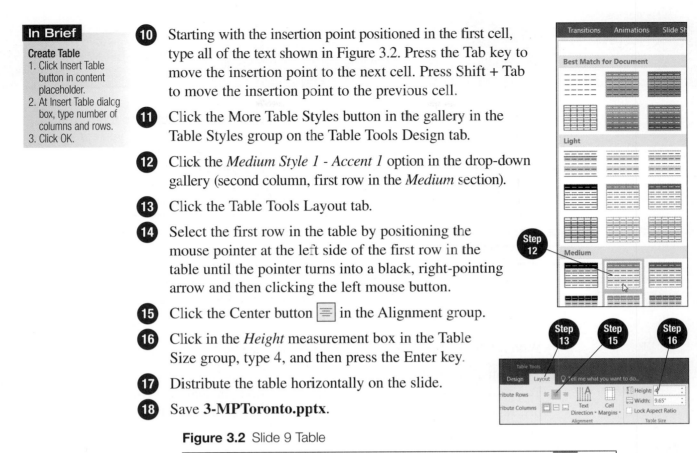

Figure 3.2 Slide 9 Table

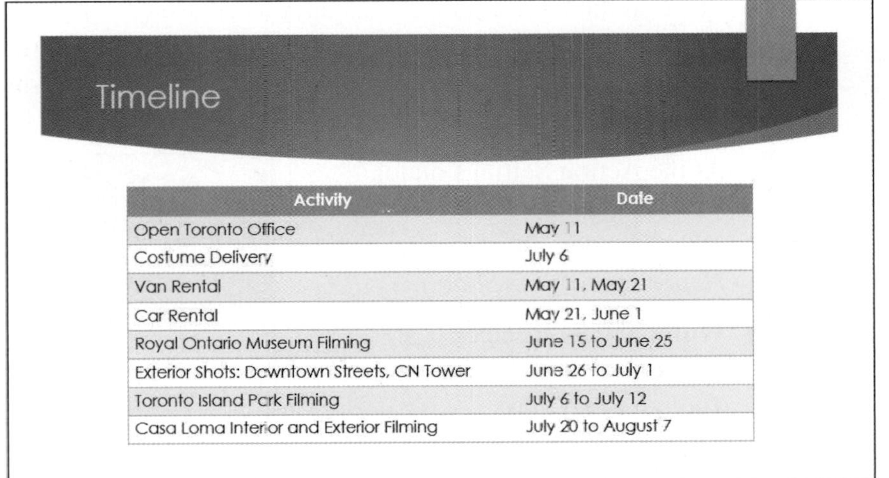

Activity	Date
Open Toronto Office	May 11
Costume Delivery	July 6
Van Rental	May 11, May 21
Car Rental	May 21, June 1
Royal Ontario Museum Filming	June 15 to June 25
Exterior Shots: Downtown Streets, CN Tower	June 26 to July 1
Toronto Island Park Filming	July 6 to July 12
Casa Loma Interior and Exterior Filming	July 20 to August 7

Check Your Work Compare your work to the model answer to ensure that you have completed the activity correctly.

In Addition

Moving and Sizing a Table

Increase or decrease the size of a table by typing the measurements in the *Height* and *Width* measurement boxes in the Table Size group on the Table Tools Layout tab. You can also drag the sizing handles that display around a table border to increase or decrease the size. When the insertion point is positioned in a table, a border containing sizing handles that display as small white circles surrounds the table. Position the mouse pointer on one of the sizing handles until the pointer displays as a two-headed arrow, click and hold down the left mouse button, and then drag to increase or decrease the size. Drag a corner sizing handle to change the size of the table proportionally. To move the table, position the mouse pointer on the table border until the pointer displays with a four-headed arrow attached and then drag to the desired position.

Activity 3.7 Inserting Action Buttons and Hyperlinks

Action buttons are drawn objects on a slide that have a routine attached to them. The routine is activated when the presenter clicks the action button. For example, you can insert an action button that displays a specific web page, a file in another program, or the next slide in the presentation. Creating an action button is a two-step process. The first step is to draw the button in the slide, and the second step is to define the action that will take place using options in the Action Settings dialog box. You can customize an action button in the same way you would customize a drawn shape. You can also insert a hyperlink in a slide that, when clicked, will display a website or open another slide show or file. Insert a hyperlink with the Hyperlink button on the Insert tab.

What You Will Do To facilitate the running of the slide show, you decide to insert an action button at the bottom of each slide that will link to the next slide or the first slide. You also decide to insert a hyperlink to a website.

Tutorial Inserting Action Buttons

Tutorial Applying an Action to an Object

Tutorial Inserting Hyperlinks

1. With **3-MPToronto.pptx** open, make Slide 1 active.
2. Insert an action button that, when clicked, will display the next slide. To begin, click the Insert tab, click the Shapes button, and then click the *Action Button: Forward or Next* option (second button in the *Action Buttons* section).
3. Position the mouse pointer (displays as crosshairs) in the lower right corner of Slide 1, click and hold down the left mouse button, drag to create a button that is approximately one-half inch square, and then release the mouse button.
4. At the Action Settings dialog box that displays, click OK. (The default setting is *Hyperlink to Next Slide*.)

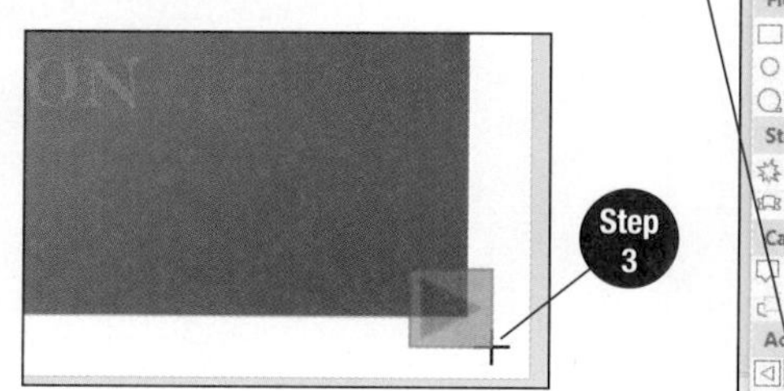

5. With the button selected, if necessary, click the Drawing Tools Format tab.
6. Select the current measurement in the *Shape Height* measurement box, type 0.5, and then press the Enter key. Select the current measurement in the *Shape Width* measurement box, type 0.5, and then press the Enter key.
7. Instead of drawing the button on each slide, you decide to copy it and then paste it in the other slides. To do this, make sure the button is selected, click the Home tab, and then click the Copy button in the Clipboard group.
8. Make Slide 2 active and then click the Paste button in the Clipboard group. Continue pasting the button in Slides 3 through 9. (Do not paste the button on the last slide, Slide 10.)
9. Make Slide 10 active and then insert an action button that will display the first slide. To begin, click the Insert tab, click the Shapes button, and then click *Action Button: Home* (fifth option in the *Action Buttons* section).

In Brief

Insert Action Button

1. Click Insert tab.
2. Click Shapes button.
3. Click action button.
4. Click or drag in slide to create button.
5. At Action Settings dialog box, click OK.

10 Position the mouse pointer in the lower right corner of Slide 10 and then click the left mouse button.

When you click in the slide, a small square shape with a home icon in the center is inserted in the slide.

11 At the Action Settings dialog box that displays, click OK. (The default setting is *Hyperlink to First Slide.*)

12 With the button selected, click in the *Shape Height* measurement box on the Drawing Tools Format tab, type 0.5, and then press the Enter key. Click in the *Shape Width* measurement box, type 0.5, and then press the Enter key.

13 Make Slide 6 active and then create a hyperlink to the museum website. To begin, select *Royal Ontario Museum*, click the Insert tab, and then click the Hyperlink button in the Links group.

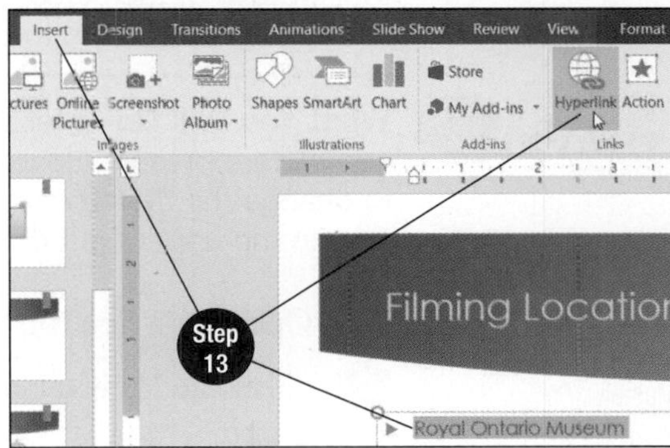

14 At the Insert Hyperlink dialog box, type www.rom.on.ca in the *Address* text box and then press the Enter key.

PowerPoint automatically inserts *http://* at the beginning of the web address. The hyperlink text displays underlined and in a different color in the slide.

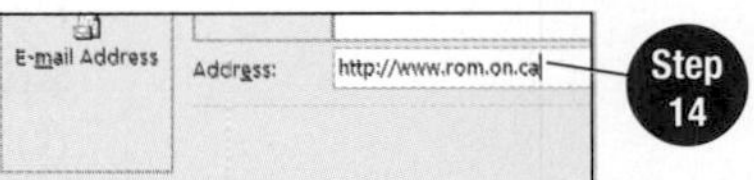

15 Run the slide show, beginning with Slide 1. Navigate through the slide show by clicking the action buttons. When Slide 6 (*Filming Locations*) displays, click the Royal Ontario Museum hyperlink.

16 After viewing the museum website, close the browser. Continue running the slide show. After viewing the slide show at least twice, press the Esc key to end the slide show.

17 Print the presentation as handouts with six slides displayed horizontally per page.

18 Save and then close **3-MPToronto.pptx**.

Check Your Work Compare your work to the model answer to ensure that you have completed the activity correctly.

In Addition

Linking with Action Buttons

You can set an action button to link to a website during a slide show. To do this, draw an Action button. At the Action Settings dialog box, click the *Hyperlink to* option, click the *Hyperlink to* option box arrow, and then click *URL* at the drop-down list. At the Hyperlink to URL dialog box, type the web address in the *URL* text box and then click OK. Click OK to close the Action Settings dialog box. Other actions you can link to using the *Hyperlink to* drop-down list include: *Next Slide*, *Previous Slide*, *First Slide*, *Last Slide*, *Last Slide Viewed*, *End Show*, *Custom Show*, *Slide*, *URL*, *Other PowerPoint Presentation*, and *Other File*. The Action Settings dialog box can also be used to run another program when the action button is selected, to run a macro, or to activate an embedded object.

Activity 3.8 Formatting with a Slide Master

If you use a PowerPoint design theme, you may choose to use the formatting provided by the theme or you may want to customize the formatting. If you customize formatting in a presentation, PowerPoint's slide master can be very helpful in reducing the steps needed to format slides. A presentation contains a slide master for each of the various slide layouts. To display slide masters, click the View tab and then click the Slide Master button in the Master Views group. The available slide masters display in the slide thumbnails pane at the left side of the screen. Apply formatting to the slide masters and then click the Close Master View button in the Close group to return to the Normal view.

What You Will Do Melissa Gehring, manager at First Choice Travel, has asked you to complete a presentation on upcoming eco-tours offered by First Choice Travel. You decide to change the theme colors and fonts of the presentation, as well as insert the company's logo in the upper right corner of all slides except the title slide.

Tutorial
Formatting with a Slide Master

1. Open **FCTEcoTours.pptx** and then save it with the name **3-FCTEcoTours**.
2. Click the View tab and then click the Slide Master button in the Master Views group.

   Hover the mouse pointer over a slide master in the slide thumbnails pane at the left side of the screen to display a ScreenTip with information about the slide layout and the number of slides in the presentation that use the layout.

3. Click the Theme Colors button in the Background group and then click *Blue* at the drop-down gallery.

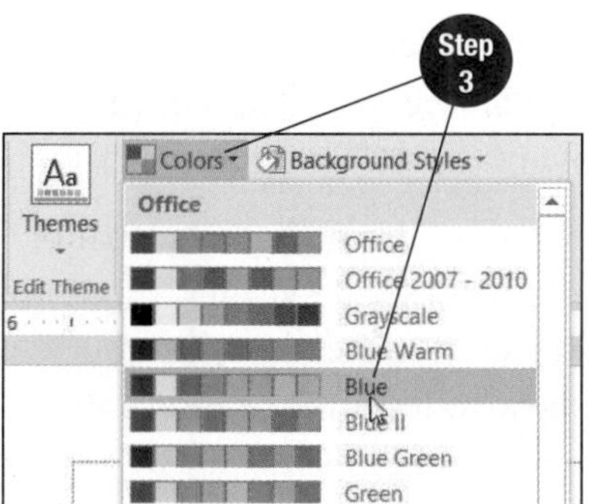

4. Click the Theme Fonts button in the Background group, scroll down the drop-down gallery, and then click *Calibri Light-Constantia.*
5. Select the *Click to edit Master title style* placeholder text in the slide in the slide pane, click the Home tab, click the Font Color button arrow, and then click the *Blue* color option (eighth option in the *Standard Colors* section).

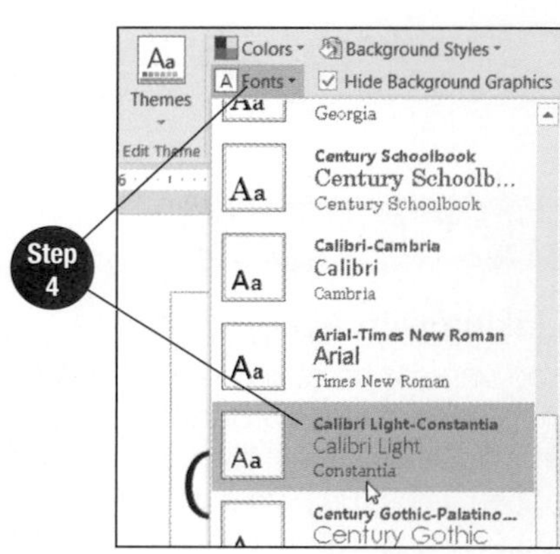

In Brief

Format in Slide Master View
1. Click View tab.
2. Click Slide Master button.
3. Make changes.
4. Click Close Master View button.

6 Click the top slide master in the slide thumbnails pane at the left side of the screen.

7 Select the *Click to edit Master title style* placeholder text, click the Home tab, and then click the Font Color button.

This applies the Blue font color.

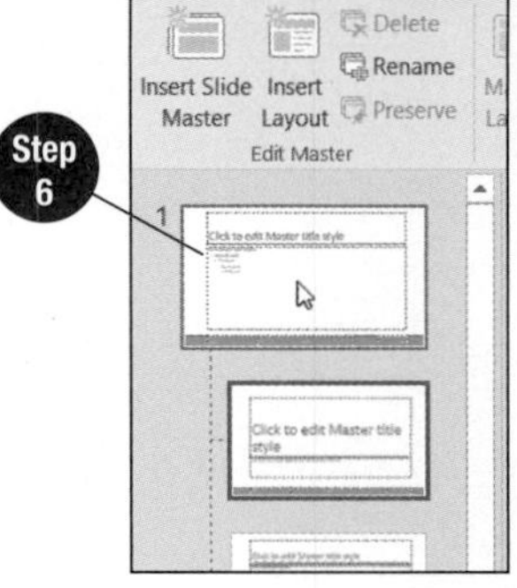

8 Insert the First Choice Travel logo in the slide master (so it prints on all slides except the first one). Begin by clicking the Insert tab and then clicking the Pictures button in the Images group.

9 Navigate to the PowerPointS3 folder on your storage medium and then double-click ***FCTLogo.jpg***.

10 Make sure the logo is selected.

11 Click in the *Shape Height* measurement box, type 0.5, and then press the Enter key.

12 Click the Align button in the Arrange group and then click the *Align Right* option at the drop-down list.

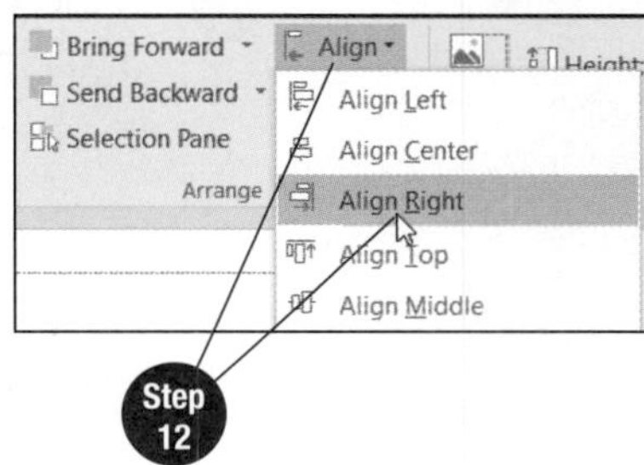

13 Click the Align button and then click the *Align Top* option.

14 Click the Slide Master tab.

15 Click the Close Master View button in the Close group on the Slide Master tab.

16 Save **3-FCTEcoTours.pptx**.

Check Your Work Compare your work to the model answer to ensure that you have completed the activity correctly.

In Addition

Applying More Than One Slide Design Theme

Each design theme applies specific formatting to slides. You can apply more than one design theme to slides in a presentation. To do this, select the specific slides and then choose the desired design theme. The design theme is applied only to the selected slides. If you apply more than one design theme to a presentation, multiple slide masters will display in Slide Master view.

Formatting Changes in Slide Master View

If you edit the formatting of text in a slide in Normal view, the link to the slide master is broken. Changes you make to a slide master in Slide Master view will not affect the individually formatted slide. For this reason, make formatting changes in Slide Master view before editing individual slides in a presentation.

Activity 3.9 Inserting Headers and Footers

Insert information you want to appear at the top or bottom of individual slides or at the top and bottom of individual printed notes and handouts pages using options at the Header and Footer dialog box. If you want the same types of information to appear on all slides, display the Header and Footer dialog box with the Slide tab selected. With options at this dialog box, you can insert the date and time, insert the slide number, and create a footer. To insert header or footer elements you want to print on all notes or handouts pages, choose options at the Header and Footer dialog box with the Notes and Handouts tab selected.

What You Will Do Melissa Gehring has asked you to insert the current date and slide numbers in the slides and to create a header for notes pages.

Tutorial
Inserting Headers and Footers

1. With **3-FCTEcoTours.pptx** open, insert a footer that prints at the bottom of each slide. To begin, click the Insert tab and then click the Header & Footer button in the Text group.

Step 1

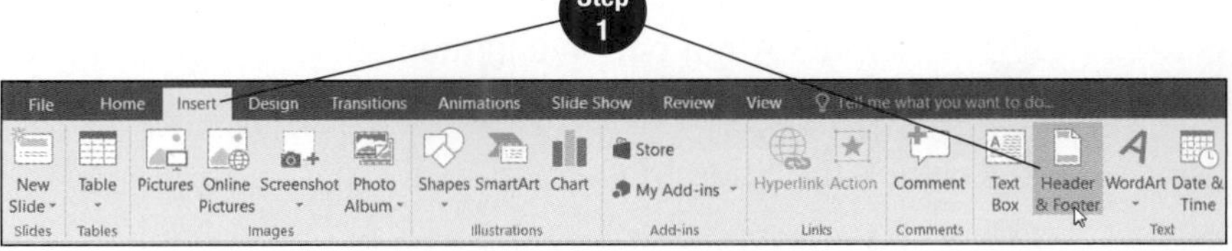

2. At the Header and Footer dialog box with the Slide tab selected, click the *Date and time* check box to insert a check mark. If necessary, click the *Update automatically* option to select it.
3. Click the *Slide number* check box to insert a check mark.
4. Click the *Footer* check box to insert a check mark and then type First Choice Travel Eco-Tours in the *Footer* text box.
5. Click the Apply to All button.
6. Make Slide 7 active.
7. Display the notes pane by clicking the Notes button on the Status bar.
8. Click in the notes pane and then type Include additional costs for airfare, local transportation, and daily tours.

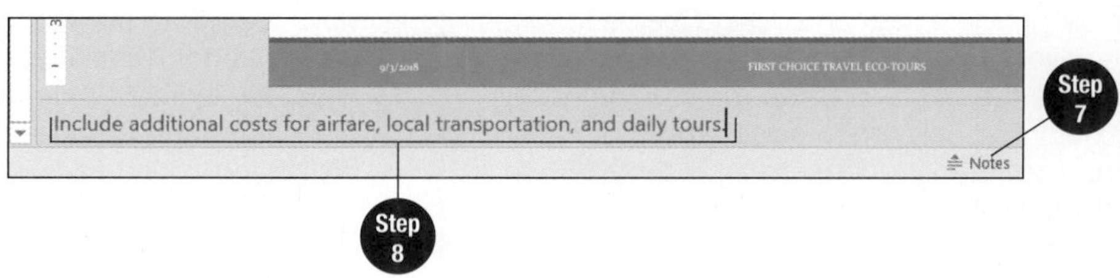

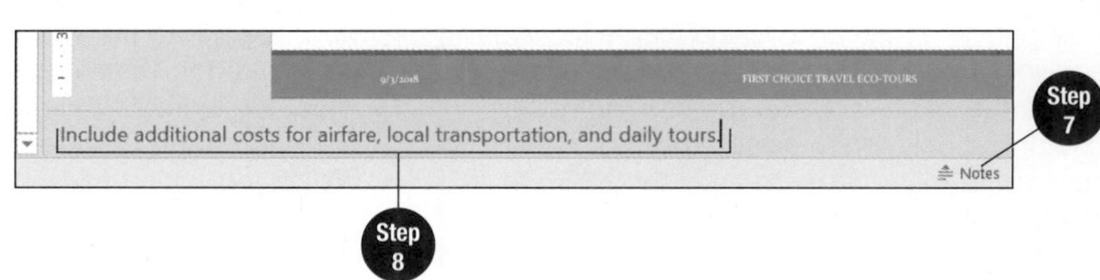

Step 7

Step 8

In Brief

Insert Header/Footer on Slide
1. Click Insert tab.
2. Click Header & Footer button.
3. At Header and Footer dialog box with Slide tab selected, choose options.
4. Click Apply to All button.

Insert Header/Footer in Notes and Handouts
1. Click Insert tab.
2. Click Header & Footer button.
3. At Header and Footer dialog box, click Notes and Handouts tab.
4. Choose options.
5. Click Apply to All button.

9. Insert a header that will display on notes and handouts pages by clicking the Header & Footer button on the Insert tab.
10. At the Header and Footer dialog box, click the Notes and Handouts tab.
11. Make sure a check mark does not display in the *Date and time* check box. If a check mark does display, click the check box to remove the check mark.
12. Click the *Header* check box to insert a check mark and then type First Choice Travel in the *Header* text box.
13. Click the *Footer* check box to insert a check mark and then type Eco-Tours in the *Footer* text box.

14. Click the Apply to All button.
15. Print the presentation as handouts with nine slides displayed horizontally per page.
16. Print Slide 7 as a notes page. To do this, click the File tab, click the *Print* option, click the second gallery (contains the text *9 Slides Horizontal*) in the *Settings* category, and then click *Notes Pages* in the *Print Layout* section.
17. Click in the *Slides* text box (located below the first gallery in the *Settings* category) and then type 7.
18. Click the Print button.

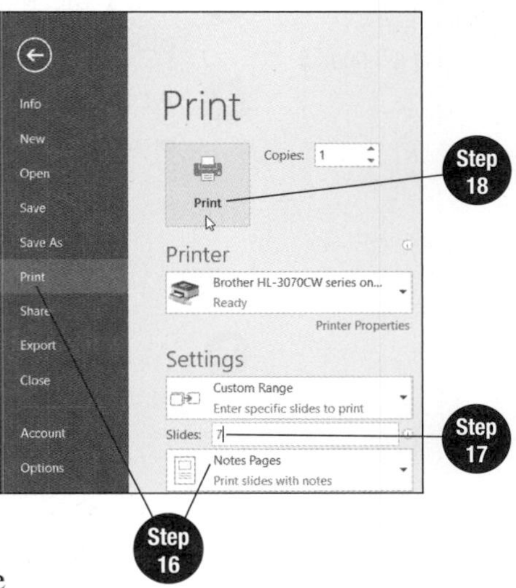

19. Click the Notes button on the Status bar to close the notes pane.
20. Save **3-FCTEcoTours.pptx**.

Check Your Work Compare your work to the model answer to ensure that you have completed the activity correctly.

In Addition

Using the Package for CD Feature

The safest way to transport a PowerPoint presentation to another computer is to use the Package for CD feature. With this feature, you can copy a presentation onto a CD or to a folder or network location and include all of the linked files and fonts, as well as the PowerPoint Viewer program in case the destination computer does not have PowerPoint installed on it. To use the Package for CD feature, click the File tab, click the *Export* option, click the *Package Presentation for CD* option, and then click the Package for CD button. At the Package for CD dialog box, type a name for the CD and then click the Copy to CD button.

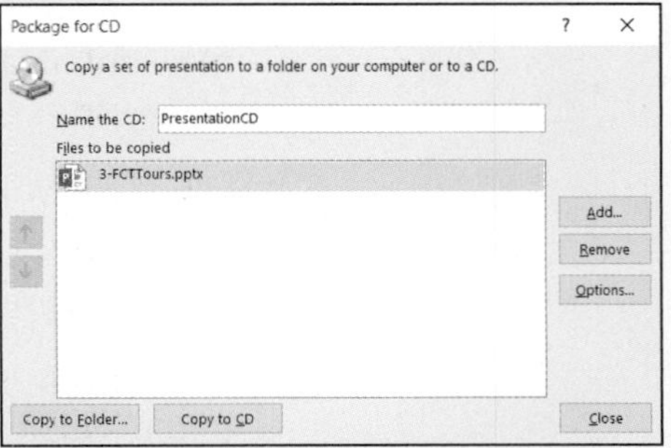

Activity 3.10 Adding Audio and Video

Adding audio and/or video effects to a presentation will turn a slide show into a true multi-media experience for your audience. Including a variety of elements in a presentation will stimulate interest in your slide show and keep the audience motivated. You can insert an audio file or video file from a folder or from the Insert Video window.

What You Will Do To add interest, you decide to experiment with adding a video file and an audio file to the presentation. The last slide of the slide show will display the video file and play an audio file. This will allow the presenter time to answer questions from the audience while the video and audio files play.

Tutorial Inserting and Modifying an Audio File

Tutorial Inserting and Modifying a Video File

1. With **3-FCTEcoTours.pptx** open, make Slide 7 active, click the Insert tab, and then click the New Slide button.
2. Click in the title placeholder and then type Let the adventure begin!
3. Click the Insert Video button in the content placeholder.

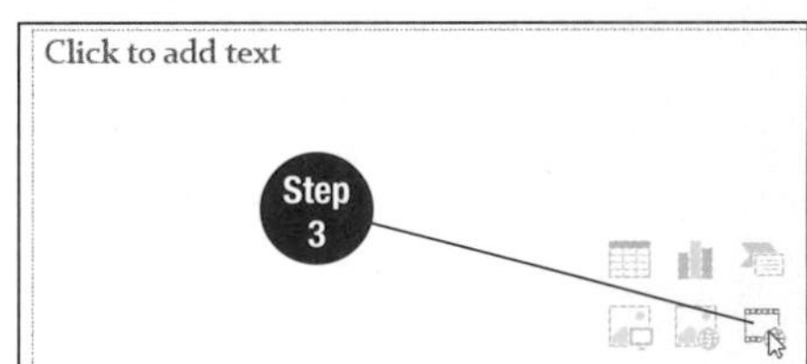

4. At the Insert Video window, click the Browse button to the right of the *From a file* option.

   You can also display the Insert Video dialog box by clicking the Insert tab, clicking the Video button in the Media group, and then clicking *Video on My PC*.

5. At the Insert Video dialog box, navigate to the PowerPointS3 folder on your storage medium and then double-click ***Wildlife.wmv***.

   This inserts the video file in a window in the slide with the Video Tools Format tab selected. Use options and buttons on this tab to preview the video file, change the brightness, contrast, and color of the video, apply a formatting style to the video window, and arrange and size the video in the slide.

6. Click the Play button in the Preview group (left side of Video Tools Format tab) to preview the video file.

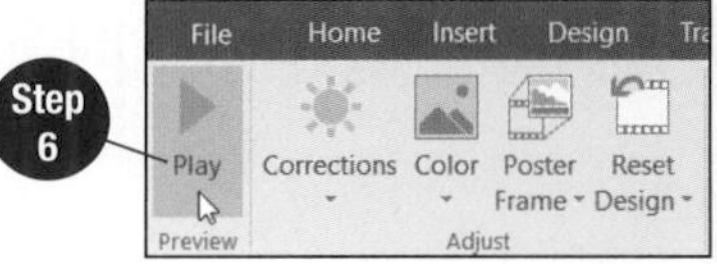

   The video plays for approximately 30 seconds.

7. After viewing the video, click the Video Tools Playback tab.
8. Click the *Fade In* measurement box up arrow in the Editing group until *01.00* displays and then click the *Fade Out* measurement box up arrow until *01.00* displays.
9. Click the Volume button in the Video Options group and then click *Low* at the drop-down list.

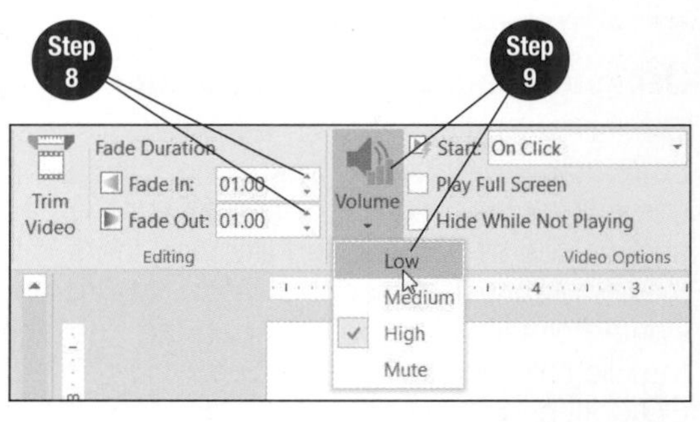

10. Click the *Loop until Stopped* check box in the Video Options group to insert a check mark.

In Brief

Insert Video Clip
1. Click Insert Video button in placeholcer.
2. Navigate to folder.
3. Double-click video file.

OR
1. Click Insert tab.
2. Click Video button arrow.
3. Click *Video on My PC.*
4. Navigate to folder.
5. Double-click video file.

Insert Audio Clip
1. Click Insert tab.
2. Click Audio button.
3. Click *Audio on My PC.*
4. Navigate to folder.
5. Double-click audio file.

11. Make Slide 1 active and then run the slide show. When the slide containing the video file displays, move the mouse pointer over the video file window and then click the Play button at the bottom left side of the window.
12. After viewing the video a couple of times, press the Esc key two times.
13. You decide that you want the video window to fill the slide, start automatically when the slide displays, and play only once. To do this, make sure Slide 8 is active, click the video file window, and then click the Video Tools Playback tab.
14. Click the *Play Full Screen* check box in the Video Options group to insert a check mark and then click the *Loop until Stopped* check box to remove the check mark.

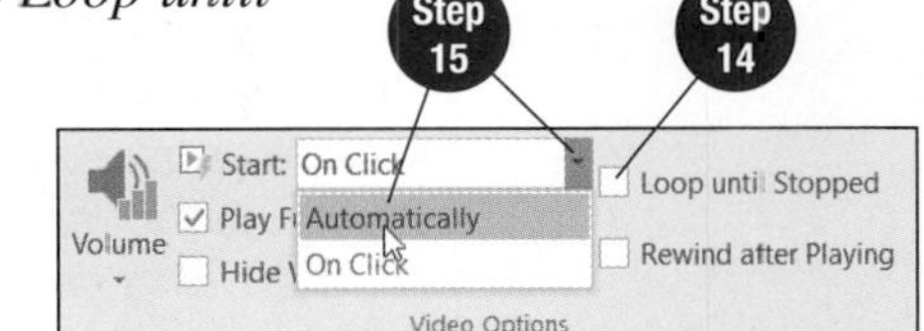

15. Click the *Start* option box arrow in the Video Options group and then click *Automatically* at the drop-down list.
16. Make Slide 1 active and then run the slide show. When the slide containing the video displays, the video will automatically begin. When the video is finished playing, press the Esc key to return to Normal view.
17. You decide that you want music to play after the presentation. Begin by making sure Slide 8 is the active slide, clicking the Insert tab, clicking the Audio button in the Media group, and then clicking *Audio on My PC* at the drop-down list.
18. At the Insert Audio dialog box, navigate to the PowerPointS3 folder on your storage medium and then double-click the file named ***FCTAudioClip-01.mid***.

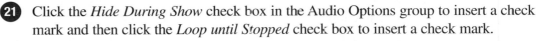

    This inserts the audio file in the slide with the Audio Tools Playback tab selected.
19. If necessary, click the Audio Tools Playback tab.
20. Click the *Start* option box down arrow in the Audio Options group and then click *Automatically* at the drop-down list.
21. Click the *Hide During Show* check box in the Audio Options group to insert a check mark and then click the *Loop until Stopped* check box to insert a check mark.
22. Make Slide 1 active and then run the slide show. When the last slide displays, watch the video, listen to the audio file for about a minute or two, and then press the Esc key to return to the Normal view.
23. Save **3-FCTEcoTours.pptx**.

Check Your Work Compare your work to the model answer to ensure that you have completed the activity correctly.

In Addition

Changing the Video Color

With the Color button in the Adjust group on the Video Tools Format tab, you can change the video color. If you want the video to play in black and white, click the Color button and then click the *Grayscale* option at the drop-down gallery. Click the *Sepia* option if you want the video to have an old-fashioned appearance when played.

Activity 3.11 Setting and Rehearsing Timings for a Slide Show

If you want a slide show to run automatically and each slide to display for a specific number of seconds, use the Rehearse Timings feature to help set the times for slides as you practice delivering the slide show. To set times for slides, click the Slide Show tab and then click the Rehearse Timings button in the Set Up group. The first slide displays in Slide Show view and the Recording toolbar displays. Use buttons on this toolbar to specify times for each slide. Use options at the Set Up Show dialog box to control the slide show. Display this dialog box by clicking the Set Up Slide Show button in the Set Up group. Use options in the *Show type* section to specify the type of slide show you want to display. If you want the slide show to be totally automatic and run continuously until you end the show, click the *Loop continuously until 'Esc'* check box to insert a check mark. In the *Advance slides* section, the *Using timings, if present* option should be selected by default. Select *Manually* if you want to advance the slides using the mouse instead of your preset times.

What You Will Do Melissa Gehring has asked you to automate the slide show so it can be run continuously at the upcoming travel conference.

Setting Timings for a Slide Show

1. With **3-FCTEcoTours.pptx** open, save it with the name **3-FCTEcoTours-Rehearsed**.
2. Make Slide 8 active, click the audio icon to select it, and then press the Delete key. Click the video window to select it and then press the Delete key.
3. Type the following information in the content placeholder:

   Call today to schedule your exciting eco-tour adventure:
   - 1-888-555-1330

   Or visit our website:
   - www.emcp.net/fc-travel

4. Select the content placeholder (make sure the border is a solid line) and then click the Bold button in the Font group on the Home tab.
5. Make Slide 1 active, click the Slide Show tab, and then click the Rehearse Timings button in the Set Up group.

   The first slide displays in Slide Show view, the Recording toolbar displays as well. The timing for the first slide begins automatically. Refer to Figure 3.3 for the names of the Recording toolbar buttons.

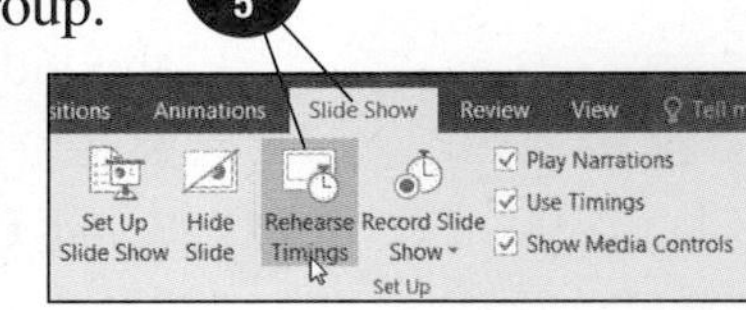

6. Wait until the time displayed for the current slide reaches four seconds and then click the Next button.

   If you miss the time, click the Repeat button to reset the clock back to zero for the current slide.

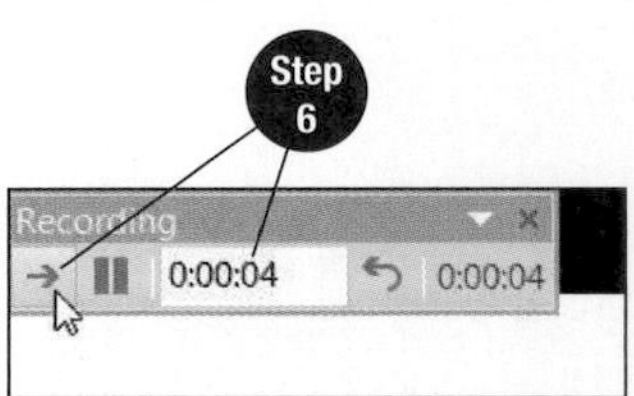

7. Set the following times for the remaining slides:

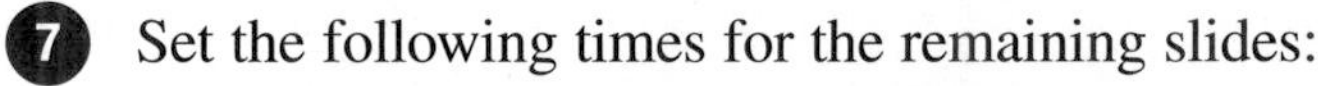

Slide 2: 5 seconds	Slide 6: 8 seconds
Slide 3: 5 seconds	Slide 7: 7 seconds
Slide 4: 4 seconds	Slide 8: 8 seconds
Slide 5: 6 seconds	

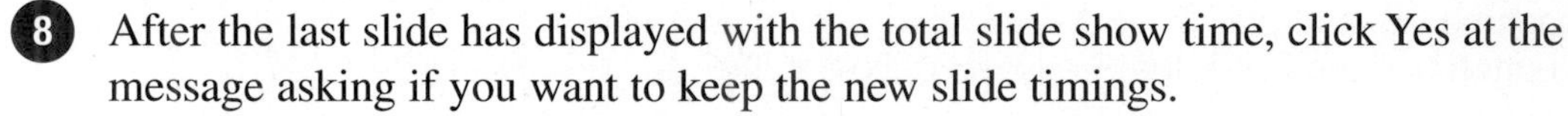

8. After the last slide has displayed with the total slide show time, click Yes at the message asking if you want to keep the new slide timings.

In Brief

Set and Rehearse Timings
1. Click Slide Show tab.
2. Click Rehearse Timings button.
3. When correct time displays, click Next button.
4. Continue until times are set for each slide.
5. Click Yes at message.

Set Up Slide Show to Run Continuously
1. Click Slide Show tab.
2. Click Set Up Slide Show button.
3. Click *Loop continuously until Esc'* check box.
4. Click OK.

9. Click the Slide Sorter button on the Status bar. Notice the slides display with the times listed below. The times that display may be off by one second.

   You can adjust the timings manually with options in the Timing group on the Transitions tab. See the In Addition below.

10. Double-click Slide 1 to change to Normal view.
11. Set up the slide show to run continuously by clicking the Set Up Slide Show button in the Set Up group on the Slide Show tab.
12. At the Set Up Show dialog box, click the *Loop continuously until 'Esc'* check box.

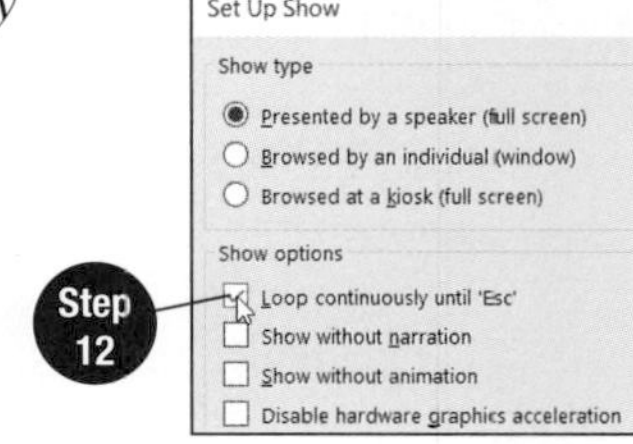

13. Click OK to close the dialog box.
14. Insert an audio file that will play continuously throughout the slide show. To begin, click the Insert tab, click the Audio button in the Media group, and then click the *Audio on My PC* option.
15. At the Insert Audio dialog box, navigate to the PowerPointS3 folder on your storage medium and then double-click the file named ***FCTAudioClip-02.mid***.
16. If necessary, click the Audio Tools Playback tab. Click the *Start* option box arrow in the Audio Options group and then click *Automatically* at the drop-down list.
17. Click the *Play Across Slides* check box in the Audio Options group to insert a check mark, click the *Loop until Stopped* check box to insert a check mark, and then click the *Hide During Show* check box to insert a check mark.
18. Drag the audio icon to the bottom center of the slide.
19. Run the slide show, beginning with Slide 1. The slide show will start and run continuously. Watch the presentation until it starts for the second time and then end the show by pressing the Esc key.
20. Print the presentation as handouts with nine slides displayed horizontally per page.
21. Save and then close **3-FCTEcoTours-Rehearsed.pptx**.

Figure 3.3 Recording Toolbar Buttons

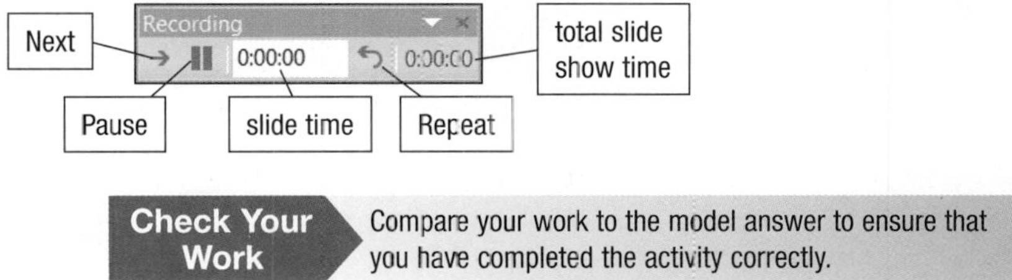

Check Your Work Compare your work to the model answer to ensure that you have completed the activity correctly.

In Addition

Setting Times Manually

The time a slide remains on the screen during a slide show can be manually set using options in the Timing group on the Transitions tab. To set manual times for slides, click the *On Mouse Click* check box to remove the check mark and then click the *After* check box to insert a check mark. Click in the *After* text box, type the desired number of seconds you want the slide to display on the screen when running the slide show, and then press the Enter key. Click the Apply To All button to apply the time to each slide in the presentation.

Features Summary

Feature	Ribbon Tab, Group	Button	Keyboard Shortcut
action button	Insert, Illustrations		
audio file	Insert, Media		
Clipboard task pane	Home, Clipboard		
draw shape	Insert, Illustrations OR Home, Drawing		
gridlines	View, Show		Shift + F9
header and footer	Insert, Text		
hyperlink	Insert, Links		Ctrl + K
rehearse timings	Slide Show, Set Up		
replace	Home, Editing	ab ac	Ctrl + H
table	Insert, Tables		
text box	Insert, Text		
video file	Insert, Media		
WordArt	Insert, Text		

Workbook Section study tools and assessment activities are available in the *Workbook* ebook. These resources are designed to help you further develop and demonstrate mastery of the skills learned in this section.

Integrating Programs SECTION 3

Word, Excel, and PowerPoint

Data Files Before beginning section work, copy the Integrating3 folder to your storage medium and then make Integrating3 the active folder.

Skills

- Export a PowerPoint presentation to a Word document
- Export a Word outline document to a PowerPoint presentation
- Link an Excel chart with a Word document and a PowerPoint presentation
- Edit a linked object
- Embed a Word table in a PowerPoint presentation
- Edit an embedded object

Precheck Check your current skills to help focus your study of the skills taught in this section.

Projects Overview

Create presentation handouts in Word for use in an annual meeting PowerPoint presentation.

Prepare a PowerPoint presentation for the Distribution Department of Worldwide Enterprises using a Word outline. Copy an Excel chart and link it to the Distribution Department meeting presentation and to a Word document and then edit the linked chart. Copy a Word table containing data on preview distribution dates, embed it in a PowerPoint slide, and then update the table.

Export a PowerPoint presentation containing information on vacation specials offered by First Choice Travel to a Word document.

Link an Excel chart containing information on department enrollments to a PowerPoint slide and then update the chart in Excel. Embed a Word table in a PowerPoint slide and then edit the table in the slide.

If you are a SNAP user, launch the Precheck and Tutorials from your Assignments page.

Model Answers Preview the model answers for an overview of the projects you will complete in the section activities.

Activity 3.1 Exporting a PowerPoint Presentation to Word

One of the benefits of a suite like Microsoft Office is that you can send data in one program to another program. For example, send Word content to a PowerPoint presentation and PowerPoint content to a Word document. To send presentation content to a document, click the File tab, click the *Export* option, click the *Create Handouts* option, and then click the Create Handouts button. At the Send to Microsoft Word dialog box, specify the layout of the content in the Word document and whether you want to paste or paste link the content and then click OK. One of the advantages to sending PowerPoint presentation content to a Word document is that you can have greater control over the formatting of the content in Word.

What You Will Do Create a Word document handout that contains slides from a PowerPoint presentation on the Theatre Arts Division at Niagara Peninsula College.

1. Open PowerPoint and then open **NPCDivPres.pptx**.
2. Save the presentation with the name **3-NPCDivPres**.
3. Click the File tab, click the *Export* option, click the *Create Handouts* option, and then click the Create Handouts button.

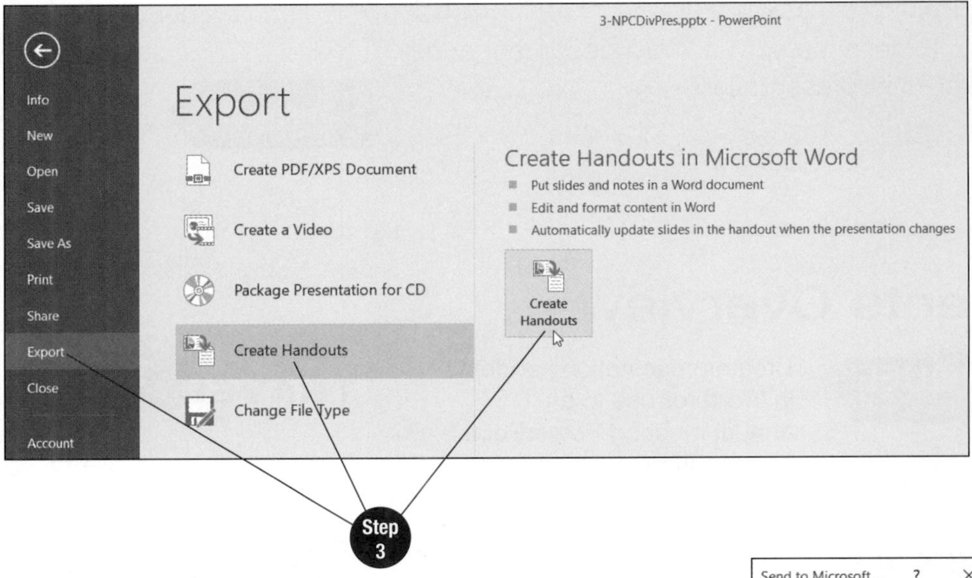

4. At the Send to Microsoft Word dialog box, click the *Blank lines next to slides* option.
5. Click the *Paste link* option in the *Add slides to Microsoft Word document* section and then click OK.

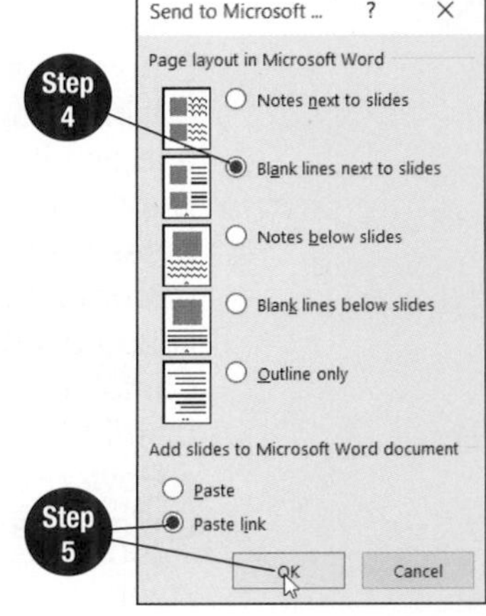

In Brief

Export PowerPoint Presentation to Word

1. Open presentation.
2. Click File tab.
3. Click *Export* option.
4. Click *Create Handouts* option.
5. Click Create Handouts button.
6. Choose options at Send to Microsoft Word dialog box.
7. Click OK.

6. If necessary, click the Word button on the taskbar.

   The slides display in a Word document as thumbnails followed by blank lines.

7. Save the Word document on your storage medium and name it **3-NPCDivPresHandout**.
8. Print and then close **3-NPCDivPresHandout.docx**.
9. Click the PowerPoint button on the taskbar.
10. Make Slide 3 active and then change *$750* to *$850*, *$350* to *$450*, and *$250* to *$300*.

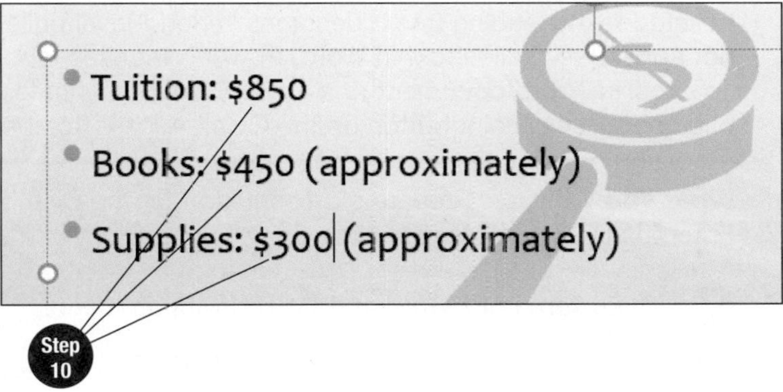

11. Save **3-NPCDivPres.pptx**.
12. Click the Word button on the taskbar and then open **3-NPCDivPresHandout.docx**. At the message asking if you want to update the document with the data from the linked files, click the Yes button.
13. Scroll through the document and notice that the dollar amounts in Slide 3 reflect the changes you made to Slide 3 in the PowerPoint presentation.
14. Save, print, and then close **3-NPCDivPresHandout.docx**.
15. Make PowerPoint active and then close **3-NPCDivPres.pptx**.

Check Your Work Compare your work to the model answer to ensure that you have completed the activity correctly.

In Addition

Pasting and Linking Data

The *Paste* option at the Send to Microsoft Word dialog box is selected by default and is available for all of the page layout options. With this option selected, the data inserted in Word is not connected or linked to the original data in the PowerPoint presentation. If you plan to update the data in the presentation and want the data to be updated in the Word document as well, select the *Paste link* option at the Send to Microsoft Word dialog box. This option is available for all of the page layout options except the *Outline only* option.

Activity 3.2 Exporting a Word Outline to a PowerPoint Presentation

As you learned in the previous activity, the Microsoft Office suite allows you to send content in one program to another program. For example, you can send Word content to a PowerPoint presentation and content in a PowerPoint presentation to a Word document. You can create text for slides in a Word outline and then export that outline to PowerPoint. PowerPoint creates new slides based on the heading styles used in the Word outline. Text formatted with a Heading 1 style become slide titles. Heading 2 text becomes first-level bulleted text, Heading 3 text becomes second-level bulleted text, and so on. If styles are not applied to outline text in Word, PowerPoint uses tabs or indents to place text on slides. To export a Word document to a PowerPoint presentation, you need to insert the Send to Microsoft PowerPoint button on the Quick Access Toolbar.

What You Will Do Prepare a presentation for the Distribution Department of Worldwide Enterprises using a Word outline.

1. Make sure both Word and PowerPoint are open.
2. With Word active, open **WEOutline.docx**.

   Text in this document has been formatted with the Heading 1 and Heading 2 styles.

3. Insert a Send to Microsoft PowerPoint button on the Quick Access Toolbar. Begin by clicking the Customize Quick Access Toolbar button at the right side of the Quick Access Toolbar.
4. Click *More Commands* at the drop-down list.

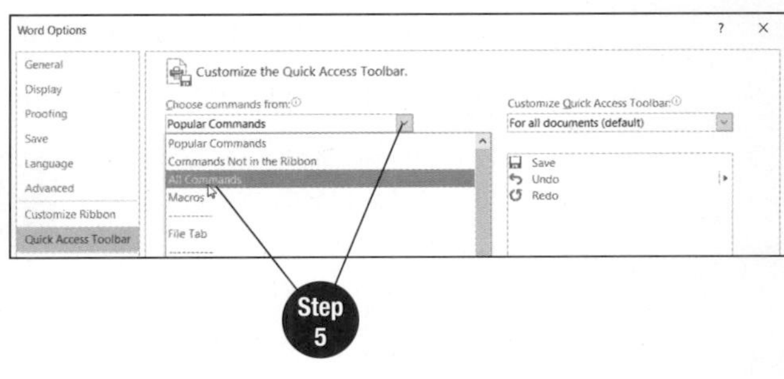

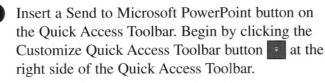

5. Click the *Choose commands from* option box arrow and then click *All Commands* at the drop-down list.
6. Scroll down the list box below the *Choose commands from* option box and then double-click *Send to Microsoft PowerPoint*.

   Items in the list box display in alphabetical order.

7. Click OK to close the Word Options dialog box.

   Notice that the Send to Microsoft PowerPoint button has been added to the Quick Access Toolbar.

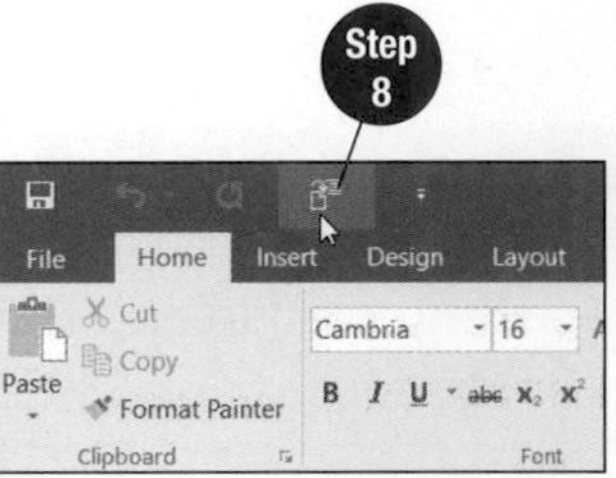

8. Send the outline to PowerPoint by clicking the Send to Microsoft PowerPoint button on the Quick Access Toolbar.
9. When the presentation displays on the screen, make sure Slide 1 is active. (If the presentation does not display, click the PowerPoint button on the taskbar.)

   The presentation is created with a blank design template.

In Brief

Insert Send to Microsoft PowerPoint Button on Quick Access Toolbar

1. Click Customize Quick Access Toolbar button on Quick Access Toolbar.
2. Click *More Commands.*
3. Click *Choose commands from* option box arrow.
4. Click *All Commands.*
5. Scroll down *Choose commands from* list box, double-click *Send to Microsoft PowerPoint.*
6. Click OK.

Send Word Outline to PowerPoint Presentation

1. Open Word document.
2. Click Send to Microsoft PowerPoint button on Quick Access Toolbar.

10. With Slide 1 active, change the layout by clicking the Layout button in the Slides group on the Home tab and then clicking the *Title Slide* option at the drop-down list.
11. Make Slide 4 active and then apply the Title Only layout. Apply the Title Only layout to Slides 5 and 6 as well.
12. Apply a design theme by clicking the Design tab, clicking the More Themes button in the Themes group, and then clicking the *Retrospect* option (shown below).

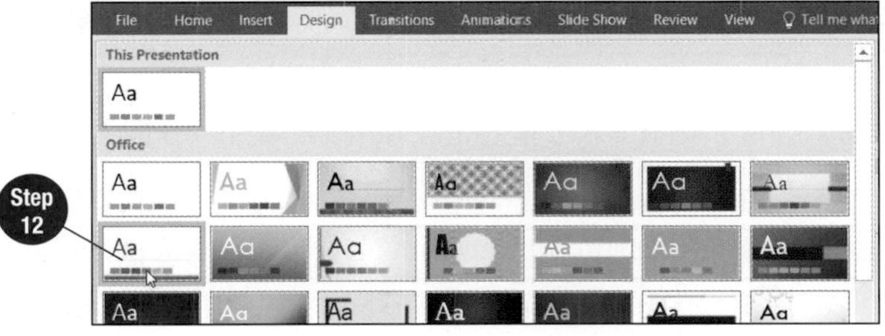

13. Click the second variant option in the Variants group (white with green).
14. Save the presentation and name it **3-WEDistDeptMtg**.
15. Close **3-WEDistDeptMtg.pptx**.
16. Click the Word button on the taskbar.
17. Right-click the Send to Microsoft PowerPoint button on the Quick Access Toolbar and then click *Remove from Quick Access Toolbar* at the shortcut menu.

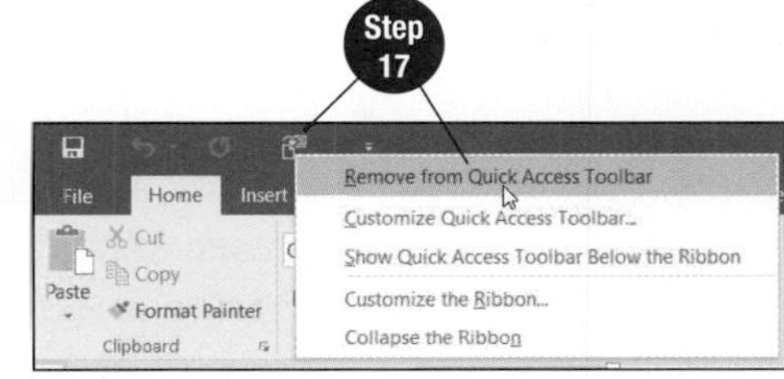

18. Close **WEOutline.docx** without saving the changes.

Check Your Work Compare your work to the model answer to ensure that you have completed the activity correctly.

In Addition

Applying a Style in Word

Heading styles were already applied to the text in **WEOutline.docx**. If you create an outline in Word that you want to export to PowerPoint, apply styles using options in the Styles group on the Home tab. A Word document contains a number of predesigned formats grouped into style sets. Click the Design tab to display the available style sets in the Document Formatting group. Choose a style set and the styles visible in the Styles group on the Home tab change to reflect your selection. To display additional available styles, click the More Styles button (contains a horizontal line and a down-pointing triangle) at the right side of the gallery in the Styles group on the Home tab. To apply a heading style, position the insertion point in the desired text, click the More Styles button, and then click the specific style at the drop-down gallery.

Activity 3.3 Linking an Excel Chart with a Word Document and a PowerPoint Presentation

You can copy and link an object such as a table or chart to files created in other programs. For example, you can copy an Excel chart and link it to a Word document and/or a PowerPoint presentation. The advantage to copying and linking over copying and pasting is that when you edit the object in the originating program, called the *source program*, the object is automatically updated in the linked file in the other program, called the *destination program*. When an object is linked, it exists in the source program but not as a separate object in the destination program. Since the object is located only in the source program, changes made to the object in the source program will be reflected in the destination program. An object can be linked to more than one destination program or file.

What You Will Do In preparation for a company meeting, you will copy an Excel chart and then link it to both the Worldwide Enterprises Distribution Department meeting presentation and to a Word document.

1. Make sure PowerPoint and Word are open and then open Excel.
2. Make Word active and then open **WERevDoc.docx**. Save the document with the name **3-WERevDoc**.
3. Make PowerPoint active, open **3-WEDistDeptMtg.pptx**, and then make Slide 6 active.
4. Make Excel active and then open **WERevChart.xlsx**. Save the workbook with the name **3-WERevChart**.
5. Copy and link the chart to the Word document and the PowerPoint presentation. Start by clicking in the chart to select it.

   Make sure you select the entire chart and not a specific chart element. To do so, try clicking just inside the chart border.

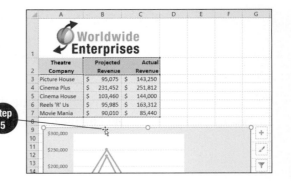

Theatre Company	Projected Revenue	Actual Revenue
Picture House	$ 95,075	$ 143,250
Cinema Plus	$ 231,452	$ 251,812
Cinema House	$ 103,460	$ 144,000
Reels 'R' Us	$ 95,985	$ 163,312
Movie Mania	$ 90,010	$ 85,440

6. With the chart selected, click the Copy button in the Clipboard group on the Home tab.
7. Click the Word button on the taskbar.
8. Press Ctrl + End to move the insertion point to the end of the document.
9. Click the Paste button arrow and then click *Paste Special* at the drop-down list.
10. At the Paste Special dialog box, click the *Paste link* option, click the *Microsoft Excel Chart Object* option in the *As* list box, and then click OK.

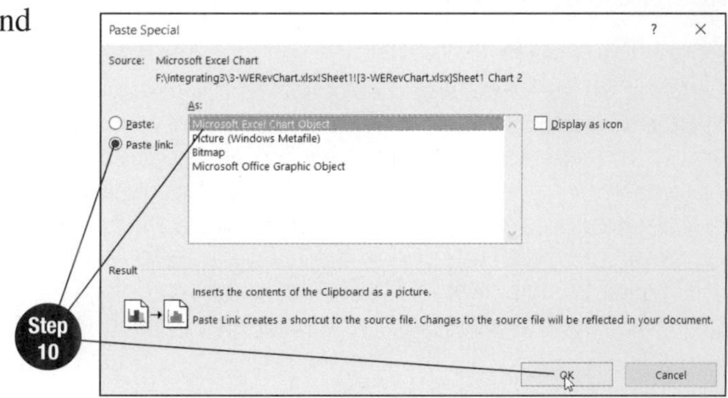

In Brief

Link Object between Programs

1. Open source program, open file containing object.
2. Select object, click Copy button.
3. Open destination program, open file into which object will be linked.
4. Click Paste button arrow, click *Paste Special*.
5. At Paste Special dialog box, click *Paste link*.
6. Click OK.

11. Select the chart and then center it by clicking the Center button in the Paragraph group on the Home tab.
12. Save, print, and then close **3-WERevDoc.docx**.
13. Click the PowerPoint button on the taskbar.
14. With Slide 6 active, make sure the Home tab is selected, click the Paste button arrow, and then click *Paste Special* at the drop-down list.
15. At the Paste Special dialog box, click the *Paste link* option, make sure *Microsoft Excel Chart Object* is selected in the *As* list box, and then click OK.
16. Increase the size of the chart so it better fills the slide and then center it on the slide, as shown in Figure 3.1.
17. Click outside the chart to deselect it.
18. Save the presentation, print only Slide 6, and then close **3-WEDistDeptMtg.pptx**.
19. Click the Excel button on the taskbar.
20. Click outside the chart to deselect it.
21. Save, print, and then close **3-WERevChart.xlsx**.

Figure 3.1 Step 16

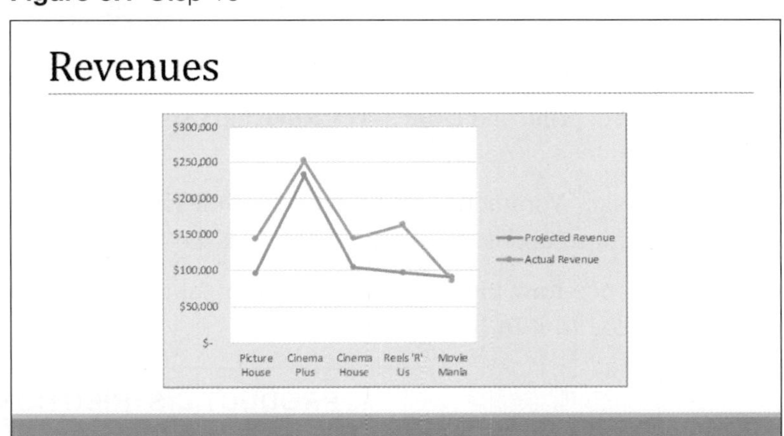

Check Your Work Compare your work to the model answer to ensure that you have completed the activity correctly.

In Addition

Linking Data or an Object within a Program

In this section, you learned to link an object between programs using the Paste Special dialog box. You can also link an object in Word using options at the Object dialog box. To do this, click the Insert tab and then click the Object button in the Text group. At the Object dialog box, click the Create from File tab. At the dialog box, type the file name in the *File name* text box or click the Browse button and then select the file from the appropriate folder. Click the *Link to file* check box to insert a check mark and then click OK.

Activity 3.4 Editing a Linked Object

The advantage to linking an object over simply copying it is that editing the object in the source program will automatically update the object in the destination program(s) as well. To edit a linked object, open the file containing the object in the source program, make edits, and then save the file. The next time the document, workbook, or presentation is opened in the destination program, the object will be updated.

What You Will Do Edit the actual and projected revenue numbers in the Worldwide Enterprises Excel worksheet and then open and print the Word document and the PowerPoint presentation that contain the linked chart.

1. Make sure Word, Excel, and PowerPoint are open.
2. Make Excel active and then open **3-WERevChart.xlsx**.
3. You discover that one theatre company was left out of the revenues chart. Add a row to the worksheet by clicking in cell A6 to make it active. Click the Insert button arrow in the Cells group on the Home tab and then click *Insert Sheet Rows* at the drop-down list.
4. Type the following data in the specified cells:
   A6: Regal Theatres
   B6: 69550
   C6: 50320
5. Click in cell A3.
6. Save, print, and close **3-WERevChart.xlsx** and then close Excel.

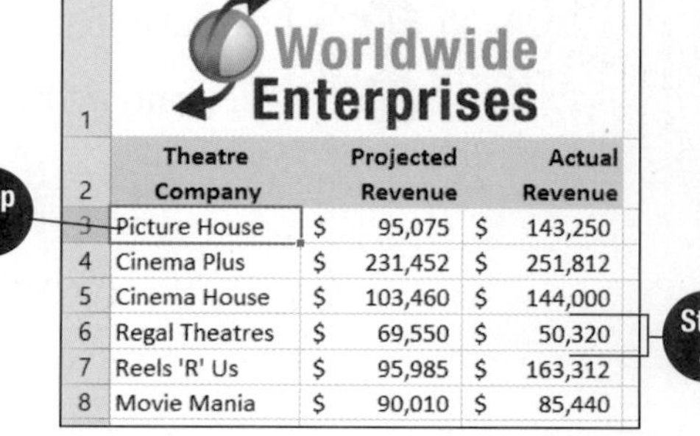

	A	B	C
1	Worldwide Enterprises		
2	Theatre Company	Projected Revenue	Actual Revenue
3	Picture House	$ 95,075	$ 143,250
4	Cinema Plus	$ 231,452	$ 251,812
5	Cinema House	$ 103,460	$ 144,000
6	Regal Theatres	$ 69,550	$ 50,320
7	Reels 'R' Us	$ 95,985	$ 163,312
8	Movie Mania	$ 90,010	$ 85,440

7. Make Word active and then open **3-WERevDoc.docx**. At the message asking if you want to update the linked file, click the Yes button.
8. Notice how the linked chart is automatically updated to reflect the changes you made to it in Excel.

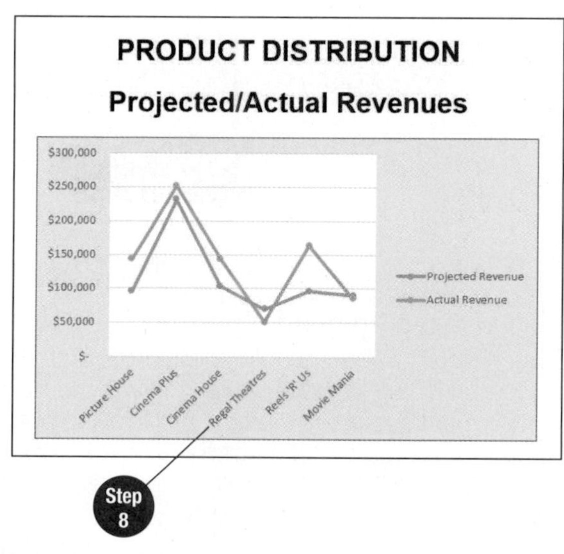

9 Save, print, and then close **3-WERevDoc.docx**.

10 Make PowerPoint active and then open **3-WEDistDeptMtg.pptx**.

11 At the message telling you that the presentation contains links, click the Update Links button.

12 Make Slide 6 active and then notice how the linked chart has been automatically updated to reflect the changes you made to it in Excel.

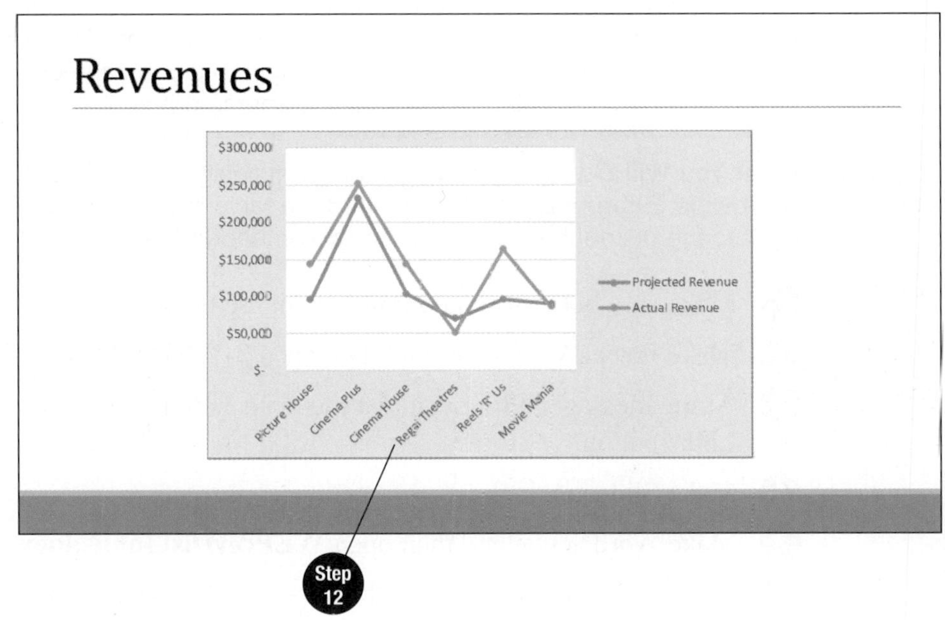

13 Save the presentation and then print only Slide 6.

14 Close **3-WEDistDeptMtg.pptx**.

Check Your Work Compare your work to the model answer to ensure that you have completed the activity correctly.

In Addition

Updating a Link Manually

You can choose to update a link manually in the destination program. To do this, open a Word document containing a linked object. Right-click the object, point to *Linked (type of object) Object*, and then click *Links*. At the Links dialog box, click the *Manual update* option and then click OK. With *Manual update* selected, the link will only be updated when you right-click the linked object and then click *Update Link* or when you display the Links dialog box, click the link in the list box, and then click the Update Now button.

Activity 3.5 Embedding and Editing a Word Table in a PowerPoint Slide

Copy and paste, copy and link, or copy and embed an object from one file into another. A linked object resides in the source program but not as a separate object in the destination program. An embedded object resides in the source program as well as in the destination program. If a change is made to an embedded object in the source program, the change will not be made to the object in the destination program. The main advantage to embedding rather than simply copying and pasting is that you can edit an embedded object in the destination program using the tools of the source program.

What You Will Do Copy a Word table containing data on preview distribution dates for Worldwide Enterprises and then embed the table in a slide in a PowerPoint presentation. Update the distribution dates for the two embedded tables.

1. Make sure both Word and PowerPoint are open.
2. Make PowerPoint active and then open **3-WEDistDeptMtg.pptx**.
3. At the message telling you that the presentation contains links, click the Update Links button.
4. Make Slide 4 active.
5. Make Word active and then open **WEPrevDistTable.docx**.
6. Click in a cell in the table and then select the table. To do this, click the Table Tools Layout tab, click the Select button in the Table group, and then click *Select Table* at the drop-down list.
7. With the table selected, click the Home tab and then click the Copy button in the Clipboard group.
8. Click the PowerPoint button on the taskbar.
9. With Slide 4 active, click the Paste button arrow and then click *Paste Special* at the drop-down list.
10. At the Paste Special dialog box, click *Microsoft Word Document Object* in the *As* list box and then click OK.

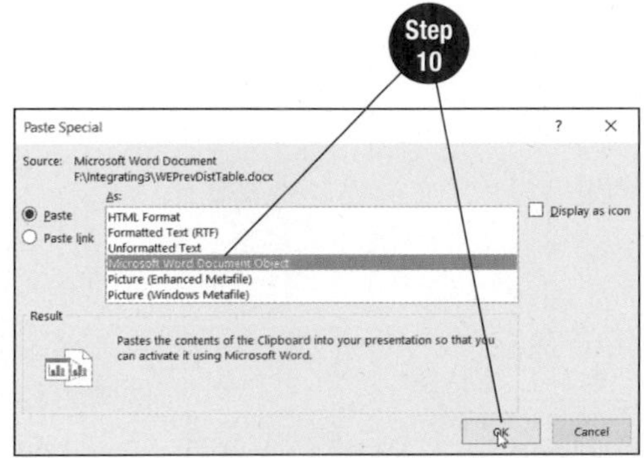

11. With the table selected in the slide, use the sizing handles to increase the size and change the position of the table as shown in Figure 3.2.
12. Click outside the table to deselect it.

In Brief

Embed Object
1. Open source program, open file containing object.
2. Select object, click Copy button.
3. Open destination program, open file into which object will be embedded.
4. Click Paste button arrow, click *Paste Special*.
5. At Paste Special dialog box, click object in *As* list box.
6. Click OK.

Edit Embedded Object
1. Open file containing embedded object.
2. Double-click object.
3. Make edits, click outside object to deselect it.

Figure 3.2 Step 11

Preview Distribution

Theatre Company	Location	Date
Cinema House	Montreal, Toronto	May 18
Cinema House	Vancouver	May 11
Cinema Plus	Los Angeles, San Diego	May 4
Cinema Plus	New York, Newark	May 11
Movie Mania	Wichita	May 25
Picture House	St. Louis	May 25
Picture House	Denver	May 18
Picture House	Salt Lake City	May 25

13 Save the presentation and then print only Slide 4.

14 Click the Word button on the taskbar and then close the document.

15 Click the PowerPoint button on the taskbar and then make Slide 5 active.

16 Make Word active and then open **WEGenDistTable.docx**.

17 Click in a cell in the table and then select the table. To do this, click the Table Tools Layout tab, click the Select button in the Table group, and then click *Select Table* at the drop-down list.

18 Click the Home tab and then click the Copy button in the Clipboard group.

19 Click the PowerPoint button on the taskbar.

20 With Slide 5 active, click the Paste button arrow and then click *Paste Special* at the drop-down list.

21 At the Paste Special dialog box, click *Microsoft Word Document Object* in the *As* list box and then click OK.

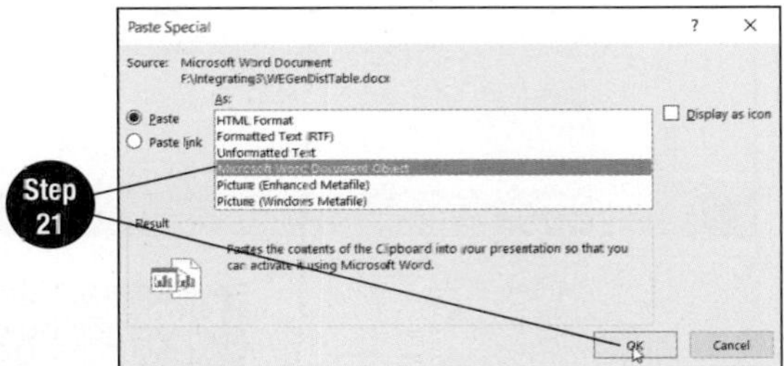

22 Increase the size and position of the table in the slide so it displays as shown in Figure 3.3 on the next page.

23 The distribution date to Cinema Plus in Sacramento and Oakland has been delayed until June 1. Edit the date by double-clicking the table in the slide.

Double-clicking the table displays the Word tabs and ribbon at the top of the screen. Horizontal and vertical rulers also display around the table.

24 Using the mouse, select *May 25* in the *Sacramento, Oakland* row and then type June 1.

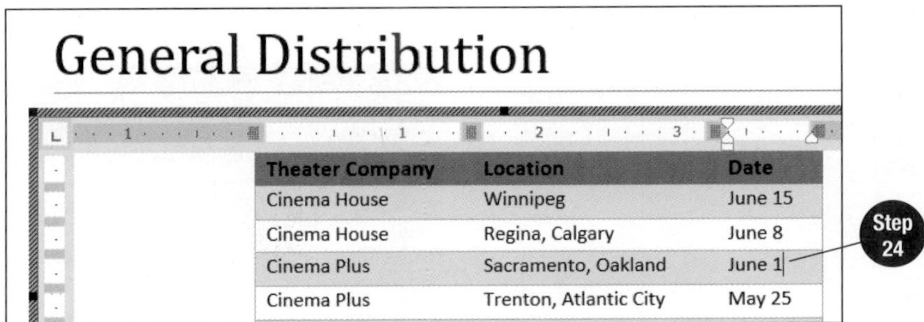

General Distribution
Theater Company | Location | Date
Cinema House | Winnipeg | June 15
Cinema House | Regina, Calgary | June 8
Cinema Plus | Sacramento, Oakland | June 1
Cinema Plus | Trenton, Atlantic City | May 25
Step 24

25 Click outside the table to deselect it.

Notice that the Word tabs disappear.

26 Print Slide 5 of the presentation.

27 Apply a transition and transition sound of your choosing to all slides in the presentation and then run the slide show.

28 Save and close **3-WEDistDeptMtg.pptx** and then close PowerPoint.

29 Click the Word button on the taskbar, close the document, and then close Word.

Figure 3.3 Step 22

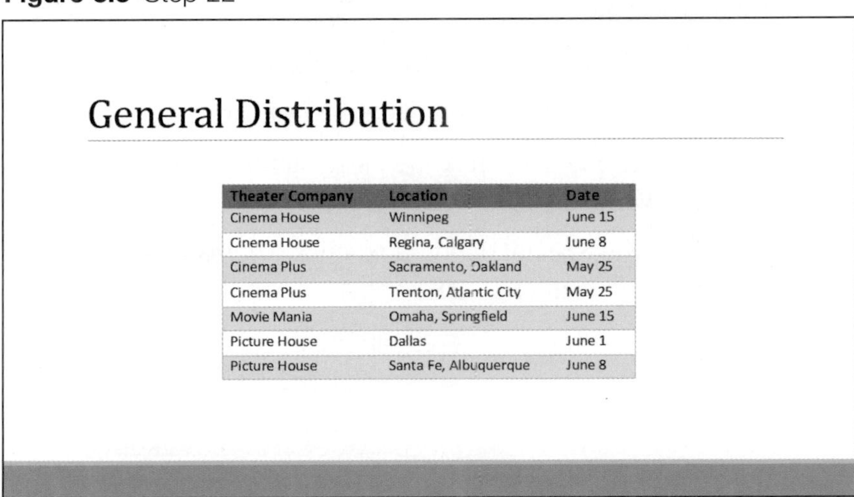

General Distribution
Theater Company | Location | Date
Cinema House | Winnipeg | June 15
Cinema House | Regina, Calgary | June 8
Cinema Plus | Sacramento, Oakland | May 25
Cinema Plus | Trenton, Atlantic City | May 25
Movie Mania | Omaha, Springfield | June 15
Picture House | Dallas | June 1
Picture House | Santa Fe, Albuquerque | June 8

Check Your Work Compare your work to the model answer to ensure that you have completed the activity correctly.

In Addition

Working with a Cropped Object

Some embedded or linked objects may appear cropped on the right or bottom side even if enough room is available to fit the image on the page or slide. A large embedded or linked object may appear cropped because Word converts the object into a Windows metafile (.wmf), which has a maximum height and width. If the embedded or linked object exceeds this maximum size, it appears cropped. To prevent an object from appearing cropped, consider reducing the size of the data by reducing the font size, column size, line spacing, and so on.

Workbook Section assessment activities are available in the *Workbook* ebook. These activities are designed to help you demonstrate mastery of the skills learned in this section.

INDEX